THE
HISTORICAL ATLAS
OF
NATIVE
AMERICANS

Inspiring | Educating | Creating | Entertaining

Brimming with creative inspiration, how-to projects, and useful information to enrich your everyday life, Quarto Knows is a favorite destination for those pursuing their interests and passions. Visit our site and dig deeper with our books into your area of interest: Quarto Creates, Quarto Cooks, Quarto Homes, Quarto Lives, Quarto Drives, Quarto Explores, Quarto Gifts, or Quarto Kids.

THE HISTORICAL ATLAS OF

OF

NATIVE AMERICANS

DR. IAN BARNES

CHARTWELL
BOOKS

CONTENTS

CHRONOLOGY

c. 50,000–1100 BC	First peoples cross to New World from Siberia.
c. 15,000–8000 BC	Clovis spear point used.
c. 3000 BC	Caral civilization, Peru.
1500–900 BC	Olmec culture.
c. 1200 BC–AD 1450	Hohokam of Sonora.
900–200 BC	Chavin culture.
100 BC–c. 1140	Anasazi.
AD 1–750	Moche civilization, Peru.
AD 300–900	Monte Albán architecture.
AD 300–1550	Classic Maya.
AD 500–1000	Tihuanaco Empire.
AD 650–800	Huari culture.
c. AD 700–1500	Amazon civilizations.
c. AD 700–c. 1550	Mississippian chiefdoms flourish through Southeast—Adena and Hopewell predecessors.
c. AD 800–1550	Mixtec culture.
c. AD 900–1150	Toltec culture.
c. AD 985–1030	Viking contact at L'Anse aux Meadows.
c. 1000–1533	Inca Empire.
c. 1100–1450	Chimú realm.
1300–1521	Aztec Empire.
1492	Columbus arrives in the Americas.
1497–98	John and Sebastian Cabot explore eastern coastline of North America for England.
1497–1503	Amerigo Vespucci explores West Indies and South American coast for Spain.
1504	European commercial fishing begins off Newfoundland and Nova Scotia.
1520s	First epidemics of European diseases hit North America and Caribbean.
1523	Ponce de Léon opens Spanish contact with Florida.
1523–24	Giovanni da Verrazzano sails Atlantic coast from Carolinas to Newfoundland; meets Wampanoag, Narragansett, and Delaware Indians.
1528	Pánfilo de Narváez leads Spanish expedition to Gulf of Mexico.
1534–41	Jacques Cartier travels up the St. Lawrence River.
1539–43	Hernando de Soto invades the Southeast; Battle of Mabila, 1540.
1540–42	Francisco Vásquez de Coronado invades New Mexico.
1578–79	Francis Drake explores Californian coast and meets Miwoks.
1583	Spanish Franciscans establish mission chains in Florida.
1584	British settlement at Roanoke Island.
1598	Juan de Oñate establishes Spanish colony in New Mexico; siezes Acoma, 1599.
1603–15	Samuel de Champlain's voyages in the Northeast; clashes with Iroquois, 1609.
1607	British settle at Jamestown, Virginia.
1616–19	Unknown disease epidemic hits New England.
1622	Opechancanough, chief of the Powhatan Indian confederacy, attacks Virginian towns.
1633–34	Smallpox epidemic affects the Northeast.
1636–37	Pequot War; tribe destroyed by colonists and Narragansett allies.
1639–45	Kieft's War against Munsee Delaware on Manhattan Island.
1644	Powhatan Indians assault Virginia again, killing 500 settlers. Opechancanough captured and murdered while a prisoner in Jamestown.
1649	Iroquois destroy Huron villages.
1655–57	Peach War: Dutch conflict with Delaware.
1659–60	First Esopus War: Dutch-Indian conflict.
1663–64	Second Esopus War: Dutch-Indian conflict.
1675–76	King Philip's War.
1680	Pueblo Revolt.
c. 1680–c. 1750	Indians acquire horses.
1681–82	René Robert Cavelier de La Salle travels down the Mississippi; claims the Mississippi Valley (Louisiana) for Louis XIV of France.
1689–97	King William's War.
1692	Francisco de Vargas reconquers New Mexico.
1700–01	Iroquois make peace with France and Britain at Montréal.
1702–13	Queen Anne's War.
1703–04	Spanish mission system in northern Florida destroyed by British and their Indian allies.
1704	Deerfield, Massachusetts, raided by French and Indians; Connecticut attacked too.
1711–13	Tuscarora War; after defeat, many Tuscaroras flee to the Iroquois.
1711–33	French wars against Fox (Mesquakie) Indians.
1715	Yamasee War; South Carolina severely damaged; start of the Creek threat.
1716–54	Creek-Cherokee Wars.
1729–33	French-Natchez War.
1730–40s	Ojibwa-Dakota Wars.
1736, 1739–40	French-Chickasaw Wars.
1738	Smallpox kills half the Cherokees.
1741	Vitus Bering and Alexei Chirikov open Russian trade with peoples in the Gulf of Alaska.

1744	Treaty of Lancaster between Six Nations and Virginia, Pennsylvania, and Maryland.
1744–48	King George's War.
1755	General Braddock defeated on the Monongahela River by French and Indians, July 9.
1755	Battle of Lake George; Johnson defeats a French, Canadian, and Indian force, and builds Fort William Henry.
1755–63	French and Indian War.
1759–61	War between Cherokees and British colonists.
1763	Treaty of Paris gives Britain Canada and New France east of the Mississippi, except for New Orleans; Indians not consulted.
1763	Pontiac's Revolt and Proclamation of Indian Territory.
1763–76	Creek-Choctaw Wars.
1769	First Franciscan mission established in California.
1774	Lord Dunmore's War between Virginia and the Shawnee.
1776–78	Captain James Cook begins British trade with people of Northwest Pacific Coast.
1776–83	American War of Independence.
1777	Battle of Oriskany, August 6.
1778	Treaty of Fort Pitt, between Delaware and United States; first U.S.-Native American treaty.
1778	Wyoming Valley Massacre, July 3.
1778	Cherry Valley Massacre, November 11.
1779	General John Sullivan, with Clinton and Brodhead, invades Iroquoia, destroying villages and crops.
1779–83	Massive smallpox epidemic from Mexico to Canada.
1780–1800	Smallpox and measles present among Indians in Texas and New Mexico.
1782	Graddenhutten Massacre of Moravian Delaware in Pennsylvania, March.
1783	Treaty of Paris: United States' independence recognized, November 30.
1784	Russians establish settlement on Kodiak Island.
1790	General Harmar enters the Ohio Valley to punish Indians for raiding and is defeated by Miami War Chief Little Turtle, near Fort Wayne, Indiana, October 18–22.
1791	General St. Clair defeated by Little Turtle, who leads a coalition of Wyandots, Iroquois, Shawnee, Miami, Delaware, Ojibwa, and Potawatomi, November 4.
1791–93	George Vancouver trades with Indian people on Pacific Coast.
1794	General Anthony Wayne defeats northwestern tribes at Battle of Fallen Timbers in Ohio, August 20.
1795	Treaty of Greenville; most of Ohio ceded to United States by Indians, August 3.
1799	Handsome Lake religion begins among the Seneca.
1804–06	Lewis and Clark expedition up the Missouri, from St. Louis to the Pacific by way of the Columbia River.
1809	Treaty of Fort Wayne: General William H. Harrison secures 2.5 million acres (1 million hectares) from Indians in Ohio and Indiana.
1811	Battle of Tippecanoe against the Shawnee, November 7.

1813	Battle of the Thames, Ontario; Tecumseh killed, October 5.
1814	Battle of Horseshoe Bend; Jackson defeats the Creeks, March 27.
1814	Treaty of Fort Jackson with Creeks, August 9.
1816–18	First Seminole War.
1819–24	Kickapoo resistance to removal from Illinois country.
1827	Winnebago uprising.
1830	Indian Removal Act.
1832	Black Hawk War.
1835–42	Second Seminole War.
1837	Smallpox epidemic among Mandan, Hidatsa, and Arikara.
1838–39	Cherokee Trail of Tears.
1842	First significant wagon train reaches Oregon.
1847–50	Cayuse Indian war in Oregon
1849	California Gold Rush.
1850–51	Mariposa War in California between miners, Miwoks, and Yokuts.
1855–58	Third Seminole War.
1855–58	Northwestern Wars against Yakama, Rogue, and Coeur d'Alene Indians.
1861–65	American Civil War.
1861–86	Apache Wars.
1862	Santee Sioux uprising.
1864	Sand Creek Massacre.
1864	Navajo Long Walk to Bosque Redondo.
1866–68	Red Cloud's War.
1867	Treaty of Medicine Lodge.
1868	Fort Laramie Treaty.
1869	First Riel uprising in the Red River region, Canada.
1872–73	Modoc War.
1876	Rosebud Campaign.
1876	Battle of the Little Bighorn: Custer's Last Stand, June 25.
1877	Chief Joseph and his Nez Perce band head for Canada.
1879	Second Riel rebellion in Canada.
1887	General Allotment Act (Dawes).
1890	Wounded Knee Massacre, December 29.
1907	Oklahoma State created.
1911	Society of American Indians formed.
1914–18	World War I.
1918	Native American Church incorporated in Oklahoma.
1924	Citizenship Act confers U.S. citizenship on Indians not already citizens.
1934	Indian Reorganization Act.
1939–45	World War II.
1958	3,000 Lumbees in North Carolina drive out Ku Klux Klan rally.
1961	National Indian Youth Council founded.
1968	American Indian Movement created.
1973	Wounded Knee Massacre site seized by Indian activists.
1977	Inuit Circumpolar Conference established.
1978	American Indian Religious Freedom Act.
1990	Native American Graves Protection and Repatriation Act.

MAP LIST

INTRODUCTION

"I beheld too, in that vision
All the secrets of the future
Of the distant days that shall be
I beheld the westward marches
Of the unknown, crowded nations
All the land was full of people,
Restless, struggling, toiling, striving,
Speaking many tongues, yet feeling
But one heart-beat in their bosoms
In the woodlands rain their axes,
Smoking their towns in all the valleys,
Over all the lakes and rivers
Rushed their great canoes of thunder."

Hiawatha,
Henry Wadsworth Longfellow (1807–82)

Any attempt to understand Native American history is normally bedeviled by images forced upon the public by films and television. Stereotypes abound—the Indian is depicted as a romantic, noble savage or a vicious, blood-soaked, scalping animal, hell-bent on rape and murder. Few people remember that the Japanese samurai and the Celts of Britain collected heads as trophies. Jay Silverheels, a Mohawk, played Tonto, the loyal Indian, in the *The Lone Ranger* TV show (1956). Since then, this classic vision has changed, new film portrayals setting the record straighter or questioning past perceptions. *Soldier Blue* (1970), *A Man Called Horse* (1970), and *Dances with Wolves* (1990) portrayed Native Americans more sympathetically. However, many Indian actors have been cast in the familiar role of the past, such as Chief Dan George (Salish) in *The Outlaw Josie Wales* (1976), or Native Americans have been played by non-natives. A turning point was the film *Smoke Signals* (1998). This was the first ever film written and directed by Indians, the two leading actors being Native American too. Written by Sherman Alexie (Spokane/Coeur d'Alene) and directed by Chris Eyre (Cheyenne/Arapaho), this road movie starred Evan Adams (Coast Salish) and Adam Beach (Saulteaux, or Ojibwa) as two young Indian men traveling from Idaho to Arizona to collect the ashes of Beach's deceased alcoholic father.

Other lesser-known, more accurate images are presented in Christian F. Feest's book, *The Cultures of Native North Americans* (Konemann, 2000). A Tlingit warrior in full wooden armor is shown on a Southeast Alaska Corporation advertising poster. Menesk, a chief of the Tsimshian Nisga'a tribe of British Columbia is depicted wearing a dance blanket, but is remarkable for his full gray beard and mustache. An 1882 photograph shows Chasi, son of Bonito, a Warm Springs Apache, using an Apache fiddle, the only stringed instrument of indigenous America. Senator Ben Nighthorse Campbell (Cheyenne) is pictured riding, in full Indian apparel, at the Tournament of Roses parade in Pasadena, Florida (1993). He was co-leader with a visiting Spanish duke, but insisted on riding ahead because Native Americans were present before the Spaniards. He repeated his ride on January 20, 1993, at the inaugural parade of President Bill Clinton.

Boundaries of consciousness require redefining, and archaeology pushes back the limits of recorded history, both in North and South America. Southern Oregon University's Laboratory of Anthropology, in partnership with Oregon State University and the Southern Oregon Historical Society, has implemented a public archaeology project at the site of Fort Lane in Jackson County. Fort Lane was built in 1853 as one of four posts constructed to protect the Indians in southern Oregon, following the discovery of gold, which led to a large influx of miners and settlers. The whites seemed intent on ethnic cleansing, and the U.S. Army was prepared to use force to stop the genocide. A contemporary report proposed placing the Indians on a reservation to ensure their survival. Captain Andrew Jackson Smith, in command of the fort, actually informed local whites that their plan to attack the reservation would result in conflict with the U.S. Army. Even so, skirmishes broke out between Takelma, Latgawa, Shasta, and Athabaskan peoples, and gold miners and other pioneers. An Indian village was attacked and its inhabitants massacred by a citizen militia led by James Lupton, recently elected southwest Oregon's representative to the territorial legislature. Some Indians moved to the 3,000-square mile (8,000-square kilometer) Table Rock Reservation, trusting in the protection of Fort Lane, where two companies of the U.S. Army's 1st Dragoons were stationed. Other local Indians started the Rogue River War, Chiefs Tecumtum and Cholcultah leading their warriors down the river, torching cabins and killing settlers.

The Army's commitment to Fort Lane was considerable, since its supplies had to be dispatched from Benecia, California, by boat to Crescent City, and then overland by pack train through the Applegate Valley. Brevet Major-General John Wool, commander of the Army of the West, and Oregon Superintendent of Indian Affairs Joel Palmer led a force to round up the insurgent Indians during 1855–56. They were marched or shipped to the Grane Ronde and Siletz Agencies on the Coast Reservation, which eventually became home to the Takelma, Latgawa, Athabaskan, Tatutni, Coos, Coquille, and Umpqua peoples of southwest Oregon. Meanwhile, Wool incurred the anger of the Rogue River settlers by condemning the aggression of citizen militias and promoting the rights of Indians. These events provide a qualification to normal generalizations concerning Native American-U.S. Army relations.

Elsewhere, archaeological evidence shows that the Amazon basin supported more than scattered populations of hunter-gatherers. This flies in the face of arguments that the Amazon had an inadequate soil base for the existence of sophisticated urban communities. Some people managed their crops so successfully that the sites of their settlements are marked by a dark, rich soil, a veritable compost heap, which punctuates the normal, orange, sandy, forest soil. It is thought that there might even have been plazas. However, one century after the arrival of the Portuguese, these stone-age chiefdoms had vanished.

Although firearms were prevalent among the Plains tribes during the second half of the nineteenth century, simpler weapons had not been abandoned. This Sioux war club from Pine Ridge, South Dakota, dates from around 1880 and has a beautifully carved chert head.

Archaeologist Clark L. Erickson, of the University of Pennsylvania, argues that the prehispanic peoples of the Amazon constructed an anthropogenic landscape through building raised fields, large settlement mounds, and causeways. Complexes of fish weirs and ponds could have produced vast quantities of fish and edible snails. An anthropologist, Michael J. Heckenberger, of the University of Florida, has identified nineteen villages in the Upper Xingu River region, all connected by roads and likely to have had populations of between 2,500 and 5,000 people each. Heckenberger cooperated with local native chiefs and a team from the Universidade Federal do Rio de Janeiro in uncovering these sites. He thinks that the settlements date to between 1200 and 1600. He says that all the villages were constructed and laid out in a common fashion, and that the roads were mathematically parallel. In places, some of these roads are 165 feet (50 meters) wide. Heckenberger believes that the roads and village plazas were versions of monuments found elsewhere, the astronomical and mathematical knowledge necessary for their construction being on a par with that needed to build the Mayan pyramids. He said, "Everyone loves the 'lost civilization in the Amazon' story. What the Upper Xingu and middle Amazon stuff shows us is that Amazon people organized in an alternative way to urbanization. We shouldn't be expecting to find lost cities. But that doesn't mean they were primitive tribes, either." Thus, more assumptions about Native Americans are disproved, because sophisticated civilizations did exist in the Amazon basin.

Elsewhere, archaeological finds are pushing back the dates of human occupation. The discovery of Caral, in the Supe Valley of Peru, and its exploration by Ruth Shady uncovered some nineteen pyramid complexes, while there are seventeen other sites in the Supe Valley. Dating back to at least 2627 BC, Caral is thought to be the mother city of the Inca civilization by Shady. The Caral communities probably traded as far as the Amazon. Archaeologist Jonathan Haas pointed out the lack of fortifications and weapons, and he believes, as does Shady, that Caral's existence was based upon trade. Wealth allowed the city of pyramids to be built, and the civilization survived without war. Shady said, "Caral was the first city with the first central government. Caral changes all our current thinking about the origins of civilization." The inhabitants of Caral experienced a thousand years of peace, suggesting that our civilizations were not always created by battle and warfare, as normally thought.

The Native American experience has impacted upon the rest of the world in the fields of agriculture, food, and medicine. Medically speaking, the Amazon rainforest is a cornucopia of delights, and its destruction could limit medical advances, since more exploration for new drugs is required there. The Incas used quinine, which can cure malaria, cramps, chills, and arhythmic problems. Ipecac can be used to treat amebic dysentery and to induce vomiting to remove poisonous foods. Curare, a toxin applied to arrow tips, is a muscle relaxant and can be utilized in abdominal surgery. Coca produces cocaine, which can be synthesized into novocaine, an important anesthetic. Occasionally, Indians employed foxglove (*Digitalis purpurea*) to treat heart conditions. Aztec medical knowledge was so vast that Spain's King Philip II ordered Francisco Hernando to record it.

Herbal remedies soon began to be used by European settlers, and Swedish botanist Peter Kalm traveled to the Middle Atlantic states (1748–50) to document Indian medicinal herbs. Among the most common remedies was witch hazel, used to treat insect bites and cuts. Leaves and roots of wintergreen contain methyl salicylate, which was utilized in various ways to alleviate rheumatic pain and muscular aches. Salicylate acid is the main component of aspirin. Northern Californian and Oregon Native Americans used the bark of cascara, Californian buckthorn, to cure constipation. Today, cascara is the most commonly known laxative, having been introduced commercially in the American pharmaceutical industry in 1878.

The paramount Native American influence lies in the types of food exported to the world. Maize, in all its colors, is now cultivated worldwide. In Africa, it has become a staple food, together with beans, peanuts, and cassava, allowing the population to survive and grow, despite the depredations of slavery. The introduction of the potato from Bolivia and Peru into Ireland and Russia permitted agriculture on really poor soil, but its monoculture in Ireland and four-year potato blight infestation, from 1845, caused mass starvation and around a million deaths. In Asia, *aloo sag* (potato and spinach) is a well-known dish, while maize and sweet potato have allowed marginal land to be brought into cultivation. Where would Mediterranean cuisine be without tomatoes and peppers? Other common Native American foods are pumpkin, squash, chocolate, vanilla, papaya, persimmon, pecan, chilli, sunflower seed, maple syrup, tapioca, avocado, pineapple, turkey, cranberry, cucumber, blueberry, asparagus, and mint.

So, Native Americans provide the historian and cartographer with an ever growing knowledge, while Indian society, with its medicine, agriculture, and food, has stocked world larders. This atlas maps the story of the Native Americans in all its glory, violence, and sadness.

Settling the Hemisphere shows how early peoples crossed into the Americas via Beringia, and gives examples of how some nations saw their own origins, such as the tale of She Who Fell From The Sky. The domestication of plants and agriculture provided the backbone of early civilizations in Central and South America, such as the Maya, Aztec, and Inca. Most Europeans, however, possess scant knowledge of Mississippian society, the Hohokam, and the Anasazi, despite the remarkable edifices and buildings they constructed. Maps show the complex communication and transport systems that developed,

Native American headdress worn by a ceremonial dancer at the Buffalo Nations Event in support of the the American bison.

while the text explores linguistic diversity, kinship, and societal patterns, especially the importance achieved by women.

First Contacts depicts Native American society on the eve of European contact. Viking encounters are explained, as are the huge industrial fishing enterprises mounted by the Basques, Normans, and Bretons, inveterate explorers and maritime risk takers. Columbus assumes his normal place, while the tales of DeLeon, Narvaez, and Cabeza de Vaca provide an overture to the savage, aggressive, and extreme cruelty of De Soto's *entrada*, and his disgraceful behavior toward Indians. The French efforts to explore the St.

An example of pictograph rock art, Navajo images show the arrival of Spaniards on horseback.

Lawrence with limited colonization are set against the 1607 British settlement at Jamestown. Whether French, British, or Spanish, the Europeans introduced new diseases that severely depleted indigenous populations. They also brought the horse, which ultimately changed some tribes' cultural and economic patterns.

Allies and Subjects: Indians in the Colonial World demonstrates the result of European-Native American relationships, which often were of a warlike nature. The struggle to control the flow of European trade goods tipped the Iroquois into a war with the Wyandot (Huron), a type of trade war that developed elsewhere between other tribes. Jamestown, with its tobacco-based agriculture, fought the Powhatan Confederacy. This British settlement is also notorious for importing African slaves. The Pequot War and King Philip's War severely damaged Indian population figures, some tribes experiencing mass enslavement. The Dutch and the Spanish experiences were similar, with messy skirmishes around New Amsterdam and the incredibly successful Pueblo Revolt, which rocked the Spanish establishment and ego. The Peace at Montréal in 1701 ended Iroquois depredations and trade wars, the Haudenosaunee promising neutrality in any future Anglo-French colonial wars.

Native Americans in Imperial Wars shows the fate of Indians torn between the policies of the imperial powers, which sometimes incited conflict between tribes when one power attempted to gain allies or prevent another power from winning friends. The civilized tribes—Creek, Choctaw, Chickasaw, and Cherokee—suffered greatly, while the socially interesting Natchez were virtually wiped out by the French. Warfare between the Ojibwa and Lakota is examined, as is the confusion and violence caused by northern Indians—Comanche and Apache—moving south. The Seven Years' War demonstrated the dangers of alliances with whites, admirably shown by the failure of the 1763 Proclamation Line, which colonial governments failed to police. White settlers encroached upon Indian hunting grounds, and land cessions were forced from such tribes as the Shawnee.

Native Americans in an Age of Revolution examines how the Indian nations responded to the American War of Independence. Employed by both the British and Americans, Native Americans made alliances with the combatants in the hope that, as a reward, they would be allowed to keep their lands without fear of further incursions by white settlers. The Treaty of Paris, which ended the conflict, ignored Indian interests, however, and the new republic began expanding rapidly westward into the Ohio Valley. There, various tribal confederations sought to stem the flow, but the efforts of Little Turtle and Tecumseh ended in failure. Matters were not improved when President Jefferson sent Meriwether Lewis and William Clark to explore westward, which helped open up the Northwest to settlement;

previously, the area had been penetrated only by fur hunters and traders, often connected to the Hudson's Bay Company.

American Nations, 1815–65 continues the tale of relentless white pressure. As European economies faced a temporary decline, migrants poured into North America, especially from the British Isles. Removals to reservations took place in the Midwest and Southeast. The civilized nations inhabited villages with European-style farms and dwellings, while the Cherokee Sequoyah had constructed a syllabary used in a Native American newspaper. Nevertheless, the Cherokee were removed, being forced to follow the Trail of Tears, an illegal act, since the Supreme Court had found in favor of the Cherokee. This fact was ignored by President Jackson, an impeachable offense under the Constitution. Black Hawk, a Sauk chief, fought against migrants, but his war was doomed in the face of increasing numbers of Americans moving westward, seeking land, gold, and furs. This relentless migration led to the extinction of several Californian tribes. Resistance by the Apache and Northwestern tribes was in vain.

Conquest, 1865–1900 illustrates the constant fight back by the Native Americans on the Plains, and in the mountains and deserts of the West, which had disastrous results for the Navajo, Nez Perce, Sioux, and Cheyenne. Even the slaughter of Custer and his troops at the Little Bighorn achieved nothing. Forts and reservations confined Native Americans, and eventually even Indian Territory was taken from them by the birth of the state of Oklahoma.

Survival and Renaissance, 1900–2002 portrays the development of tribal economic enterprises, the Native American contribution to America's wars, and the birth of Indian political activism. A growth in the Native American population has coincided with its participation in the professions, politics, the arts, and education. As Native American standards of living rise, there is hope that general poverty and ill health among Indians will decline, and that they will reacquire status in their own land.

The remaining adobe walls of Citadel Pueblo in Wupatki National Monument, Arizona. Built around AD 1100 by the Anasazi, the fortress-like structure stands on a bluff overlooking the surrounding countryside.

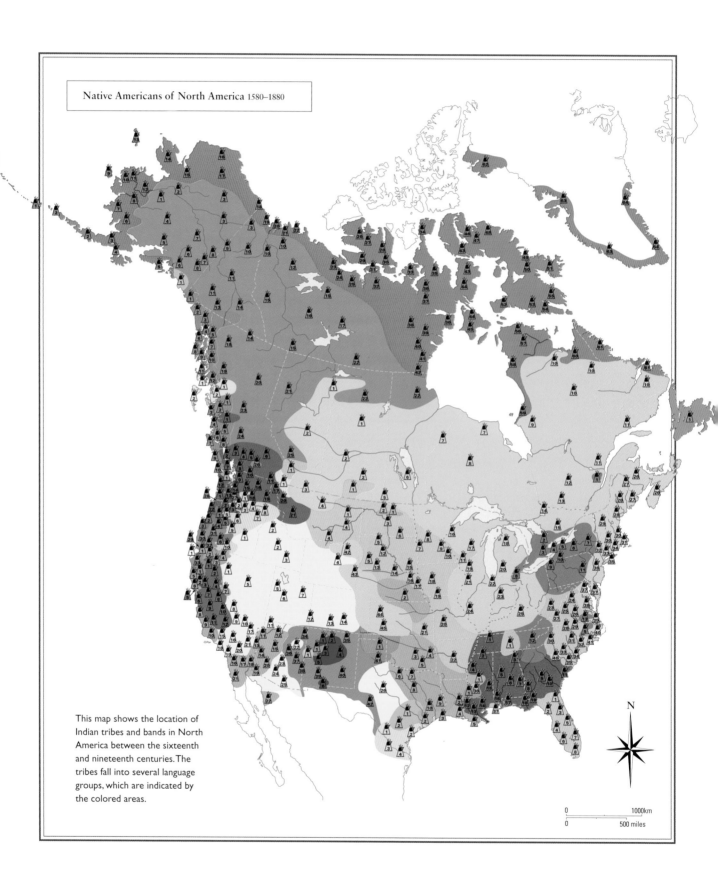

Native Americans of North America 1580–1880

This map shows the location of Indian tribes and bands in North America between the sixteenth and nineteenth centuries. The tribes fall into several language groups, which are indicated by the colored areas.

N

0   1000km
0   500 miles

Native Americans of North America 1580–1880

 Algonkian

1 Woods Cree
2 Plains Cree
3 Blackfeet
4 Atsina (Gros Ventre)
5 Plains Ojibwa (Bungi)
6 Saulteaux
7 Swampy Cree (Westmain Cree)
8 Northern Ojibwa
9 East Cree (Eastmain Cree)
10 Nascapi
11 Montagnais
12 Tetes du Boule (Attikamek)
13 Algonkin
14 Nipissing
15 Mississauga
16 Chippewa (Southern Ojibwa)
17 Menomini
18 Ottawa
19 Fox
   Sauk
20 Mascouten
21 Kickapoo
22 Potawatomi
23 Miami-Wea
24 Illini-Peoria
25 Shawnee
26 Micmac
27 Malecite-Passamaquoddy
28 Eastern Abenaki-Penobscot
29 Western Abenaki-Sokoki
30 Massachusett-Nipmuc
31 Wampanoag-Nauset
32 Mahican (Mohican) Wapping (Wappinger)
33 Southern New England (Quiripi)-Paugussett,
   Quinnipiac, Tunxis
34 Mohegan-Pequot
   Narraganset-Niantic
35 Eastern Long Island (Unquachog)-Shinnecock,
   Poosepatuck, Montauk
36 Delaware-Munsee, Unami
37 Nanticoke-Conoy
38 Powhatan-Pamunkey, Mattapony, Chickahominy,
   Nansemond, Potomac, Rappahannock
39 Chowanoc, Weapemeoc
40 Hatteras, Machapunga, Pamlico
41 Coree
42 Northern Cheyenne
43 Northern Arapaho
44 Southern Cheyenne
45 Southern Arapaho
46 Saluda

 Athabascan

1 Ingalik – Holikachuk
2 Koyukon
3 Kutchin
4 Kolchan
5 Tanaina
6 Ahtena
7 Tanana
8 Nabesna
9 Han
10 Kutchin
11 Tutchone
12 Hare
13 Tagish
14 Kaska – Pelly River
15 Slavey
16 Dogrib
17 Yellowknife
18 Tahltan
19 Tsetsaut
20 Sekani
21 Beaver
22 Chipewyan
23 Carrier
24 Chilcotin
25 Sarsi
26 Nicola
27 Kwalhioqua
28 Clatskanie
29 Tolowa
30 Chetco, Galice Creek, Tututni
31 Umpqua, Upper Coquille
32 Applegate Creek, Chastacosta
33 Chilula, Hupa, Kato, Lassik, Mattole,
   Nongatl, Sinkyone, Wailaki, Whilkut
34 Navajo
35 Jicarilla Apache
36 Tonto – Northern & Southern
37 Cibecue
38 Western Apache, White Mountain
39 Chiricahua Apache
40 Mescalero Apache
41 Kiowa Apache
42 Lipan

 Beothuk

1 Beothuk

 Caddoan

1 Arikara
2 Pawnee
3 Yscani
4 Tawehash
5 Wichita
6 Kichai or Kitsai
7 Waco
8 Tawakoni
9 Adia, Eyeish, Kadohadacho, Natchitoches
10 Hasinai

 California Penutian

1 Nomlaki, Wintu, Wintun
2 Konkow, Maidu
3 Patwin, Plains Miwok
4 Nisenan, Northern Miwok
5 Coast Miwok
6 Costano
7 Central Miwok
8 Southern Miwok
9 Northern Valley Yokuts
10 Chukchansi, Foothills Yokuts, Kings River
11 Southern Valley Yokuts, Tachi
12 Kaweah River, Poso Creek, Tule River

 Chimakum

1 Chimakum, Quileute, Hoh

 Chinook

1 Cathlamet, Chinook, Clatsop
2 Cathlapotle, Chilluckittequaw, Clackamas
   Clowwewalla, Multnomah, Skilloot, Watlala
3 Wasco, Wishram

 Coahuiltecan

1 Coahuilteco
2 Karankawa
3 Borrado
4 Comecrudo, Cotoname

Native Americans of North America 1580–1880

 Eskimo Aleut

1 Atka
2 Unalaska
3 Aglemiut
4 Kaniagmiut
5 Chugachigmiut
6 Nushagamiut
7 Togiamiut
8 Kuskwogmiut
9 Nunivagiut
10 Kalaligmiut
11 Magemuit
12 Ikogmiut
13 St. Lawerence Island Eskimo
14 Bering Strait Eskimo
15 Kotzebue Eskimo
16 North Alaskan Eskimo
17 Northern Interior Eskimo
18 Kigirktayuk
19 Kigirktarugmmiut
19 Kupugmiut
20 Novorugmiut
21 Kittegaryumiut
22 Avvagmiut
23 Nuvungmiut
24 Kogluktomuit
24 Agiarmiut
25 Kilsusktormiut
26 Kanghiryuatjagmiut
27 Kanghiryuarmiut
28 Copper Eskimo
29 Nagjuktormiut
   Puivilirmiut
30 Ikaluktukmiut
31 Ahiarmiut
32 Umingmaktormiut
33 Giqiqtarmiut
34 Arviqtuurmiut
35 Netsilingmiut
36 Netsilik Eskimo
37 Utkuhikhalingmiut
38 Caribou Eskimo
39 Qairnirmiut
40 Harvaqtuurmiut
41 Padlimiut
42 Ahiarmiut
43 Iglulik Eskimo
44 Aivilingmiut
45 Sadlermiut
46 Tununirmiut
47 Tununirusirmiut

48 Akudnirmiut
49 Padlimiut
50 Baffin Island Eskimo
51 Oqomuit
52 Sikosuilarmiut
53 Akuliarmiut
54 Qaumauangmiut
55 Nugumiut
56 Tarramiut
57 Eskimo of Quebec
58 Itivimiut
59 Qikirmuit
60 Siqinirmuit
61 Labrador Eskimo
62 Polar Eskimo
63 West Greenland Eskimo
64 East Greenland Eskimo

 Eyak

1 Eyak

 Keres

1 Keres

 Kiowa

1 Kiowa

 Kutenai

1 Kutenai

 Muskogian

1 Kaskinampo
2 Chickasaw
3 Koasati
4 Chakchiuma, Ibitoupa, Taposa
5 Napochi
6 Alabama
7 Apalachicola, Muklasa, Tuskegee
8 Muskogee, Sawokli
9 Chiaha, Oconee, Okmulgee
10 Hitchiti, Yamasee, Tamathli
11 Cusabo
12 Okelousa, Houma
13 Bayogoula, Quinipissa, Tangipahoa
14 Acolapissa
15 Choctaw
16 Mobile, Pascagoula, Tohome

17 Pensacola
18 Apalachee, Chatot
19 Osochi

 Natchez

1 Natchez, Taensa
2 Avoyel

 Oregon Penutian

1 Atfalati, Lakmiut, Yamel
2 Alsea, Kuitsh, Siuslaw, Yaquina
3 Coos or Hanis, Miluk
4 Calapodya, Chelamela, Yoncalla
5 Marys River
6 Latgawa, Takelma

 Salishan

1 Bellacoola
2 Comox, Puntlatch
3 Seechelt
4 Lillooet, Squawmish
5 Thompson
6 Shuswap
7 Cowichan, Nanaimo, Songish
8 Lummi, Semiahmoo, Stalo
9 Chelan, Nooksack, Samish, Skagit
   Snohomish, Suquamish, Swallah, Swinomish
10 Methow, Okanagan
11 Senijextee (Lakes)
12 Clallam, Copalis, Humptulips, Queets, Quinault
   Satsop, Skokomish, Twana, Wynoochee
13 Cowlitz, Lower Chehalis, Upper Chehalis
14 Duwamish, Muckleshoot, Nisqually, Puyallup
   Skyomish, Snoqualmie, Squaxon
15 Columbia, Wenatchee
16 Colville, Nespelem, Sanpoil, Sinkakaius, Spokan
17 Lower Kalispel
18 Moses - Columbia
19 Coeur d'Alene
20 Upper Kalispel
21 Flathead

Native Americans of North America 1580–1880

 Shapwailuta

1 Mical, Pshwanwapam, Taidnapam, Waptailmin
2 Atanum, Klickitat, Topinish, Yakima
3 Skin, Waiam
4 Chimnapum, Wanapam
5 Tenino, Tyigh
6 Cayuse, John Day or Tukspush
7 Umatilla, Wallawalla (Walula)
8 Nez Perce
9 Molala
10 Klamath, Modoc

 Siouan

1 Assiniboine
2 Hidatsa
3 Mandan
4 Crow
5 Lakota
6 Nakota, Yanktonai
7 Dakota
8 Sisseton, Mdewakanton
9 Wahpekute
10 Wahpeton
11 Winnebago
12 Miniconjou
13 Brule, Oglala
14 Ponca
15 Yankton
16 Omaha
17 Oto
18 Iowa
19 Missouri
20 Osage
21 Kansa
22 Quapaw
23 Moneton
24 Manahoac, Saponi
25 Nahyssan
26 Monacan
27 Tutelo
28 Eno - Adshusheer, Occaneechi
29 Shakori, Shoccoree
30 Cheraw - Yadkin
31 Keyauwee, Sissipahaw, Sugaree, Waxhaw, Woccon
32 Cape Fear
33 Catawba, Congaree, Wateree
34 Pedee, Waccamaw, Winyaw
35 Santee, Sewee
36 Ofo
37 Biloxi-Moctobi

 Tanoan

1 Jemez
2 Picuris, Taos
3 Nambe, Pojoaque, San Ildefonso, San Juan Santa Clara, Tesuque
4 Pecos
5 Isleta, Piro, Sandia, Tigua
6 Manso

 Timucua

1 Icafui Yui, Saturiwa, Tacatacuru
2 Potano, Yustaga
3 Acuera, Freshwater Indians, Ocale, Utina
4 Mococo, Pohoy, Tocobaga
5 Surruque
6 Calusa
7 Ais, Guacata
8 Tekesta

 Tonkawan

1 Tonkawa
2 Aranama

 Tsimshian

1 Gitksan, Niska
2 Tsimshian

 Tlingit

1 Yakutat
2 Gonaho
3 Chilkat
4 Auk
5 Taku
6 Huna
7 Killisnoo
8 Sitka
9 Kake
10 Stikine
11 Henya, Klawak, Kuju
12 Sanya, Tongas

 Tunican

1 Grigra, Koroa, Tiou, Tunica, Yazoo
2 Akokisa, Bidai
3 Atakapa
4 Chitimacha, Opelousa
5 Chawasha Washa

 Uto-Aztecan

1 Northern Paiute
2 Northern Shoshone – Lemhi
3 Bannock
4 Eastern Shoshone (Wind River)
5 Western Shoshone – Gosiute
6 Pahvant
7 Yampa
8 Mono or Owens Valley Paiute
9 Tübatulabal
10 Panamint
11 Southern Paiute
12 Wiminuche
13 Muache
14 Capote
15 Tataviam
16 Alliklik, Kawaiisu, Kitanemuk
17 Chemehuevi
18 Fernandeño, Gabrielino
19 Juaneño, Luiseño
20 Cahuilla, Cupeño, Serrano
21 Vanyume
22 Hopi
23 Pima
24 Quahatika, Sobaipuri
25 Papago
26 Comanche Sobaipuri

 Wakashan

1 Kitamat, Kitlope
2 China Hat
3 Bella Bella
4 Wikeno
5 Nohuntsitk, Somehulitk
6 Kwakiutl
7 Koskimo, Nawiti
8 Nimpkish
9 Nootka
10 Makah, Ozette

 Yuchi

1 Yuchi

 Yuki

1 Coast Yuki, Huchnom, Yuki
2 Lile'ek, Wappo

Zuni

1 Zuni

SETTLING THE HEMISPHERE

"WHEN WE SAW SO MANY CITIES AND VILLAGES BUILT BOTH
ON THE WATER AND DRY LAND ... WE COULD NOT RESIST OUR
ADMIRATION ... BECAUSE OF THE HIGH TOWERS, CUES (PYRAMIDS)
AND OTHER BUILDINGS, ALL OF MASONRY, WHICH ROSE FROM
THE WATER. SOME OF OUR SOLDIERS ASKED IF (IT) WAS A DREAM."
BERNAL DIAZ, WITH CORTES, VIEWING TENOCHTITLAN IN 1519.

Recent archaeological finds have forced historians to reassess the past in South America. The various Mississippian mound civilizations in North America are well known, as are the Hohokam and the Anasazi cultures. Olmec, Maya, Zapotec, Teotihuacan, Toltec, and Aztec cultures of Mesoamerica are likewise well documented. This area, which covered southeast Mexico, Guatemala, Belize, El Salvador, and parts of Honduras, Nicaragua, and Costa Rica, was a region of cultural interaction despite differences in topography that range from volcanic heights to coastal plains, and humid rainforest to dry northern deserts. The ethnic jigsaw of the area borrowed ideas and designs from its several components in complex sequential, and parallel social and political developments. Monumental architecture, building design, and urbanization characterize Mesoamerica. Human sacrifice coexisted with sophisticated astronomical observations and hieroglyphic writing.

Similarly, the various Andean civilizations are well known: Chavin, Moche, Huari, Chimu, and Inca. However, new archaeological finds show that historians still have much to uncover.

New discoveries at Huanca de la Luna, a citadel at the heart of the Moche empire, led Santiago Uceda, director of the Museum of Trujillo, to state, "We believe we have come across the legacy of what can be called the earliest and most sophisticated of the pre-Columbian peoples." However, an

archaeological dig at Caral in the Supe Valley, 120 miles (193 kilometers) north of Lima, uncovered a number of sites dating back to 2670 BC. Other mysteries are unfolding elsewhere according to an exhibition on Amazonian civilization at the British Museum. Furthermore, over 153 square miles (500 square kilometers) of artificial earthworks, identified as fish weirs, have been uncovered by Dr. Clark L. Erickson of the University of Pennsylvania. These are situated at Baures in the eastern lowlands of Bolivia, known as the Llanos de Mojos.

The ancient city of Caral in the Supe Valley, Peru. In the foreground are the temple and amphitheater, while in the background, several pyramids wait to give up their secrets. This amazing site is providing archaeologists with a new insight into South American peoples.

Firstly, Caral. The site occupies a 150–170-acre (60–70-hectare) site comprising six platform mounds surrounding a huge plaza. The largest mound is 500 feet (150 meters) long, 450 feet (140 meters) wide, and 60 feet (20 meters) tall. The architecture has courtyards, rooms, and sunken plazas, suggesting a ritual center. Symmetrical staircases exist, and there is a residential area consisting of 110 acres (45 hectares). Caral is as large as any other world third-millennium site, excluding Sumeria. The carbon dating suggests that Caral arose at the same time as ancient Egypt and Sumer. Caral is so old that it might be called "the mother city," which fed all later Andean civilizations up to the Incas. The buildings show no sign of there being kings, but some class society probably developed to organize the monumental architecture. The mounds and sunken plazas are found frequently in younger South American sites. Caral is important

A mural depicting a Moche decapitator, discovered at Huaca de la Luna, Peru.

because of its size and nearby contemporary sites suggesting a large population in the Supe Valley. Caral itself might have housed as many as 3,000 people.

The Supe Valley is easy to irrigate, which may account for Caral's location. Agriculture produced squash, beans, and cotton. Remains of guava, peppers, avocados, and potatoes have been unearthed too. However, the civilization was pre-ceramic, and neither pottery nor grain have been found, suggesting that Caral was economically different to later civilizations. Instead, anchovy and sardine traces have been discovered in desiccated human feces.

Apparently, cotton was traded with coastal dwellers in exchange for fish and clams. The cotton would be woven into fishing nets. Evidence suggests that Caral was a trading center based upon an early division of labor. Caral supports the theories of archaeologist Michael Moseley, who argued that complex societies evolved first in coastal areas; the orthodox view is that civilizations did not arise until the ceramic period allowed grain cultivation, and seeds to be cooked and stored in pottery vessels. Mollusc shells from the Amazonian rainforests are present, and in one sunken plaza, capable of holding hundreds of people, were found thirty-two flutes made from pelican and condor bones, and thirty-seven cornets carved from deer and llama bones.

Much of Caral is still buried, and some archaeologists think that the Supe culture could be older than 3000 BC. Caral arose at the same time as Middle Eastern civilizations in a parallel development of class societies emerging from tribal ones. Interestingly, no weapons have been found at Caral. Jonathan Haas, curator of anthropology at the Field Museum of Natural History in Chicago, claims, "What we are learning from Caral is going to rewrite the way we think about the development of early Andean civilization."

The desert empire of the Moche flourished on Peru's northern coast from approximately AD 1 to 750. Early Moche developed in the coastal valleys around Trujillo, and by AD 400 reached from Chira Valley in the north to the Huarney Valley in the south. About 15,000 Moche inhabited the civilization, and they built monumental adobe structures, irrigation canals, and terraced fields. The Pyramid of the Sun (Huaca del Sol) is 131 feet (40 meters) high and some 1,148 feet (350 meters) long. Moche artisans wrought fine gold, silver, and copper artifacts, while ceramics often involved stirrup-spout vessels.

Moche religion involved art and iconography, which was painted on walls and illustrated ceremonial sacrifices. Ritual coca leaf chewing is depicted, as are battle scenes and the victims of beheading. The major god of the Moche had feline canines and a belt with snake heads. Moche civilization ended perhaps due to inundations by a sand sheet or an abrupt climatic change, like those associated with El Niño, the warm-water currents from the Pacific that bring raised temperatures and torrential rain. In

1996, the remains of seventy men, women, and children were found in a mass grave; this may have been a ritual killing by priests to appease the rain gods.

Moche finds suggest that Mexican Aztecs, Peruvian Incas, and Guatemalan Mayas were no more advanced than the Moche. Santiago Uceda's archaeologists began digging a new pyramid-citadel at Sipan and, after two years, they unearthed walls decorated with geometric figures, ornate jewelry, gold, and cloaks studded with precious stones. Sixty plates, vases, and jars used in funeral rites were found. Other aspects of moche life were displayed. The tombs of three warriors were opened, and their inhabitants were at least 6 feet (2 meters) tall, whereas the average height of a Moche man was between 4 feet 9 inches and 5 feet 7 inches (1.45 and 1.70 meters). Apparently, elite tall warriors were chosen to fight ritually while being revered as deities. The loser was killed, and the victor given the right to wear a cloak made from puma hides, decorated with feathers, emeralds, other precious stones, and gold shields. The greatest warriors could wear bat masks. The Moche also ate human flesh and drank the victim's blood, mixed with rainwater, to prolong life. Murals display a warrior with the title, "Ai-Apaec" (Strangler), who was always present when priests beheaded and cut up human bodies as offerings to the gods.

The third archaeological development has been the recent assessment of the landscape in the Llanos de Mojos. There, one can find the apparent remains of transportation canals, pyramid-style mounds, elevated causeways, raised agricultural fields, and groups of unusual, zigzag ridges dispersed over the savannah. Several contemporary researchers, among them Clark Erickson, believe these

The Court of the Thousand Columns at Chichén Itzá, in the Yucatan Peninsula, Mexico. These Mayan ruins originally supported a roof for what is thought to have been a great meeting hall.

supported relatively dense populations and elaborate cultures. These earthworks were abandoned by unknown peoples between AD 1400 and 1700. Perhaps European diseases, possibly smallpox, filtered in and destroyed the populations.

The Llanos contains deep alluvial deposits from which a series of mounds were built near Baures and joined by causeways. One forested mound (loma), Ibibaté, is 20 feet (6 meters) higher than the surrounding land. Its soil is filled with pottery fragments; some lomas contain 10–30 feet (3–10 meters) of sherds. Ibibaté is a pair of mounds connected by a short earth wall. Earthen causeways radiate out like roads from the mound toward other mounds. These causeways are about 3 feet (1 meter) high, up to 15 feet (5 meters) wide, are perfectly straight, and are bordered by narrow canals. The lomas were probably small in the beginning, but grew through accumulated garbage and collapsed houses, much like mounds in Palestine.

Erickson claims that these Llanos communities began 3,000–5,000 years ago, and the village cultures built thousands of miles of artificial earth walls and canals, supported by a sophisticated farming system. Around Baures, a series of long, low, zigzag walls were built some 2–2.5 miles (3–5 kilometers) long. Erickson believes these to be fish weirs that were used when the rainy season covered the savannah with up to 2 feet (0.6 meter) of standing water. Narrow channels up to 9 feet (3 meters) long open at angles in the zigzag. Erickson says that woven nets could be used to harvest fish and shellfish at these points. The openings also funneled fish into manmade ponds up to 98 feet (30 meters) across. The weirs are piled high with apple snail shells; the ponds still fill up with fish, which seethe in the dry season.

Erickson's ideas have generated heated debate among archaeologists. Betty Meggers claims that large, complex societies could not exist in Amazonia. Others state that the mounds were made by natural forces, and some claim that the earthworks were probably constructed by a higher culture, likely Andean. Erickson has been criticized because the earthen structures could only be built by a coercive, centralized power with a hierarchical division of labor. He contends that horizontally-linked societies with bonds of kinship, alliances, and informal modes of cooperation could build such earthworks over generations of time. Archaeologist Anna C. Roosevelt believes that fish, and an abundance of fruit, nuts, and edible palm could create a more egalitarian society, such as Native American cultures in the Pacific Northwest and California. Erickson also criticizes Meggers for extrapolating interpretations after fixating on one site at a time, whereas he argues that the entire landscape should be treated as an artifact. In England, long, raised, parallel ridges over miles of lowland can be seen, the result of Anglo-Saxon plowing techniques. Here, the English landscape is indeed an archaeological landscape. As Erickson says about the Llanos, "The raised fields are all aligned in a north–south direction. The landscape is telling us something."

Finally, evidence now exists of a fully operational forest civilization on the Brazilian Amazon. This highly developed Stone Age culture has left few remains except skeletons stored in humanoid ceramic jars. Also evident are decorated tangas, ceramic covers like bikini bottoms, tied on with cords. This civilization lasted some 8,000 years and ended after Europeans arrived in the sixteenth century. Several million people lived here and worked in the rainforest without destroying it; they even managed certain tree varieties according to archaeologists. Stands of the same tree appear around rich, black soil deposits

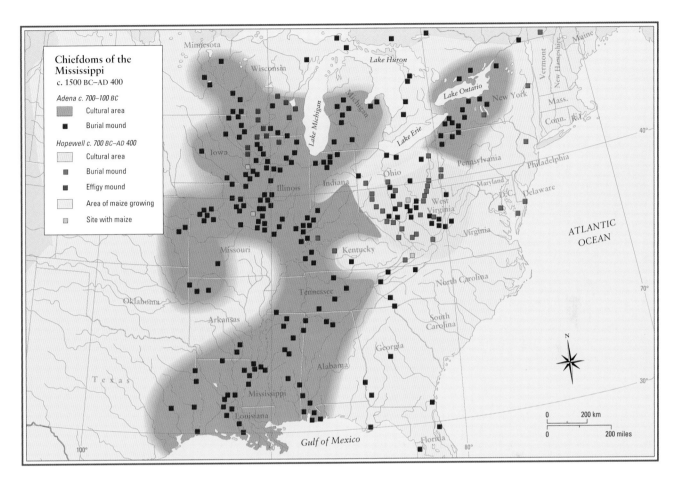

Chiefdoms of the Mississippi
c. 1500 BC–AD 400

Adena c. 700–100 BC

◼ Cultural area

■ Burial mound

Hopewell c. 700 BC–AD 400

◩ Cultural area

■ Burial mound

■ Effigy mound

▨ Area of maize growing

□ Site with maize

where villages once existed, and where incoming Brazilian farmers like to raise crops.

The population spread thickly along the rivers. Archaeologist Eduardo Neves thinks that towns were often horseshoe-shaped arrangements of thatched wooden dwellings that were aligned north–south to face eastward-flowing rivers. Most villages were located on bluffs, raising them above potential floodwaters and facilitating defense. Roosevelt runs a long-term research project on the region and maintains that Santarém was the center of a great chiefdom in the heart of Amazonia, which acquired power over a large territory between the tenth and sixteenth centuries. Her view is that several chiefs unified and ruled an area of approximately 8,880 square miles (23,000 square kilometers). Riverine chiefdoms were linked together to exchange ideas and trade goods, which might explain the stylistic similarities seen between Santarém pottery and other types from areas of northern South America.

Early European accounts of the Amazon, especially Portuguese, tell of very large and numerous villages, and admit that Amazonian political and territorial power bases with authority over surrounding areas were well constructed. They also admired the sophistication of the pottery. Thus, it seems that from early European encounters, the civilizations were well established, with a developed social order, well-organized leadership, a strong belief system, and an efficient manner of exploiting local resources. So, these Amazonian peoples existed, but possessed no written history save for myth and oral tradition. Then, European diseases struck and the people were wiped out.

Rivers provided early civilizations with "highways" and essential trade routes. In North America, the mighty Mississippi and its tributaries allowed the spread of the Adena and Hopewell.

THE COMPETING THEORIES OF MIGRATION

WHILE MOST EXPERTS BELIEVE THAT HUMANS ARRIVED IN NORTH AMERICA BY LAND BRIDGE FROM ASIA, THERE ARE DIFFERENT OPINIONS AS TO EXACTLY WHEN THIS OCCURRED.

H istorians and geologists suggest that a bridge—the Bering Land Bridge—connected Siberia and North America at various times during the Ice Ages. Such a link would have allowed animals and prehistoric peoples to cross from one continent to the other. This thesis applying to people was first mooted by the sixteenth-century Jesuit missionary José de Acosta. Most anthropologists, historical linguists, and archaeologists accept that Native Americans are descended from northeastern Asians, but argue about when the migrations occurred. Some are of the opinion that an initial colonization took place less than 15,000 years ago—that is the main Amerind group, followed by Na-Dene (Athapascan speakers), and then Inuit and Aleut. However, other scholars maintain that human beings arrived earlier in America, but there is no concrete evidence to support this, other than disputed archaeological finds. Biological anthropologists have studied blood groups and dental characteristics, and agree with the three migration waves. These Paleo-Indians were fully modern when they arrived with their Stone-Age toolkits; no evidence has ever been found to support the presence of Neanderthal or other humanoid types. So far, the earliest distinctive American-style artifacts are the Clovis stone blades.

Arguments continue, since campfire remains in

Thor Heyerdahl's Ra II showed that Egyptians could have crossed the Atlantic.

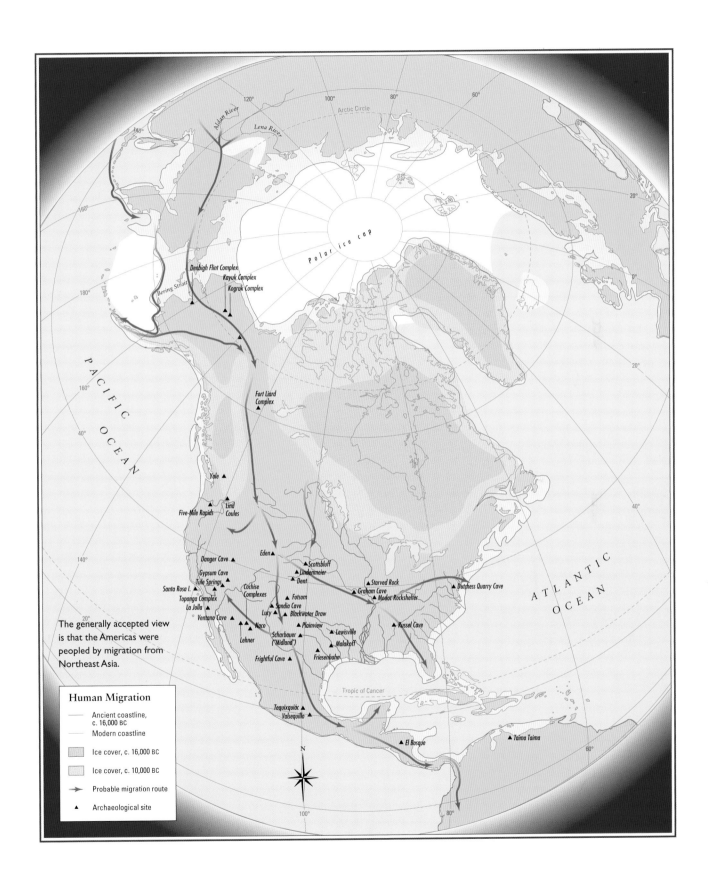

The generally accepted view is that the Americas were peopled by migration from Northeast Asia.

Human Migration

Ancient coastline, c. 16,000 BC

Modern coastline

Ice cover, c. 16,000 BC

Ice cover, c. 10,000 BC

Probable migration route

Archaeological site

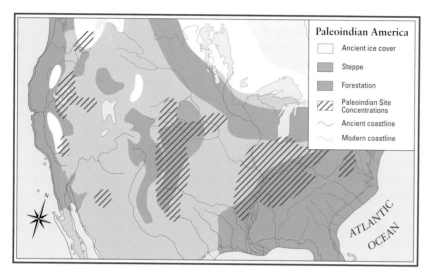

Paleoindian America
- Ancient ice cover
- Steppe
- Forestation
- Paleoindian Site Concentrations
- Ancient coastline
- Modern coastline

Nomadic groups known as paleoindians were the first to populate North America. They spread across the continent.

The various Mississippian cultures are characterized by the mounds they built. These have been found throughout the eastern half of the country.

Adena, Hopewell, and Mississippi Mounds

▲ Major Adena or Hopewell mounds, 1000 BC–AD 1000

▲ Major Mississippian mounds, AD 700–1700

the Valley of Mexico have been radiocarbon dated to 21,000 BC, and bone tools found in the Yukon, Canada, date to 22,000 BC. To confuse matters further, the British Broadcasting Corporation (BBC) showed an archaeological TV documentary that argued that Negroid Australian aborigine types existed in Latin America, especially in Tierra del Fuego, where such genes are to be found, as if an earlier or even later group arriving by sea had been pushed southward to near extinction.

The presence of Vikings at L'Anse aux Meadows, in Newfoundland, demonstrates early transoceanic contact, while Thor Heyerdahl displayed other possibilities in his *Kon-tiki* and *Ra* expeditions. The balsa raft *Kon-tiki* was sailed from Peru to Polynesia, and the *Ra II* was a papyrus vessel that voyaged from North Africa to Barbados in 57 days. The trip was undertaken to support a theory that ancient Egyptians could have reached South America to found Latin American civilizations. The voyage would also please those sceptics who feel that no Native Americans could have developed the Adena and Hopewell Mound cultures.

Other theories of contacts and culture mixes have been suggested. The physical features of Northwest Pacific coast peoples are more Oriental than elsewhere, and notions exist that Japanese could have reached America via the Japanese Current or Hawaii. Also, Tlingit warrior armor has a Japanese appearance. Japanese Jomon pottery resembles Ecuadorean Valdivia pottery. Even the Indus Valley has been linked to Middle America through the similarities between the Asian game Parcheesi and Patolli. The Atlantic, some argue, might have been crossed by Egyptians, Libyans, and Phoenicians, owing to apparent language and inscription similarities. African arrivals in the Olmec culture region could explain the Negroid aspect of Olmec sculpture. Even the Basques are alleged to have reached Pennsylvania and the Gulf of St. Lawrence, because ancient grave markers resemble certain Native American ones.

More unusual contacts are alleged. Clearly, the Lost Tribe of Israel theory is nonsense, but the sixth-century Irish monk St. Brendan was believed to have landed in America. More recently, in 1996, two young men found a human skull and bones at Kennewick in Washington State. The local coroner ordered radiocarbon and DNA analysis of the nearly complete skeleton. The man was 40–55 years old, about 5 feet 9 inches (1.76 meters) tall, and allegedly his skull was of Caucasian style rather than Native American. However, the dental characteristics showed a possible relationship with south Asian peoples. The man had a stone spear point in his hip, and radiocarbon dating of the bone showed its age to be 9,200–9,500 years.

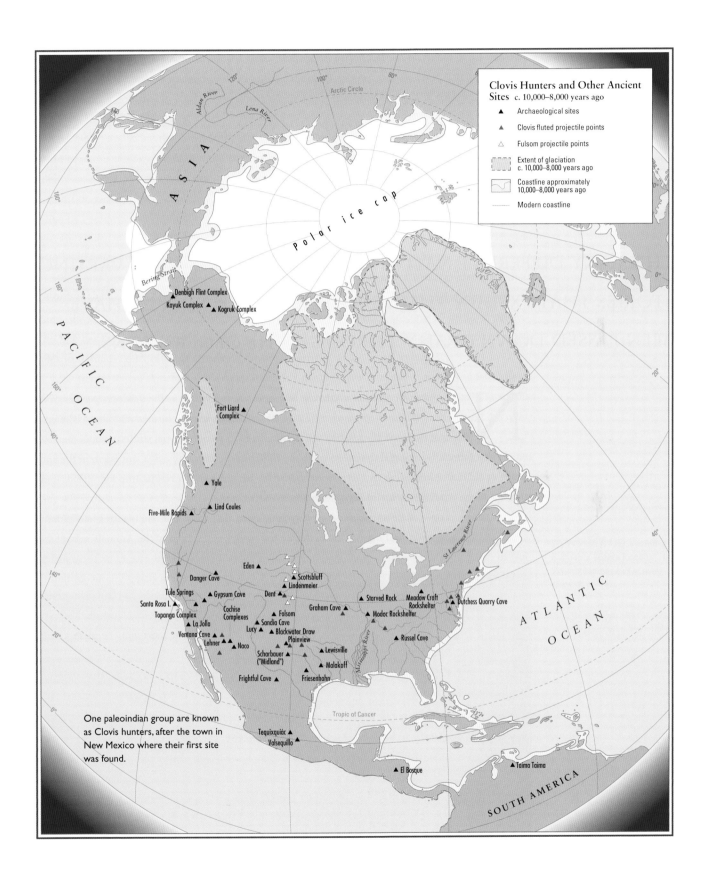

Clovis Hunters and Other Ancient Sites c. 10,000–8,000 years ago

▲ Archaeological sites

▲ Clovis fluted projectile points

△ Fulsom projectile points

⬚ Extent of glaciation c. 10,000–8,000 years ago

⬚ Coastline approximately 10,000–8,000 years ago

--- Modern coastline

ASIA

Aldan River

Lena River

Arctic Circle

Polar ice cap

Bering Strait

PACIFIC OCEAN

Denbigh Flint Complex
Kayuk Complex ▲ Kogruk Complex

Fort Liard Complex

Yale

Five-Mile Rapids ▲ ▲ Lind Coules

Eden ▲
Scottsbluff
Danger Cave ▲ Lindenmeier
Tule Springs ▲ Gypsum Cave ▲ Dent ▲ ▲
Santa Rosa I. ▲ Cochise Complexes ▲ Graham Cave ▲ Starved Rock
Topanga Complex ▲ Folsom ▲ ▲ Modoc Rockshelter Meadow Croft Rockshelter
▲ La Jolla Sandia Cave ▲ Dutchess Quarry Cave
Ventana Cave ▲ Lucy ▲ Blackwater Draw
Lehner ▲ ▲ Naco ▲ Plainview ▲ Russel Cave
Scharbauer ("Midland") ▲ Lewisville
Frightful Cave ▲ ▲ Molakoff
Friesenhahn

St Lawrence River

Mississippi River

ATLANTIC OCEAN

Tropic of Cancer

Tequixquiac ▲
Valsequillo ▲

El Bosque ▲ ▲ Taima Taima

SOUTH AMERICA

One paleoindian group are known as Clovis hunters, after the town in New Mexico where their first site was found.

THE RISE OF AGRICULTURE

THE DEVELOPMENT OF AGRICULTURE AMONG NATIVE AMERICANS GAVE RISE TO PERMANENT SETTLEMENTS AND THE DEVELOPMENT OF IMPORTANT TECHNIQUES, SUCH AS IRRIGATION.

The transition from hunting and gathering plants to growing crops for food took place over thousands of years, and occurred during the Archaic Period, c. 7000–2000 BC. By 7000 BC, Mesoamerican nomadic hunters were growing vegetables like squash and chillis near campsites. Dry cave sites at Tehuacan and Romero's Cave at Tamaulipas provide evidence of cultivated beans, pumpkins, and gourds as far back as 7000 BC, while maize can be dated to around 3000 BC. Gradually, 1-inch (2.5-centimeter) maize cobs were developed into more modern variants, and Mesoamerican civilizations flourished around this food supply.

By 3000 BC, Native Americans in North America were cultivating local plants, such as sunflower, goosefoot, pigweed, knotweed, maygrass, and marsh elder. These provided seeds, starchy flour, and tubers. Gourds and squash, native to the Eastern Woodlands, were grown too. Between 2500 BC and AD 400, Native North Americans seriously began to propagate and produce plants. This was principally a woman's job and probably enhanced female status. Quite when Mesoamerican plants spread into the Southwest is debatable. Bat Cave evidence suggests 3500 BC, but other sites are consistent with 1500 BC. Certainly, the Hohokam tradition may have been established by 300 BC, and the Mogollon by AD 700. The Anasazi were established by 185 BC, so Archaic hunter-gatherers changed into the Pueblo societies of the Southwest.

Southwestern farmers grew maize, squash, and several bean species, all originating in Mexico, as did cotton and amaranth seeds from pigweed. Indians also cultivated agave, little barley grass, tobacco, cholla, dropseed, lamb's quarter, panic grass, and devil's claw cactus, the last being used for basketry. Irrigation was essential for germination and cultivation. Furthermore, effective food storage techniques were developed.

The Eastern Woodlands farmers (2000–1500 BC) had domesticated lamb's quarter, marsh elder, squash, and sunflower before maize was introduced from the Southwest around AD 200. Maize became increasingly important between AD 800 and 1100, and this culture shift was accompanied by the growth of towns, class societies, and fortified civic ceremonial centers, especially among members of the Mississippian culture.

Eventually, maize cultivation was adopted from Florida to the Great Lakes, and the north benefited from a maize variety requiring a shorter growing season. The shift to maize in the northern regions was accepted between AD 1000 and 1500, and varied in time from sub-region to sub-region. These so-called "Oneota" groups, Indian bands involved in the transition, established fortified agricultural villages along lake shores, major waterways, and wetlands. However, agriculture was just one economic strategy. Archaeological evidence indicates the hunting of buffalo, elk, deer, and sometimes raccoon, muskrat, and beaver. Agriculture allowed population increases and resource competition between villages. Thus, pressure existed to confederate to secure zones of influence; the Iroquois are one example. Areas such as Maryland and Virginia developed small economic village units, some of which were organized into the Powhatan paramount state.

Some qualifications should be made about farming. In the East, calories and nutrients came from domesticated plants, while in the Southwest, the most nutritious food was provided by wild plants. Also, the East, with its temperate climate, was easy to farm. The arid Southwest needed constant water management by means of canals, ditches, reservoirs, and dams. These were used to irrigate mulched gardens, terraced gardens, and fields. Also, the differing regions developed various methods of crop protection. The Mohawks and others drenched their seeds with hellebore to poison crows, while the Navajo dribbled squash with a mixture of urine and goat's milk to protect plants from the depredations of clinch bugs and cockroaches. With the domestication of maize came religious rites to secure harvests; here was the Hopi Niman Kachina ceremony, and the Iroquois Green Corn Ceremony.

An early illustration depicting the cultivation of maize (sometimes called Indian corn). In the Southwest, maize became an important ingredient of the Native American diet.

THE INCA EMPIRE

THE INCAS CREATED A SOPHISTICATED SOCIETY, NOTED FOR ITS WORK ETHIC, ITS ARCHITECTURE, ITS AGRICULTURAL PRACTICES, AND ITS CRAFTSMANSHIP.

Opposite: Huayna Picchu towers above the ruins of the Incas' famed mountain fortress of Machu Picchu.

The Inca Empire spread along the Pacific Coast of South America and was centered on the Andes.

U ntil recently, the world acknowledged the Inca Empire as the most important historical Andean civilization. Interest has focused on the Temple of the Sun at Cuzco, or the mountain fortress of Machu Picchu, with its temple-pyramid, houses, and terraced fields. The Incas, therefore, are the terminal point in a long process, accepted by conventional wisdom, that began about 2500 BC. Apparently, hunter-gatherer groups, who occupied seasonal fishing villages, established permanent settlements along the Peruvian coast and coastal valleys. These isolated communities were unified occasionally by the Chavin culture (900–200 BC), the Moche (c. AD 1–750), the Huari (AD 650–800), the Chimu in the fourteenth and fifteenth centuries, and then the expansionist Inca.

However, an archaeological dig at Caral, in the Supe Valley, 120 miles (190 kilometers) north of Lima, uncovered a number of new sites. Caral dates from 2600 BC and occupies a 200-acre (80-hectare) site comprising six platform mounds surrounding a huge plaza. The architecture has stairs, rooms, and courtyards. Agriculture produced squash, beans, and cotton, all grown with the aid of irrigation. Remains of peppers, avocados, and potatoes were unearthed too. Apparently, cotton was woven into fishing nets and traded with coastal people for sardines, anchovies, and clams. Pottery and grain were not present, suggesting that Caral was a trading center based upon an early division of labor. Mollusc shells from the Amazonian rainforests were also present, as were flutes made from pelican and condor bones. Much of Caral is still buried, and some archaeologists think that the Supe culture could be older than 3000 BC. Dating suggests that Caral arose at the same time as ancient Egypt and Sumeria in a parallel development of class societies emerging from tribal ones. Finally, no weapons have yet been found at Caral.

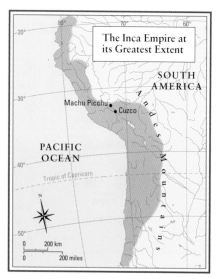

The Inca Empire at its Greatest Extent

SOUTH AMERICA

Machu Picchu
Cuzco

PACIFIC OCEAN

Tropic of Capricorn

Andes Mountains

0   200 km
0   200 miles

Caral, then, may be the "mother city" that led to all later Andean civilizations up to the Incas. The latter were a small, aggressive tribe living in central Peru until moving to the Cuzco Valley around AD 1000. They sought to dominate neighboring tribes until the fifteenth century, when they began rapid expansion, conquering and accepting tribute from one valley tribe after another. Pachacuti Inca Yupanqui started the process, which reached its heyday under Huayna Capac (reigned 1493–1525). The multitribal and multilingual empire, using Quechua as a common tongue, stretched from southern Colombia, across Ecuador and Peru, to Bolivia, and northern parts of Argentina and Chile. In 1532, the Spaniard Francisco Pizarro landed in Peru with 180 men during a civil war between contenders for the Inca throne. Pizarro conquered the empire by controlling the Sapa Inca Atahualpa, whom he had strangled in 1533. The Spanish then built Lima as a capital, supplanting Cuzco.

At its height, the Inca Empire was noteworthy for its sophisticated political and administrative system. Its hierarchical society, an agricultural theocracy ruled by the Sapa Inca, the "incarnation" of the sun, placed all subjects under strict control—laziness could be punished by death, because work was being stolen from the Sapa Inca. State records of grain stores, population, troops, and taxes were kept by quipas, a set of color-coded cords with knots tied for accounting divisions. The empire was also characterized by irrigation and aqueducts, monumental stone architecture, and a road network that included suspension bridges, sometimes as long as 330 feet (100 meters).

The Incas grew maize, potatoes, yucca roots, peppers, avocados, peanuts, and lima beans. Notable in Inca society was medicine. Priest-doctors could cure dysentery, ulcers, eye problems, toothache, and lice infestations. Herbal remedies, including quinine, were highly effective. Surgeon-priests could amputate when necessary, after patients were anesthetized by chewing coca leaves, hypnosis, or drinking chicha beer. Even blood transfusions were performed, aided by the fact that all Incas were O rhesus positive.

Inca craftsmen were known for their jewelry—especially large ear-spools—pottery, and metalsmithing in silver and gold. Animals were used for pack transport, wool, and food (llama, alpaca, and the guinea pig). Weavers employed cotton and wool from the llama and alpaca, and from the wild vicuña or guanaco.

THE ANASAZI

IN THE FOUR CORNERS REGION, WHERE THE STATES OF UTAH, COLORADO, ARIZONA, AND NEW MEXICO MEET, LIVED THE ANASAZI, WHO BECAME VERY INFLUENTIAL IN THE SOUTHWEST.

At about 100 BC, the Anasazi culture became distinct from the Mogollon and Hohokam. Up to AD 750, they lived in pithouses while they developed and refined their agricultural and ceramic skills. Absorbing others' traditions, they produced a startling black-on-white pottery style, making drinking cups with handles, wide-shouldered water jars (*ollas*), animal effigies, and plates. Their baskets were beautifully crafted, and the name Basketmaker Culture was applied to the early Anasazi. Sometimes, Yucca fibers were interwoven with other plant materials to create geometric designs. Some baskets were painted, while others were covered with a layer of pitch or resin to make watertight containers.

After AD 750, the Anasazi began building above-ground structures, but kept the pithouse as a kiva, used by men for ceremonial and social purposes. The pueblo appeared, buildings being constructed from stone and adobe cement, or just adobe bricks. Houses began to have shared walls and were built on top of each other, the inhabitants moving from one level to another by ladders. As levels were stepped back in terraces, the roof of one could be used as the front yard of another. The most well-known Anasazi sites are at Mesa Verde, Canyon de Chelly, and Chaco Canyon.

The Chaco Canyon settlements spread over 53,000 square miles (137,000 square kilometers) of the San Juan water system and comprised 125 known planned towns. Many of these were connected by roads, and all were served by an extensive irrigation system that watered squash, bean, and cornfields. Archaeologists have argued that Chaco Canyon controlled trade in food and turquoise, and that the population gradually accumulated wealth with bought goods and resources. Social distinctions grew, those living in large houses being distinct from those inhabiting scattered, small villages.

An Anasazi "black-on-white" *olla* and redware bowl. This Southwestern culture developed significant ceramic skills.

Communications were provided not only by roads, which sometimes ran 50 miles (80 kilometers) into the interior, but also by signal stations on the mesa tops, using fire, smoke, or reflected light. The Chacoans also built causeways and cut stairways into sheer cliffs. The large Chaco towns were spiritual and ritual centers of pilgrimage, as well as trade centers.

The most impressive town is Pueblo Bonito. Built in a D-shape and covering 2.5 acres (1 hectare), it once contained 800 rooms and thirty kivas. The pueblo, which is linked to seventy-five other settlements, may have been home to 1,200 people. The town comprised four stories within a protective wall, and the different levels could aid defense.

The kiva reflects a belief that people emerged from a former world, which was symbolized by occupants leaving the kiva into full view of the plaza. People descended into this underground world by ladder through the roof smokehole. Set into the floor would be a round, shallow, navel-like *sipapu*, a representation of the place where spiritual access to a deeper world below was possible,

Three major cultures developed in the Southwest: the Anasazi, Hohokam, and Mogollon.

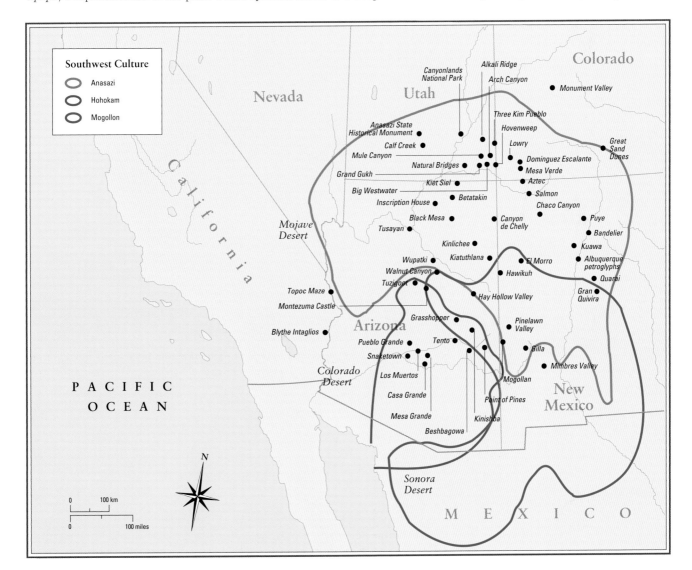

and where Corn Mothers emerged into the world. The Great Kiva at Chetro Ketl, near Pueblo Bonito, is 50 feet (15 meters) across, with an encircling bench, a raised fire container, and masonry vaults.

An Anasazi pueblo in southwestern Colorado, near Cowboy Wash, which dates from the twelfth century, sparked a heated archaeological debate. Seven bodies at the site had been dismembered, the bones being strewn about. Cut marks were found on the bones, suggesting that human flesh had been butchered for cannibal meals. Some bones had burn marks, allegedly from cooking. A coprolite (dried human excrement) contained a protein, myoglobin, apparently from human flesh. No archaeologist has yet provided a totally plausible or acceptable reason for the finds—hunger, site desecration, an isolated incident?

Chaco Canyon had been abandoned by AD 1140, tree-ring tests showing that no new building took place after that date. Severe drought conditions probably drove the people away. A later migration from Mesa Verde to Chaco occurred a century later, but was short-lived; then the Diné (Navajo) moved in during the eighteenth century. The Hopi and Zuni peoples are thought to be descendants of the Anasazi.

Opposite: The ruins of Pueblo Bonito in Chaco Canyon. Spreading over 2.5 acres (1 hectare), the pueblo had around 800 rooms and thirty kivas (pithouses).

Chaco Canyon is thought to have been the political and economic center of the Anasazi culture. It contained a number of settlements spread over an an area of 53,000 square miles (137,00 square kilometers).

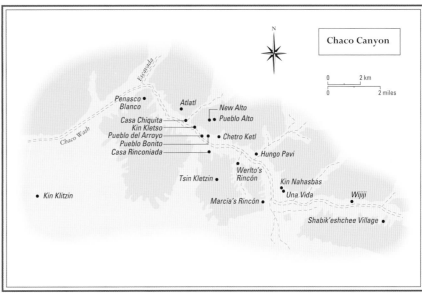

THE MISSISSIPPIANS

CENTERED ON THE GREAT RIVER THAT FLOWS SOUTHWARD
THROUGH THE USA, THE MISSISSIPPIAN CULTURE IS
DISTINGUISHED BY THE FLAT-TOPPED MOUNDS IT ERECTED
WHEN BUILDING ITS TOWNS.

Opposite: Mississippian cultures
spread throughout the drainage
of the great river.

Black burnish pottery
discovered at Moundville.

The Mississippian or Mound Builder Culture flourished between AD 750 and 1500 (or even later) and is characterized by certain distinguishing features. Its pottery was usually tempered with crushed mussel shell, horticulture was maize based, and the major towns comprise series of large, flat-topped mounds, often surrounding a plaza. The organization needed to build the towns was immense, involving a stratified, hierarchical society, probably with hereditary offices. Evidence of this can be found in the records of the Natchez, later destroyed by the French.

The civilization spread along both banks of the Mississippi, from the Gulf of Mexico to Minnesota, and also along such tributaries as the Ohio, Missouri, Tennessee, Arkansas, and Red rivers. The remainder of the region was contained by other river basins along the Gulf and Carolina coasts, from the Neches River in Texas to the Carolina Pee Dee River.

The largest and most interesting Mississippian centers were Cahokia in Illinois; Etowah and Ocmulgee in Georgia; Moundville in Alabama, Spiro in Oklahoma, SunWatch in Ohio; and Nanih Waiya in Mississippi. The entire culture was based on maize production, together with beans and squash. The fields were managed by women, whose main tool was a hoe with a stone, bone, wood, or shell blade.

All of the major settlements have large mounds; Cahokia's Monks Mound covers 16 acres (6.5 hectares) and is 72 feet (22 meters) high.

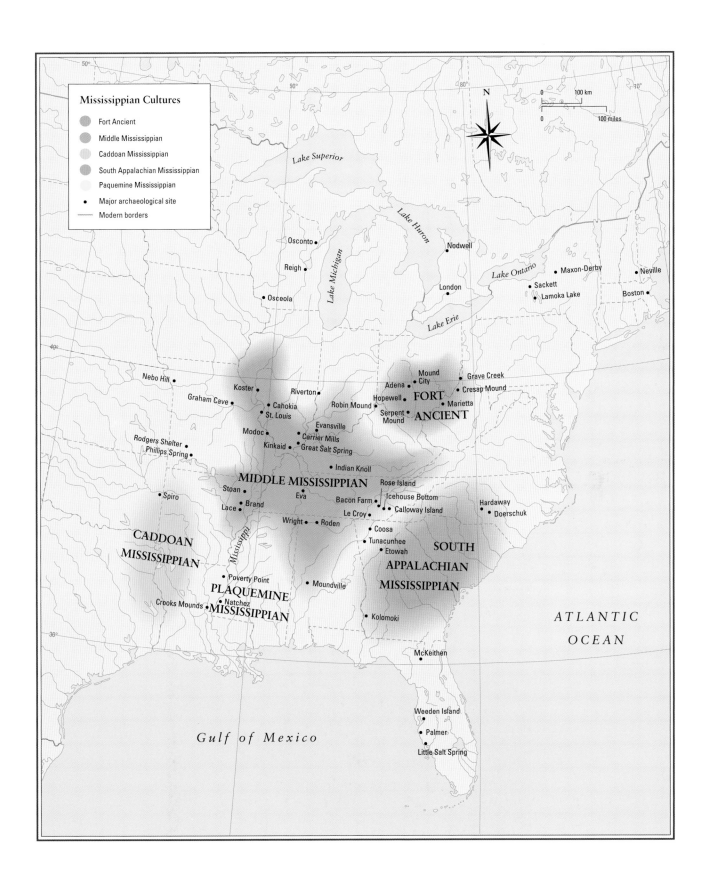

Mississippian Cultures

- Fort Ancient
- Middle Mississippian
- Caddoan Mississippian
- South Appalachian Mississippian
- Paquemine Mississippian
- Major archaeological site
- Modern borders

N

0   100 km
0   100 miles

Lake Superior

Lake Huron

Lake Michigan

Lake Ontario

Lake Erie

Osconto

Reigh

Osceola

Nodwell

London

Maxon-Derby

Sackett

Lamoka Lake

Neville

Boston

Nebo Hill

Koster

Riverton

Mound City

Adena

Grave Creek

Graham Cave

Hopewell

Cresap Mound

Cahokia

Robin Mound

FORT

St. Louis

Serpent Mound

Marietta

ANCIENT

Evansville

Modoc

Carrier Mills

Rodgers Shelter

Kinkaid

Great Salt Spring

Phillips Spring

Indian Knoll

MIDDLE MISSISSIPPIAN

Stoan

Rose Island

Spiro

Eva

Bacon Farm

Icehouse Bottom

Lace

Brand

Hardaway

Le Croy

Calloway Island

Doerschuk

Wright

Roden

Coosa

CADDOAN

Tunacunhee

MISSISSIPPIAN

Etowah

SOUTH

APPALACHIAN

Poverty Point

Moundville

MISSISSIPPIAN

PLAQUEMINE

Crooks Mounds

Natchez

MISSISSIPPIAN

Kolomoki

Mississippi

Mc Keithen

ATLANTIC

OCEAN

Gulf of Mexico

Weeden Island

Palmer

Little Salt Spring

The settlements ranged from under 10 acres (4 hectares) to more than 100 acres (40 hectares), often being surrounded by a fortified palisade and ditch. Encircled by smaller family homes, the wall could separate the social elite from the commoners outside. The mound centers were the focuses of socio-political power; the plazas could encompass feasts, ceremonies, and rituals designed to socially integrate the population. Cahokia is estimated to have held 20–40,000 people. The buildings on mound tops could have been palaces or temples, or have had mortuary functions. Undoubtedly, important leader/priests would have ensured the correct sequences of annual rites to maintain social harmony, respect for the dead, and such forces in the world as the sun and Corn Mothers.

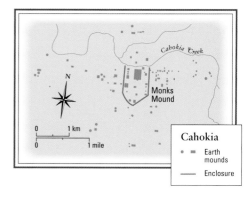

The chief has often been compared with the supreme ruler, the Great Sun of the Natchez, who lived on one mound. Others living on high would have been his mother, the White Woman; his brothers, the Suns, from whom were chosen the war chief and head priests; and his sisters, Woman Suns. Under these select few were the nobles and commoners. When a chief died, his palace would have been razed, more earth added to the mound, and a new building for the next chief constructed. The kinship ties and ritual provided legitimacy and authority over the town, territory, and its people.

The Mississippian culture was also linked by a network of trade routes along the interconnecting river systems. Goods would be readily transported by canoe. Prestige products were important to the elites. Among these were freshwater pearls; Great Lakes and southern Appalachian copper;

The Great Temple Mound at Etowah, Georgia, another major Mississippian site. It was built between AD 1000 and 1500.

hematite; silver from Ontario; chert, a stone capable of producing a sharp edge; galena from the upper Mississippi to make white pigment; Appalachian mica; Ohio flint stones and soapstone pipes; Arkansas quartz; obsidian; bears' teeth; shell beads and shells; shark and alligator teeth; turtle shells; and pottery. Copper was crafted into ritual objects for the elites. Trade in utilitarian tools and everyday objects appears lacking.

Cahokia provides an example of rise and decline between AD 900 and 1400. Covering 5 square miles (13 square kilometers) and incorporating a hundred mounds, the town appears to have one major and several subcommunities. The central enclosed area covers 205 acres (83 hectares) and was fortified. Cahokia was the largest population center north of Mexico.

The people of Cahokia were adept with the bow and arrow, which supplanted the spear and spear thrower, the *atlatl*. The military strength of the culture prevented conquest by Spain, but by the early seventeenth century, Mississippian centers had been abandoned. Overpopulation, climatic deterioration, disease, soil depletion, or warfare might explain the decline; as yet, no archaeologist knows.

Large mounds at Cahokia. There are a hundred in all within an area of 5 square miles (13 square kilometers).

Built by the Hopewell culture on the banks of the Little Miami River, Fort Ancient contains mounds and earth walls.

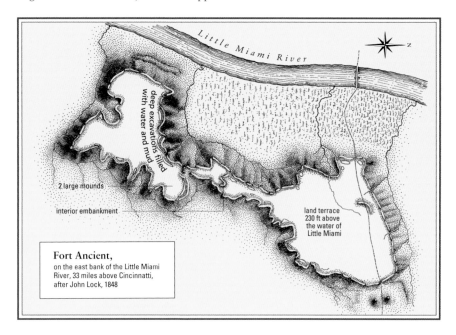

Fort Ancient,
on the east bank of the Little Miami River, 33 miles above Cincinnatti, after John Lock, 1848

People of the Salmon

In the Pacific Northwest, Native peoples utilized wood for housing and other essential items, living on the region's rich diversity of fish, particularly salmon.

The first record of contact between Pacific Northwest Coast Indians and Europeans occurred in 1741, when a Russian explorer, Chirikov, sailed to southeast Alaska. Later, the Spaniard Juan Perez reached the Queen Charlotte Islands in 1774 and traded with Haida Indians. Spaniards arrived in the following year, while James Cook, the British explorer, was there in 1778.

Historians estimate that the Northwest Coast contained a population of at least 130,000 by 1492, making it one of the most populated areas of North America. These Indians were divided into three main groups, but with tremendous linguistic variation between them all. The Tlingit peoples inhabited the far north of the Northwest Coast and its islands. To the south were the Tsimshian Indians along the fjorded coast of British Columbia. Haida-speakers dwelt on the Queen Charlotte Islands and part of Prince of Wales Island. Further south were the various Kwakiutl groups. Elsewhere, Nootkan and other tribes, such as the Makah, hunted whales and seals in the open sea for their meat, using oil rendered from the blubber as a food and food preservative. The Salishan-speakers along the British Columbian coast, and in Washington and western Montana developed twenty-three interlinked languages, split by the Cascade Mountain range into sixteen coastal and seven inland divisions.

All of these tribes benefited from mild winters and large forested areas, which provided wood for board houses and a range of canoe types; by as early as AD 500, wedges and mauls were being used to split boards from red cedars. The large population was supported by runs of Pacific salmon. Five salmon species spawn in upstream rivers, while herring, smelt, and oil-rich candle fish were plentiful, as were shellfish and sea mammals. Society became increasingly stratified, which was marked by material wealth. Some archaeological sites, notably the Makah site at Ozette and that on the Hoko River of the Olympic Peninsula have shown evidence of a rich culture prior to the post-Columbian period.

The Northwest peoples possessed a highly sophisticated knowledge of local woods for house and boat building, weapons, helmets, bowls, canoe paddles, combs, dance helmets, and spirit masks. The Ozette site even shows that the Makah used steel tools before 1492; these probably reached North America by way of Asian vessels that were wrecked after being carried across the Pacific by the Japan current.

The development of a hierarchal society was expressed visually in terms of architectural embellishments and other forms of artwork, such as heraldic totem poles, blankets, basketry hats and containers, and highly-decorated dance capes with mother-of-pearl buttons and cloth appliqué designs, such as whales. Canoes could be painted with heraldic designs; Haida canoe prows bore the images of the Thunderbird, the victor of the heavens and helper of the people, or the Killer Whale, lord of the sea and underworld.

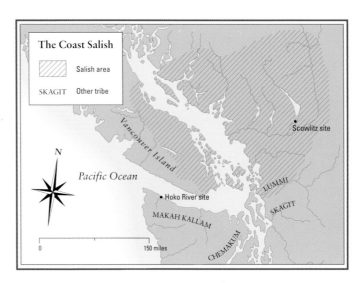

Salishan speakers occupying the region of southwest coast of British Columbia and Washington around Puget Sound are known as the Coast Salish. They speak many languages and dialects.

Spirit masks were naturalistic, portraying specific individuals, or were given moving parts for visual impact. Many naturalistic images, such as the raven, eagle, whale, moon, and weather, have been taken as clan or family crests. Winter was the time for dance societies to celebrate theatrical rites and depict myths through transformation masks, which had strings that revealed a mask within a mask when pulled, allowing Wolf to become Man.

The most well-known art form is the totem pole. These include house posts, commemoration works, and poles that show family and clan crests or historical figures; they might also represent family wealth. Another practice was the potlatch, a ceremony of gift giving that involved feats and dances, which conferred status on the givers and redistributed wealth to improve social harmony; the custom probably originated in marriage gifts and death rituals.

Tlingit totem poles. These ornate, carved structures are a visual embodiment of the tribe's hierarchical society.

Trade Routes and Transport

AS NATIVE AMERICAN CIVILIZATIONS FLOURISHED, THEY BEGAN TO TRADE WITH ONE ANOTHER, USING WATERWAYS AND OTHER TRAILS TO CRISSCROSS THE CONTINENT.

The travois was a popular means of carrying loads. Before the arrival of the horse, Indians used dogs to pull them.

Several long, north–south routes developed in the Mississippi Valley, with links to the regional trade systems of the Pacific, Gulf, and Atlantic coasts. Certain areas, like the western desert and plateau areas, were poor in land routes, while the California mountains largely prevented long journeys. North America was crisscrossed by watercourses, allowing travel by canoes, which were easily portaged around rapids and waterfalls. Land trails followed river valleys or ridges, and it is thought that some were used by animals first.

The Mississippi is the dominant north–south route, and its tributaries provide links between the areas east and west of the river. For example, the Wisconsin, Illinois, and Ohio rivers enter from the east, while the Minnesota, Missouri, and Arkansas rivers flow in from the west. A major east–west route ran down the St. Lawrence, through the Great Lakes to the Grand Portage and onto the Lake of the Woods. Westward from this lake, connections existed via the Yellowstone and Missouri rivers, which eventually reached the Columbia River to the Pacific coast. A nodal point on this route was the Straits of Mackinac, where southward travel was possible across Lakes Huron and Erie. Then, travelers could use the Sandusky and Scioto rivers to reach the Ohio, or could ascend the Maumee, portage to the Wabash, and descend to the Ohio. Moving southward from the Ohio to the Tennessee River, a trader might leave the latter where it bends eastward and follow the trail south to Mobile Bay. Converging north of the bay are the Tombigbee and Alabama rivers, home to many pre-Columbian civilizations, notably the Mobiles at Mauvila, where de Soto slaughtered so many Native Americans.

In the East, a trail ran the length of the Appalachians, from New York to Georgia, while there was a route from the St. Lawrence to New York and the Atlantic via the Richelieu River, Lake Champlain, and the Hudson River. This became an important campaign route during the Anglo-French imperial wars and the American Revolution. Further south, Cuba was linked to Tampa Bay, where a trail ran around Apalachee Bay to Mobile. From there, the Natchez Indians could be reached, also the Arkansas River.

In the Southwest, the Pueblo villages were important focal points near the Rio Grande River. From Texas, a difficult trail followed the Colorado River, then crossed the dry plains. Routes also followed the Red and Arkansas-Canadian rivers to a pass through the Sangria Mountains, which then reached the head of the Rio Grande, with a trail south to Mexico. Trails in today's Idaho and Dakotas were difficult, only becoming really easy with the availability of horses.

Movements into California and the Pacific Coast from the Plains were possible along three routes. In the south, a desert crossing led to the San Diego/Los Angeles region. In the center, passes around Lake Tahoe were used, and in the north, the Klamath River Valley led to the Sacramento River and San Francisco Bay. In the Northwest, the Columbia River was a trading hub; with the Fraser River, it

The canoe was a vital means of transport throughout North America. There were two types: frame and dugout. In the Pacific Northwest, large, seagoing canoes with raised prows were built by the Haida. This painting, Spreading the Canoe, by Bill Holm (1992) depicts a large dugout canoe being shaped by means of steam.

provided access to a huge hinterland. The Willamette River allowed entry into today's Oregon, while
Northwest Pacific Coast Indians used large seagoing canoes to reach other coastal areas and islands.

Modes of transport included the travois and canoe. The travois was an A-frame, the point of which
was fastened to the shoulders of a dog. Netting spread across the frame held household, hunting, or
trade goods. Two basic canoe types are found in North America. Frame canoes were covered by birch
or elder bark, or animal hides. These could be designed to carry between three and forty people. The
other type is the dugout, used along the Northwest Pacific Coast and in eastern woodlands. These were
hollowed out and shaped by steam. Frame canoes were lightweight and relatively easy to portage; after
European trade began, they became the preferred form of water transport. The Pacific Coast dugouts
are particularly exemplified by the red cedar Haida canoes, which had raised, projecting prows that
made them suitable for sea travel and whaling. Swinomish warriors were known to make canoes that
were 50 feet (15 meters) long.

Native Americans fishing from
a frame canoe. These simple
vessels could be covered with
birch or elder bark, or animal
hides. Their light weight made
them easy to carry around falls
and rapids.

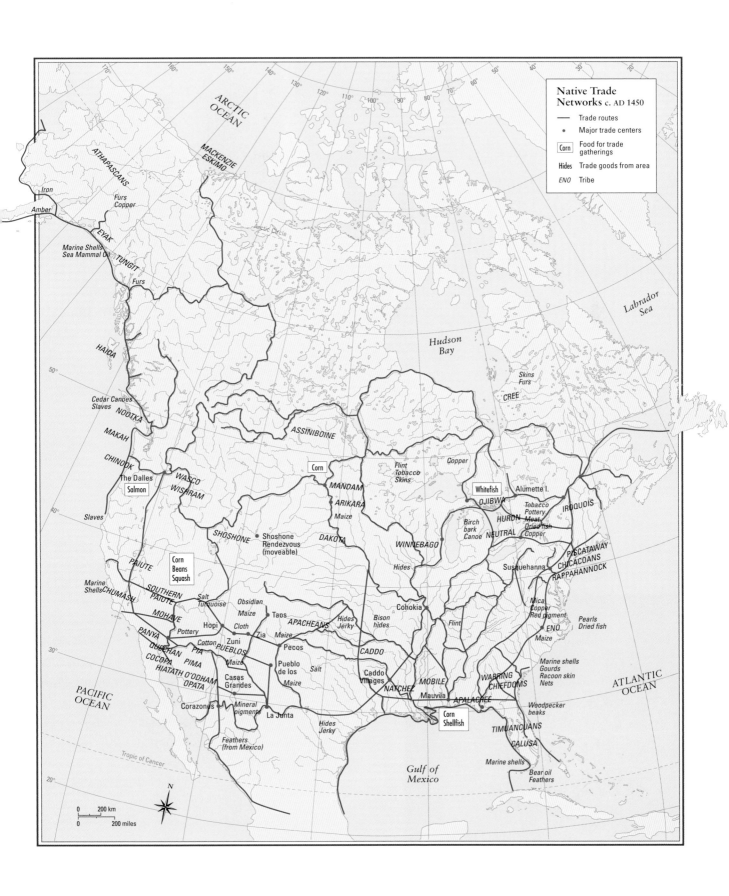

Native Trade Networks c. AD 1450

— Trade routes

• Major trade centers

Corn   Food for trade gatherings

Hides   Trade goods from area

ENO   Tribe

ARCTIC OCEAN

ATHAPASCANS

MACKENZIE ESKIMO

Iron

Amber

Furs
Copper

EYAK

Marine Shells
Sea Mammal Oil

TUNGIT

Furs

HAIDA

Arctic Circle

Hudson
Bay

Labrador
Sea

Skins
Furs

CREE

MAKAH

Cedar Canoes
Slaves

NOOTKA

CHINOOK

ASSINIBOINE

Copper

The Dalles

Salmon

WASCO
WISHRAM

Corn

Flint
Tobacco
Skins

MANDAN

Whitefish

Alumette I.

ARIKARA

OJIBWA

Tobacco
Pottery
Meat
Dried fish
Copper

IROQUOIS

Slaves

Maize

HURON

NEUTRAL

SHOSHONE

Shoshone
Rendezvous
(moveable)

DAKOTA

Birch
bark
Canoe

PAIUTE

Corn
Beans
Squash

WINNEBAGO

Hides

PISCATAWAY

CHICACOANS

Susquehanna

RAPPAHANNOCK

Marine
Shells

CHUMASH

SOUTHERN
PAIUTE

Salt
Turquoise

Obsidian

Maize

Taos

APACHEANS

Hides
Jerky

Bison
hides

Cohokia

Mica
Copper
Red pigment

Pearls
Dried fish

MOHAVE

Pottery

Hopi

Cloth

Zia

Maize

Flint

ENO

Maize

PANYA

Cotton

Zuni

PUEBLOS

Pecos

CADDO

QUECHAN

PIA

PIMA

Maize

Pueblo
de los

Salt

Caddo
Villages

MOBILE

WARRING
CHIEFDOMS

Marine shells
Gourds
Racoon skin
Nets

ATLANTIC
OCEAN

COCOPA

HIATATH O'ODHAM
OPATA

Cases
Grandes

Maize

NATCHEZ

Mauvila

APALACHEE

Woodpecker
beaks

PACIFIC
OCEAN

Corazones

Mineral
pigments

La Junta

Hides
Jerky

Corn
Shellfish

TIMUANCUANS

Feathers
(from Mexico)

CALUSA

Tropic of Cancer

Marine shells

Bear oil
Feathers

Gulf of
Mexico

0   200 km

0   200 miles

N

ART

ALTHOUGH "ART" WAS A FOREIGN CONCEPT TO PRE-CONTACT
NATIVE AMERICANS, THEIR ARTISTIC SKILLS WERE APPARENT IN
THE ADORNMENT OF THE EVERYDAY OBJECTS THEY MADE.

Accepted concepts of art do not apply to pre-contact Native American artifacts. Indian life was motivated by subsistence, and items essential for survival and daily use. Life was circumscribed by ritual, which might have involved collecting materials to make something, or be linked to dance and religion. All aspects came together in a totality that could also embrace religion and shamanism. No Native American language possesses a word meaning "art" in an accepted sense.

Indians used all sorts of symbols from the spiritual and physical worlds to adorn their daily lives and rituals. Symbols could portray power in the world, especially the natural world, demonstrating the interconnection between humanity, animals, and plants. Thus, Native Americans were concerned with and were aware of the cosmos, which occasionally was represented by a mandala, itself influenced by the shape of a circle, a common image in nature. The circular Aztec calendar was a timekeeping device and a religious symbol. Like Tibetan monks, the Navajo create sand paintings and sand mandalas representing the impermanence of life. Some mandalas are like labyrinths, but with no way out. Medicine wheels and dreamcatchers are two artifacts that exemplify the mandala, linking utensils, religion, and psychology. The hooped willow twig scooping spiders' webs is a form of mandala used by many modern children when out walking on a frosty or dewy morning, when webs are easy to spot. The schematic nature of the patterns in all mandalas depicts the balance of forces within a symbolic universe.

Native Americans, both North and South, have spent thousands of years in relationships with natural forces and life. This understanding

A gold headdress of the Mochica culture from the North Coast of Peru.

has generated rituals for specific purposes at important points in time—hunting, cultivating, harvesting, marriage ceremonies, funerary rites, and going to war. The cosmos or world view, however, can be variously depicted by different tribes in differing geographical locations. The Plains and Woodlands societies divided cosmic space into sky, the earth's surface, and places below land and water. Local space was projected as circular, with four quadrant zones representing the cardinal directions of north, south, east, and west in associated colors of red, yellow, white, and black, hues common to many tribes. On the Northwest Pacific Coast, the realms of life were the sea or river, then forests and mountains. All regions of the cosmos were linked to a central vertical axis connecting zones of power and acting as a conduit for prayers. The axis might be represented by a tree of life, especially in modern Navajo blankets or in paintings. The axis could also be a pole, or the space between hearth stones and

A carved Aztec calendar stone, a combination of time keeping device and religious symbol.

the overhead smokehole. The cosmic zones were peopled by spirits like the Pueblo kachinas, or the great spirits were represented by etching into stone, pottery, or wood pictures of the Thunderbird, the Underwater Panther, the Eagle, and the Killer Whale. Dreams and vision quests were all part of the all-embracing perceptions in the Native American mind.

How these views are projected into art, perhaps a utensil that is well made and interestingly decorated, can only be seen by observing artifacts that differ according to the cultural region under consideration. The Woodlands communities carved stone and hammered copper with animal symbols. Geometric motifs were common. Porcupine quills were softened and dyed, being used for quilling; shells were another decorative material. Personal adornment could involve tattoos. The Plains tribes employed decorative materials like the Woodland peoples, but increasingly used richly decorated clothing as a way of greeting the gods. Hide paintings might show a tribe's or warrior's history and exploits. The art of the Western Great Basin and Plateau focused on basketry. However, the attempted extermination of the native population by white Americans virtually wiped out their artistic record.

The Navajo are renowned for sand painting. Pictures are made by pouring colored sands onto a surface. They are often used for ritual purposes.

Along the Northwest Pacific Coast, kinship and a hierarchical social system allowed status to be displayed in architecture, totem poles, spirit masks with moving features, and blankets. The masks were important in theater. Southwestern art was also extremely visual, with incredibly beautiful pottery, jewelry, and carefully decorated cotton clothing. Architecturally, the Anasazi were amazing, producing finely wrought pueblos and kivas, while their basketry, textiles, and pottery often depicted animal or astral symbols with an emphasis on contrasting colors.

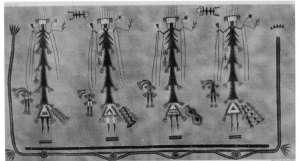

POPULATION

THE NUMBER OF NATIVE AMERICANS ON THE CONTINENT PRIOR
TO EUROPEAN CONTACT IS SUBJECT TO MUCH DEBATE. WHAT IS
CLEAR IS THAT AFTER 1492, IT WENT INTO SERIOUS DECLINE.

It has been estimated that there were 75 million Native Americans in both North and South America prior to the arrival of Europeans, the majority living south of the Rio Grande in central Mexico and some of the countries comprising Central and South America. The population north of Mexico, excluding Greenland, has been estimated as being between one and 18 million. Smithsonian Institution anthropologist Douglas Ubelaker states that the generally accepted total for central Mexico, the most densely populated region, is 10–12 million. Peru could have held nine million, while Canada and the United States had two million.

In the early twentieth century, James Mooney concluded that there were only 1.5 million American Indians, Inuit, and Aleuts at the time of the first European contact, but this could vary from the early 1500s to 1845, depending upon the region. In 1966, anthropologist Henry Dobyns argued that European diseases may have wiped out many Native Americans prior to settler contact. For example, illness may have raced down the trade routes from the Labrador fisheries. Also, de Soto found many empty villages during his *entrada*, the result of disease being transported from Spanish Cuba to Florida by local Native American traders. Thus, logically, populations must have been higher than those estimated by Mooney. Dobyns used mortality rates from epidemics and estimates of environmental capabilities for supporting populations in various regions, suggesting that, by 1492, perhaps 18 million lived north of Mesoamerica. Eventually, Ubelaker revised his northern estimate to seven million—five million in the United States' mainland and two million in Alaska, Canada, and Greenland. All scholars agree, however, that 1492 introduced factors that caused population decline for the following 400 years, after which it began to climb.

Whatever the actual population figures, early Americans lived in communities that ranged in size from small villages to cities as large and sophisticated as anywhere else in the world. A minority were nomadic. The densest populations could be found along the coasts and river valleys, around the Great Lakes, in

Mexico, Florida, and the Caribbean Islands, and on the Northwest Pacific Coast. Some 600 languages were spoken, and different communities included bands, chiefdoms, city states, and nations. Native American kings, emperors, prophets, sculptors and poets, scientists, artisans and architects, mathematicians, and doctors could be found. Land, river, and coastal trade routes linked the continent, allowing the spread of ideas and cultural influences among the various peoples. Medicine, surgery, sport, military service, art, diplomatic skills, religion, and dance could all be avenues for social promotion. However, regional distinctions due to climate and environment produced various identities, creating alternative social trajectories, such as the maintenance of tradition, or those of militarization and imperial expansion, as with civilizations in Mesoamerica and the Andes.

Native American cultural areas can be designated in a number of ways. A common system identifies ten regions according to certain characteristics based on climate, land type, and the biological population, and shows how humans adapted to these conditions. The Eastern Woodlands, the Southeast, the Southwest, the Plains, the Californian Inter-mountain region, the Plateau, the Great Basin, the sub-Arctic, the Northwest Pacific Coast, and the Arctic all exist in North America. In addition, to the south were the Mesoamerican and Circum-Caribbean culture areas, and beyond them, the Andean and Amazonian regions. Typical of the various regions were the farmers and fishermen of the woodlands, such as the Iroquoian peoples, who inhabited longhouses, while the Southeast offers the Mound Builders and their civilized tribal heirs. The Southwest is commonly identified with the Pueblos and their Athapascan invaders; the Great Basin was the home of gatherers. California supported a hundred dialects in a food-abundant region, and the Plains were lightly peopled by nomadic hunters. The sub-Arctic peoples comprised small bands of hunters and fishermen, while the Arctic is exemplified by specialized clothing and seal hunting. Mesoamerica and the Andes are commonly represented by the Mayan, Aztec, and Inca civilizations.

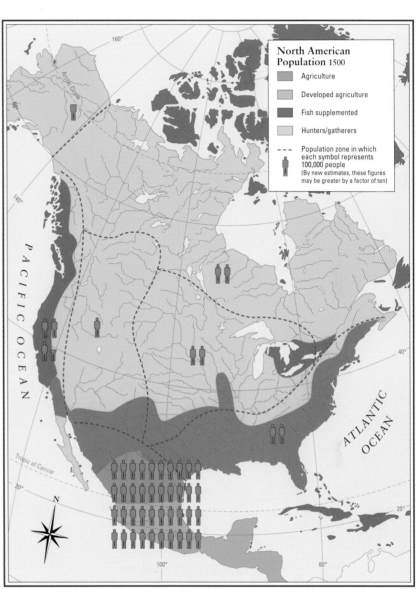

At the time of European contact, the majority of Native Americans in North America occupied Mesoamerica.

LANGUAGES

WHEN EUROPEANS FIRST MADE CONTACT WITH NATIVE
AMERICANS, THEY ENCOUNTERED AN ENORMOUS DIVERSITY OF
LANGUAGES AND CULTURES.

An original page from the *Codex Borbonicus* showing the Aztecs' sacred calendar. The Aztecs developed picture writing and produced many books, although few of them have survived.

As many as 2,000 tongues have been estimated in the Americas as a whole. It is not surprising that over thousands of years, languages diversified as people moved, separated, and evolved different cultures. In a few places along the geographically divided Pacific Coast, six mutually unintelligible languages could be spoken in a county-sized area, as in Humboldt County, California.

Students of language development suggest that the first wave of Native American progenitors arriving across Beringia shared a common language or group of closely related languages. This theory argues that a second wave of migrants from northeast Asia settled Alaska and regions of British Columbia; their descendants moved south to become Navajo and Apache, members of the Athabaskan language group, itself belonging to the Na-Dene family. The first wave had moved further south. A third wave became the Aleut/Inuit group. Other theorists argue differently, proffering alternative linguistic classifications. They claim to have identified some sixty-two language families in North America. Some tongues do not fit into a family, however, like the now-extinct Timucuam language of Florida.

Some languages were wiped out by disease and European brutality. Small Indian communities were vulnerable to British linguistic imperialism, as manifested in the Bureau of Indian Affairs boarding schools. Languages likely to survive are Cherokee, Choctaw, Seminole, and some Southwestern tongues, such as Tiwa, Navajo, and Zuni. Algonquian languages are under threat, except perhaps in Canadian Cree and Ojibwa communities. The small groups of Indians in Oregon and California face extinction, such as the Takelma, Yana, Salinan, and Chumash. Efforts to preserve Indian languages result from political and cultural activism, legislation to set up Indian language programs in public schools, tribal-controlled colleges, and through the increasing number of Native Americans entering the broad teaching profession. The national Endowment for the Humanities made a grant to the Makah tribe of Neah Bay, Washington, for the purpose of preserving and teaching their language. Furthermore, written forms of the languages are being used for poetry, narrative, and lexicographic essays on language in Native American tongues, especially in Micmac, Navajo, Winnebago, Miskitu, and Quiché Mayan.

Early European contacts and anthropologists have often regarded

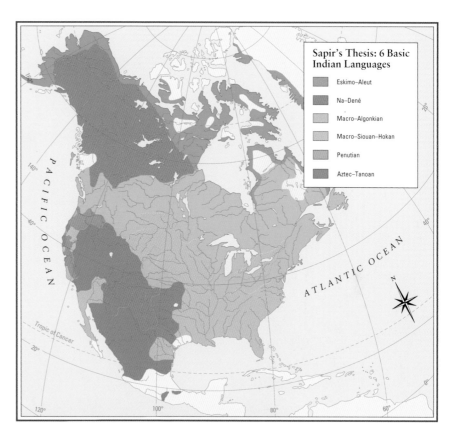

Sapir's Thesis: 6 Basic Indian Languages

- Eskimo–Aleut
- Na–Dené
- Macro–Algonkian
- Macro–Siouan–Hokan
- Penutian
- Aztec–Tanoan

Edward Sapir (1884–1939) was an American anthropologist and linguist. His theory was that there were six basic Native American languages, their spread being shown by this map.

Petroglyphs on Newspaper Rock in southern Utah. This rock has one of the largest known collections of petroglyphs, some of which date to prehistoric times.

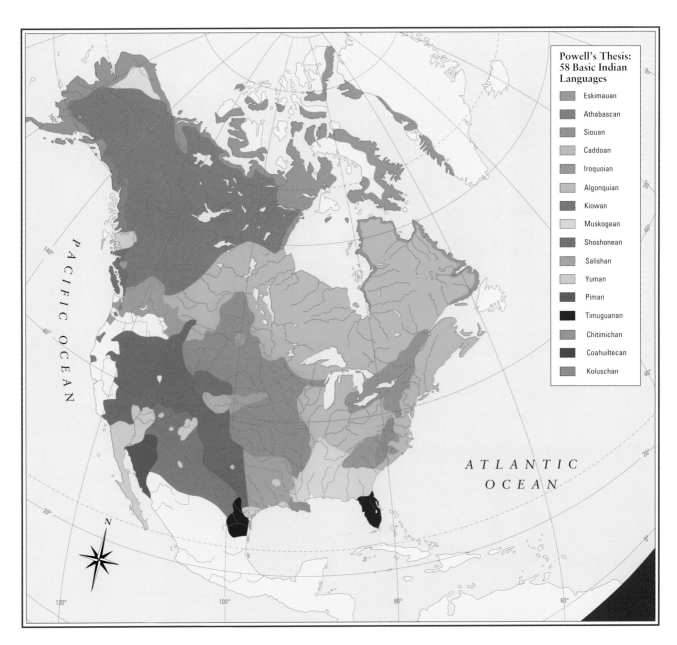

Powell's Thesis: 58 Basic Indian Languages

- Eskimauan
- Athabascan
- Siouan
- Caddoan
- Iroquoian
- Algonquian
- Kiowan
- Muskogean
- Shoshonean
- Salishan
- Yuman
- Piman
- Timuguanan
- Chitimichan
- Coahuiltecan
- Koluschan

John Wesley Powell (1834–1902) was a soldier, geologist, and explorer of the American West. He became a director of the U.S. Geological Survey and of the Bureau of Ethnology at the Smithsonian Institution. He was responsible for an influential classification of North American Indian languages.

Native Americans as barbaric savages, as witnessed by their lack of written works, despite the fact that most Europeans did not receive an elementary education until the nineteenth century. However, there is evidence for written communication systems. The Olmecs produced plaques and seals marked with glyphs, perhaps a mother culture for the Maya and Aztecs with their similar work. The Iroquois created pictographs in wampum belts to remind oral historians of events, as well as to seal treaties and diplomatic negotiations. The Aztecs and Mayans used picture-writing, but thousands of handwritten Mayan books were burned by fearful Spanish religious zealots; only four remain. Early descriptions of Peruvian languages compiled dictionaries of Incan words, some meaning "to write," "paper," and "letters." A writing system existed with ten consonants. Native American art often recounts stories through images, such as those on rock (petroglyphs) cut by the ancestors of the Pueblo people 600 years ago at Galisteo, New Mexico. They depict an arrow-swallower, a kachina, and a shield.

An early North American written language took the form of hieroglyphics marked on birch bark or animal hides, noticed in the late seventeenth century by a missionary, Father la Clerq, while among the Micmac. He used them to translate holy texts. The Ojibwa etched pictographs into birch-bark scrolls, preserving their sacred songs. The symbols represented sounds, an idea picked up from European contact. A fascinating story recounts how the Cherokee Sequoyah (c. 1770–1843) constructed a syllabary, each Cherokee sound unit being represented by a symbol. Eighty-five symbols represented six vowels, the consonant "s," and seventy-

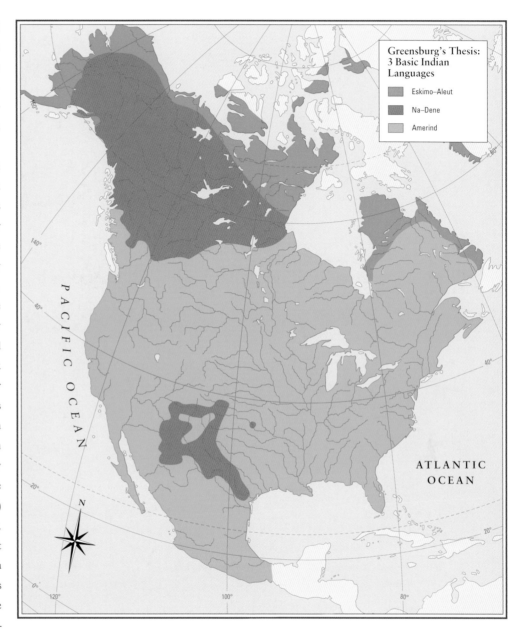

eight consonant-vowel units. Capable of being mastered in a few days, the syllabary was typeset to allow the printing of the Bible. Cherokee literacy blossomed; within three years, three-quarters of Cherokee people could read. The *Cherokee Phoenix and Indian Advocate* newspaper was published in bilingual form between 1828 and 1835, when the State of Georgia banned it for advocating Indian rights to their lands in Georgia.

Many words from Indian languages have been absorbed into English, often referring to place names and geographical features. They include the Manhattan cocktail (after a tribe that inhabited the New York region), chocolate, anorak, shark, avocado, and kayak. All have enriched the dominant language's word stock.

Having studied over 1,500 American Indian languages, Joseph Greensburg claimed that all could be placed into one of three groups. His work, plus studies done on blood types and teeth, suggests that there were three separate migrations from Asia into the Americas.

KINSHIP

MATRILINEAL DESCENT IS A COMMON ASPECT OF KINSHIP IN MANY NATIVE AMERICAN SOCIETIES, AND WOMEN PLAYED A MUCH MORE IMPORTANT ROLE THAN EUROPEANS REALIZED.

Cherokee Nan'yehi (Nancy Ward), from a drawing by renowned artist George Catlin. Nan'yehi was a famed Native American warrior and diplomat.

Europeans were confused when they first attempted to understand Native American marriage and kinship relations. Women were seen as being exploited by men or were romanticized as being free—the Pocahontas syndrome. Europeans were raised in patrilineal societies and failed to appreciate the role women played in tribal society. Descent through the male line might describe the Ojibwa (Anishinaabe) or Lakota, whose women were not allowed to talk to strangers, but would be inappropriate for the Iroquois, Cherokee, and Pueblo societies. In fact, women were property owners, decision makers, diplomats, and warriors, such as Navajo Annie Wauneka and Chiricahua Apache woman fighter Lozen. Well known is Cherokee Nan'yehi (Nancy Ward, 1738–1824), renowned for her bravery and skill in combat, and her diplomacy. She was called Ghighua, or Beloved Woman (also translates as War Woman), a distinction given to exceptional Cherokee women. In matrilineal Cherokee society, marriages with white traders and diplomats could ratify an alliance or gain commercial advantage. The children of such unions were classed as Cherokee and would blend into tribal life.

Kinship patterns are extremely complex and as diverse as the number of tribes, but the matrilineal societies of the Iroquois (Haudenosaunee) in New York State, and the Arizona Hopi provide clues as to how society was organized. An Iroquois clan mother with her hearth led the system, and all her sons, daughters, and their children for ever were members of the same uterine family and could never inter-marry. The clan mother's husband was the father, but his children were obviously members of his wife's clan by right. Chieftainships (fifty in all) were passed through the female side, and the headwomen chose male representatives to voice clan issues at tribal meetings. If a clan woman moved geographically, she took her clan name with her (Frog, Turtle, Wolf). Her descendants would be related to the mother clan, share its name, and would not inter-marry within it. A collection of such dispersed clans comprised a *phratry*. If a clan member, say Wolf, traveled among the tribes of the

Iroquois League, whether Oneida, Onondaga, Cayuga, or Seneca, he or she would receive hospitality from any constituent Wolf clan. The Iroquois believed that the strength of the nation was built from the collection of individuals from all hearths and clans, and that tribal power was weakened when a member died. Thus, population numbers could be maintained by adoption or by capturing people in war. The whole complex system originated with Onondaga Hiawatha, the legendary figure who assisted the Peacemaker in bringing the tribes together. Also helping the federation to unite was a woman chief, Jikohnsaseh, who crowned the first chairman of the Iroquois League, thereby proclaiming and symbolizing women's power.

The Hopi inhabited the summits of the mesas of the Arizona desert, crowding together into large villages. Previously, when being forced south by Apache bands, natal men, those born of a matrilineal or matrilocal society, moved away to marry. Subsequently, these men would live elsewhere in the village or return to their natal home after a divorce, a fairly common occurrence. Land went with the homes and was owned by women. Men might help with agricultural labor, but the crops remained with the women, to be distributed to household members as the women deemed fit. Another important feature of women was their responsibility for guarding the household fetishes of animals or plants, and to hand their custodianship to a daughter. Interestingly, religious ceremonies were conducted by men, giving a religious basis to a group of descendants through ritual property. The houses were named after natural manifestations—Rabbit, Sun, Corn, Moon. The named houses became the basis for clan development. Like the Iroquois, a daughter might leave the original house, but would take the house name with her. Thus, a number

of households would grow, but all would be attached to the same fetish and house/clan name. If a household died out, its lands would be inherited by another related household.

The Hopi community was further strengthened by the Hopi Way, a covenant between their god Masawu and the first Hopi. The community was all, with all relations and clan mothers guiding and inspiring the tribal membership in a spirit of discipline, cooperation, and reciprocity. The kivas, kachina dolls, and religious leaders provided a social cement. The lifestyle of this peaceful people, self-designated as the Hopitou, with its corn-based economy, continues with a yearly cycle of rites and ceremonies.

A kachina doll from the late nineteenth century. The dolls play an important role in Hopi and Pueblo cultures, and can represent anything that exists in the natural world. The name itself means "life bringer".

Annie Wauneka, Navajo leader and chairwoman of the Navajo Tribal Fair, presents a blanket as prize in a fry bread making contest in 1963.

First Contacts

"... WHEN THE SKRAELINGS SAW THE MILK THEY WANTED TO BUY

NOTHING ELSE. AND SO THE OUTCOME OF THEIR TRADING ...

WAS THAT THE SKRAELINGS CARRIED THEIR PURCHASES AWAY IN

THEIR BELLIES, AND LEFT THEIR PACKS AND FURS ..."

GRAENLENDINGA SAGA (1382–95), ABOUT VOYAGES TO AMERICA.

Native Americans made their first long-term contacts with Europeans on lands near the Newfoundland and Labrador fishing banks. The earlier Norse/Viking contact was probably short-lived and minimal. Apart from meetings with fishermen, various other types of encounter took place. Firstly, accidental contacts occurred along the American coastline, involving explorers, traders, pirates, shipwrecked sailors, and the crews of ships seeking shelter from storms. Secondly, European explorers and potential colonists wintered among Indians and met nations in the interior. Thirdly, Native Americans in the North met Mesoamericans and Caribbean peoples accompanying de Soto's and Coronado's entradas. Fourthly, there was the missionary experience. Fifthly, trading relationships were made through the early fur business. Finally, contacts were made with colonists from Portugal, France, Spain, and England.

The various early contacts occurred at a time when Native American society was undergoing considerable change. The Iroquoian groups had increased their population owing to the development of a corn-based economy to such an extent that they probably began to develop small alliances, later to become the Iroquois Confederacy, the Five Nations of the Long House (Haudenosaunee). Further south, the late Mississippian society was disintegrating, and tribes were coalescing into new units or confederacies, such as the Creek, Cherokee, Choctaw, and Catawba. On the Atlantic coasts, new "states," based upon overbearing chiefdoms, were being created, like the Virginian-based Powhatans and the Georgia Coosas. In the Southeast, large-scale societies developed in Florida—Calusa and Timucuan—and they bore the brunt of early Spanish incursions. Into this range of societies came a number of different European groups, each with a separate, inchoate agenda. Initially, the St. Lawrence and Labrador tribes met Basque and Breton fishermen, many of whom dried fish on land and established amicable minor trading relations with the Micmac and Montagnais, although the Beothuk were fairly hostile. Added to these encounters were occasional meetings with pirates, traders, and the crews of ships seeking secure harbors. Among these was Giovanni da Verrazzano (1524), an Italian navigator employed by France, who found New York and Narragansett bays. Other examples were Cartier (1534), Diaz (1539), and Cabrillo (1542–43), who eventually explored the Californian coast.

The second manner of contact occurred when the Spanish pushed into Florida and the Southeast, spending winters among Native Americans. Here, Pánfilo de Narváez landed in Tampa Bay in 1528; his expedition was recounted in 1542 by survivor Alvar Núñez Cabeza de Vaca, which stimulated the de Soto (1539–43) and Coronado (1540–42) entradas. These leaders arrived with servants of Caribbean, African, and mestizo origin. De Soto entered the Mississippi region, while Coronado explored the Southwest.

The French impact did not involve large-scale "invasion" forces, but was a bid for mastery of parts of North America to counterbalance Spain. King Francis I sent the Sieur de Roberval (1540–43) to follow up Cartier's earlier exploration of the St. Lawrence. The failure of these expeditions ended French interest in the Americas until Champlain established a presence on the river after his 1604 expedition to the Bay of Fundy.

A most significant series of contacts were those implemented by missionaries, often Franciscan or Dominican friars, who accompanied early Spanish incursions. Such missionary activity began in

A contemporary illustration depicting Samuel de Champlain aiding a war party of Montagnais, Algonkin, and Huron warriors in an attack on the Iroquois. Champlain's activities in this respect would eventually lead to a Franco-British war.

NATIONS AND TRIBES, c. 1450

NATIVE AMERICAN HISTORY BEFORE MAJOR EUROPEAN CONTACT IS DIFFICULT TO ASCERTAIN, BUT ARCHAEOLOGICAL RESEARCH GIVES AN IDEA OF THEIR DISTRIBUTION.

ALEUTS

Native American history before major European contact is difficult to ascertain. European records begin in the late fifteenth and early sixteenth centuries, and tend to be maps or lists of place names. Only a small body of written documents provides eyewitness accounts of European-Indian contacts. Whalers and fishermen who frequented the Canadian coast provide no evidence, although commercial fisheries were large-scale ventures. When records do emerge of Spanish entradas, Francis Drake on the Pacific Coast, and French penetration of the St. Lawrence, together with their meetings with Indians, they merely provide snapshots of immediate locales, rather than the interior. However, information and supposition allow some estimate to be made of where various nations lived; the first map of North America was compiled in 1500 by Juan de la Cosa, a colleague of Columbus. The history of Central America can be judged from rich archaeological evidence, early Spanish records of the Aztecs, and from Mayan books, such as the *Codex Tro-Cortesianus*.

Elsewhere, in the Northeast, two language groups existed, the Algonquian and the Iroquoian. The former inhabited Nova Scotia to New England, through the Hudson Valley, Long Island, and the Delaware Valley, and included Micmac, Abenaki, Pequot, Narragansett, and Wampanoag. A further group lived around the Great Lakes, exemplified by the Algonkin, Menominee, Ottowa, and Potawatomi. A third branch were the Prairie Algonkin, the Illinois, Kickapoo, Miami, Sauk, and Shawnee. The Iroquoian dwelt in New York State, Québec, and Ontario; some of them formed the League of Five Nations. Some evidence of the area can be discovered in the records left by the explorers Verrazzano, Gomez, and Cartier.

The distribution of Indian nations in the early sixteenth century.

Indian Culture Areas, North America c. 1500

- Arctic
- Subarctic
- Northwest Coast
- Plateau
- Great Basin
- California
- Southwest
- Plains
- Eastern Woodlands Northeast
- Eastern Woodlands Southeast

ESKIMOS

INGALIKS
ANAINAS
KUTCHINS

Victoria Island

Great Bear Lake

DOGRIBS

Great Slave Lake

ESKIMOS

Baffin Island

KASKAS

SLAVEYS

CHIPPEWYANS

TLINGITS
TAIMSHIAN
DAS

BEAVERS

SARAIS

Hudson Bay

ESKIMOS

NASKAPIS

KWAKIUTIS
NOOTKAS
SALISHS

CREES

CREES

MONTAGNAIS

MICMACS

BEOTHUKS
Newfoundland

SHUSWAPS

BLACKFEET

GROS VENTRE

ASSINIBOINS

L. Winnipeg

ABENAKIS

St. Lawrence R.

CHINOOKS
THOMPSONS
SANPOILS
YAKIMAS
NEZ PERCÉS
FLATHEADS

OJIBWAS

SIOUX

OTTAWAS

HURONS

Lake Superior

CROWS

MANDANS

ARIKARAS

SACS
FOXES

WINNEBAGOS

Lake Michigan

Lake Huron

L. Ontario

IROQUOIS

Lake Erie

SUSQUEHANNOCKS

MASSACHUSETTS
WAMPANOAGS
NARRAGANSETTS
PEQUOTS

YUROKAS
POMOS

WASHOS

SHOSHONES

CHEYENNES

MIAMIS

ERIES

DELAWARES

YOKUTS
CHUMASH

PAIUTES

PAWNEES

ILLINOIS

SHAWNEES

Missouri R.

ATLANTIC OCEAN

LUISEÑOS

UTES

Colorado R.

ARAPAHOS

Arkansas R.

OSAGES

WICHITAS

POWHATANS

TUSCARORAS

WALAPAIS
MOHAVES
YUMAS
PAPAGOS

HOPIS

NAVAJOS

ZUNIS

RIO GRANDE
PUEBLOS
APACHES

KIOWAS

CHEROKEES

CHICKASAWS

CATAWBAS

PIMAS

CREEKS

CHOCTAWS

GUALES
(YAMASEES)

CADDOS

NATCHEZ

MOBILES

Rio Grande

Mississippi R.

COAHULTECS

Gulf of Mexico

CALUSAS

Tropic of Cancer

N

0   400 km

0   400 miles

The concept of Indian "nations" stems largely from the desire of European governments to negotiate with other governments. In fact, the tribes were mainly language groups comprising a number of largely independent bands with little or no centralized control. This map shows the location of the "nations" at the beginning of the seventeenth century.

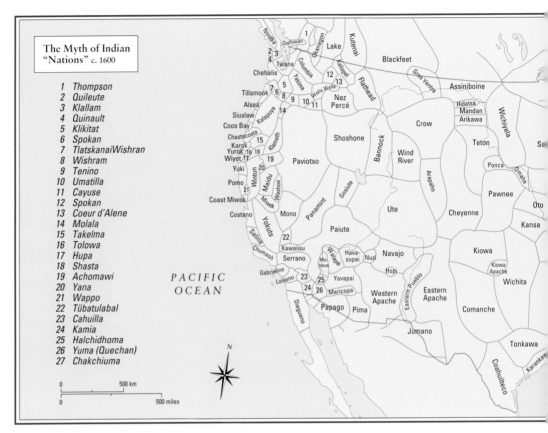

The Myth of Indian "Nations" c. 1600

1 Thompson
2 Quileute
3 Klallam
4 Quinault
5 Klikitat
6 Spokan
7 TlatskanaiWishran
8 Wishram
9 Tenino
10 Umatilla
11 Cayuse
12 Spokan
13 Coeur d'Alene
14 Molala
15 Takelma
16 Tolowa
17 Hupa
18 Shasta
19 Achomawi
20 Yana
21 Wappo
22 Tübatulabal
23 Cahuilla
24 Kamia
25 Halchidhoma
26 Yuma (Quechan)
27 Chakchiuma

PACIFIC OCEAN

0 ___ 500 km
0 ___ 500 miles

In the Southwest, populations began collecting around the Zuni and Pecos Pueblos, evidenced by the spreading Kachina cult, and the region became a nodal trade point. The Southeast comprised a number of farming, fishing, and hunting communities: from north to south, there were Iroquoians (Meherrin, Nottaway, and Tuscarora); Algonquian sharing the same lands (Powhatan, Secotan, and Weapemeoc), and some of these were merging into larger units, such as the so-called Powhatan Confederacy. Next were Muskogean speakers, who included Apalachee, Choctaw, Chickasaw, and Creek. The Cherokee were related more to the Iroquois, but were distinct. These peoples, with the unrelated Natchez, Caddo, and Atakapa, were restructuring after the erosion of the Mound Culture and the impact of European disease. Although these civilizations were robust, they felt the impact of Spanish entradas. The Florida tribes of the Calusa, Tekesta, and Timucua are clearly described in Spanish records, and they suffered the devastating impact of European sickness and warfare before other nations.

The vast Great Plains area was sparsely inhabited. The Blackfeet and Shoshone hunted buffalo, but the Siouan Mandan and Hidatsa, and the Caddoan Caddo, Wichita, Pawnee, and Arikara settled in farming villages in river valleys. Brief contacts were made with Europeans via the Cabeza de Vaca and Coronado incursions.

California was occupied by diverse tribes with many differing tongues, each relating to a particular environment. Bands such as the Miwok met Drake in 1579, while the Spanish expeditions of Unamuno (1587) and Cirmenho (1590) had little impact. The Plateau was sparsely populated along river valleys

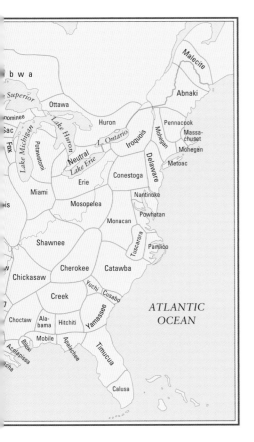

by such tribes as the Klamath, Modoc, Nez Perce, Cayuse, and Walla Walla to the South, and by the Salish and Spokane to the North. The Great Basin is a desert characterized by the Great Salt Lake. There, tribes lived by gathering and hunting small game, the main tribal groups being Paiute, Shoshone, and Ute.

The Northwest might be a narrow strip of land, but it contains many isolated microenvironments, the rich conditions of which allowed up to 200,000 inhabitants—such as the Tlingit, Haida, and Chinook—to develop many cultures and languages. These tribes probably encountered Europeans centuries after those in Florida. The Arctic was inhabited by Inuit and Aleut; British Captain Frobisher was shot at with an iron-headed arrow during his 1576–78 expedition. The Subarctic incorporated the vast territory from Alaska to Newfoundland, and was home to Athabaskan and Algonquian tribes. The former included the Ahtena, Beaver, Hare, Ingalik, and Tagish, while the latter comprised Cree, Montagnais, Naskapi, and northern Ojibwa among others. The Newfoundland Beothuk appear unrelated to these two groups

Fort Yukon, established in Alaska in 1847 by Alexander Murray. It acted as a trading post among the Kutchin people, an Athabaskan tribal group.

Food and Nutrition, 1450

BEFORE CONTACT WITH EUROPEANS, NATIVE AMERICANS THROUGHOUT THE CONTINENT HAD ACCESS TO A WIDE VARIETY OF FOODS, MANY OF WHICH ARE STILL EATEN TODAY.

Native Americans used a vast range of domesticated and wild plants. The New York and Ohio valley regions provided many fruits, such as grapes, plums, thorn apples, cherries, strawberries, bear berries, blackberries, blueberries, elderberries, and sumac berries. Nuts included acorns, butternuts, hickory nuts, walnuts, hazelnuts, and beechnuts. The Northeast witnessed the domestication of sunflowers for seed and tubers (Jerusalem artichokes), sumpweed, goosefoot, maygrass, and giant ragweed. Throughout the area, as elsewhere, corn, beans, and squash became staple foods.

The Great Lakes provided wild rice in shallow waters, and the Ojibwa fought hard to hold and increase control of these rice lands. A common food for hunting expeditions and traveling was pemmican, pounded dried meat mixed with fat and berries. Spring greens were commonly grown, and the Delaware are reported to have harvested young dandelion, milkweed, pokeweed, lamb's quarters, mustard, dock, and watercress, mixing them with cooked meat.

Corn was immensely important, and many varieties were developed to suit diverse growing conditions. Originally the small seeds of a wild grass, teosinte, the 1450 varieties could produce a crop in the short northern growing season or have deep roots to suit Southwest conditions. Through selected breeding, the Navajo developed white, red, black and white, and the usual yellow corn. The botanical treasure store of Central and South America also produced pineapples, avocado, papaya, cocoa, beans, tomatoes, chillis, potatoes, sweet potatoes, peanuts, cashews, vanilla, and manioc, but many of these never traveled north.

The Southwest provided corn, squash, and bean varieties, including the protein-rich tepary. Wild foods included seeds—amaranth, lamb's quarter, saguaro, mustard and pigweed; fruits—cholla and prickly pear; and nuts—black walnuts and piñon. Interestingly, corn provides 348 calories per 3.5 ounces (100 grams), whereas the same weight of piñon nuts gives 635 calories.

Over time, beans, squash, and corn became the most important crops; when beans and corn are cooked together, by virtue of their amino acids, they produce complete protein. Added to these were sweeteners in the form of wild honey, dried and fresh fruit, and maple syrup. The last was commonly used by the Great Lakes nations. Indian cuisine tended to comprise a soup or stew accompanied by some type of bread, or roasted meat or fish. Boiling food was achieved with the aid of ceramic vessels in the Southwest and East; on the Plains, a cleaned buffalo paunch could be held by sticks and filled with water, into which hot stones were dropped.

Protein was readily available. Eastern coastal regions provided deer, wild geese, lobsters, clams, mussels, bass, cod, and squid. Wild turkeys and, occasionally, dogs were also eaten. The Plains provided buffalo in vast herds. The Northwest gave up salmon, halibut, and whales. Flesh could be dried, smoked, or preserved in rendered whale and seal oil. In fact, fats were important for all Native Americans, and bears provided a sustainable source. California and the Great Basin were rich in plants and small game.

Native Americans also employed wild and cultivated plants for social and religious purposes. South Americans had the coca leaf, the origin of cocaine, while tobacco was used throughout North America, with the exception of the extreme north. Tobacco was a feature of social rituals and could be smoked, eaten, used as snuff, or burned for incense. Alcohol was widely imbibed in certain areas before Europeans arrived. Mexicans produced forty different beverages, ranging from corn beer to fermented honey. The Southwest had a cactus wine, and the Southeast persimmon wine. The Aztecs used intoxication for meditation and to aid prophecy. Papagos and Pimas believed drinking alcohol would bring rain. In Northern Mexico and along the Rio Grande, the people valued the hallucinogenic properties of peyote buttons. Certain Mexican tribes and Apaches took them to suppress hunger and thirst or for religious purposes to induce psychedelic experiences, which later might be expressed in art. Comanche raids spread peyote to the Kiowa, Cheyenne, and Arapaho. Other drugs used were mescal and certain mushrooms, such as the teonanacatl.

A Pima woman grinding corn. Although this photograph was taken in 1913, the technique used is ancient. The kernels of corn are placed on a flat rock known as a *matate* and then a smaller rock, a *mano*, is rolled over them. Years of use would gradually create a depression in the *matate*.

Opposite: Vikings voyaged to North America from Greenland, establishing at least one settlement, at L'Anse aux Meadows on the coast of present-day Newfoundland. It is possible that they journeyed further south.

Inuit-Norse contact has resulted in Norse objects being found in Inuit archaeological sites; much would have been stripped out of Norse farms when their inhabitants left. Chain mail, woolen cloth, metal clinch nails, and a comb have been discovered in northwestern Greenland and on Ellesmere Island. The relations between the Inuit and the Norsemen probably ranged from trade to warfare. Greenlanders were dependent on Iceland and Europe for grain, lumber, and luxury goods; they would have been purchased with walrus, polar bear, and other skins. Also useful was walrus and narwhal ivory, and records show that vast quantities of this material were sold. However, it could only be obtained 300 miles (500 kilometers) north of the Greenland settlements. Logic suggests that the Norsemen would have traded with the Inuit for ivory to ensure a ready and continuous supply.

Dating from 1741, this etching by J.M. Fosie depicts Inuit dwellings in Greenland. They would have employed similar structures elsewhere.

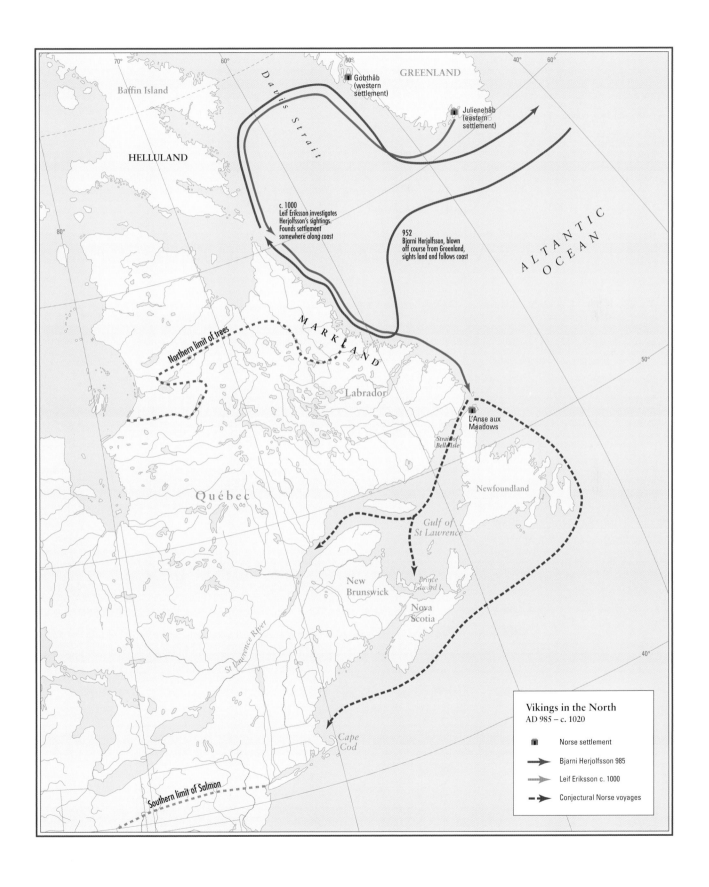

Baffin Island

Davis Strait

GREENLAND

Gobthåb
(western
settlement)

Julienehåb
(eastern
settlement)

HELLULAND

ATLANTIC
OCEAN

c. 1000
Leif Eriksson investigates
Herjolfsson's sightings.
Founds settlement
somewhere along coast

952
Bjarni Herjolfsson, blown
off course from Greenland,
sights land and follows coast

Northern limit of trees

MARKLAND

Labrador

L'Anse aux
Meadows

Strait of
Belle Isle

Québec

Newfoundland

Gulf of
St Lawrence

St Lawrence River

New
Brunswick

Prince
Edward I.

Nova
Scotia

Cape
Cod

Southern limit of Salmon

Vikings in the North
AD 985 – c. 1020

🏠 Norse settlement

→ Bjarni Herjolfsson 985

→ Leif Eriksson c. 1000

- - → Conjectural Norse voyages

Commercial Fisheries: The Basques and French

ATTRACTED TO THE NORTH AMERICAN COAST BY THE PROMISE OF GOOD FISHING, THE BASQUES AND FRENCH DEVELOPED SUBSTANTIAL FISHERIES IN THE REGION, AND PAVED THE WAY FOR COLONIZATION.

Newfoundland fish are recorded as having been landed in England in 1504, and in 1506, Portugal was levying customs duties on American cod. Normans were fishing in American waters in 1504, and Bretons in 1511, followed by the Basques in 1512. Ships crossed the Atlantic each summer and engaged in one of two practices. Wet fishing involved salting a catch and returning to Europe immediately, whereas dry fishing involved landing the catch in North America, where it was gutted, salted, washed, and dried on racks, before sailing back to Europe to sell the product.

The Portuguese and Spanish Basques fished off the south and east coasts of Newfoundland, while the Bretons sailed into the Belle Isle Straits, fishing off Cape Breton and the nearby Nova Scotian coasts. By 1540, Spanish and French Basques controlled the Belle Isle Straits, and hunted bowhead and right whales off the coast of Newfoundland. Dead whales were towed to rendering stations established around the edge of Red Bay, Labrador. The flukes and flippers were removed, then strips of skin and blubber were cut into chunks and boiled down in large copper cauldrons, the oil being stored in wooden casks before being shipped to Europe. Bones of whales killed by Basques still litter the beaches of Red Bay Harbor. As many as 1,000 Basques were engaged in the whaling industry at one time, sailing ships of up to 600 tons.

By the 1570s, British fishermen had taken control of the eastern Avalon Peninsula of Newfoundland, while Spanish and French Basques fished waters in the Gulf of St. Lawrence and off the rest of Newfoundland. By 1578, between 300 and 350 ships were engaged in these fisheries. Those operating the dry fisheries and whaling landed thousands of Europeans on the northeastern coasts of North America, perhaps as many as 20,000 by 1580. These fishermen met Beothuks, Montagnais, and Micmac Indians. Conflict could occur over competition for fishing sites and because the Europeans felled timber to produce flakes for drying fires. When Europeans returned home, the Indians would dismantle the fishing installations to reuse iron nails and other goods. In general, though, the Indians would accept gifts, help in processing fish, and occasionally engage in treading animal skins. Basque-Montagnais relations were amicable, such that small boats could be left in Labrador over the winter and remain untouched for the following season. The Beothuks were recorded as being cruel, however, and boats and gear needed guarding against attack.

The European fishermen were a valuable asset to be exploited by the Indians—a source of new technologies and metal. Thus, Indians would compete among themselves violently to control the flow of goods. Moreover, inter-European rivalries could cause competition and aggression over the control of the fishing waters.

Much evidence for the fisheries was discovered by historical geographer Selma Barkham in Spanish Basque archives. Thousands of documents established the importance of the Red Bay whaling settlement. Papers showed that a Basque whaler, the *San Juan*, had sunk with 1,000 barrels of newly processed whale oil. Underwater archaeologists found this ship in 24 feet (7 meters) of water, together with the remains of other sunken ships. Adzes, axes, knives, harpoons, and pitchers were recovered from the *San Juan*. Graves of European seamen were also discovered in the area, men presumably killed in the whale hunt.

A detail from a 1721 map of North America by Herman Moll, showing cod being dressed and dried in Newfoundland. There were extensive fishing grounds off the northeast coast of North America, which drew boats from France, Spain, and England.

The result of such commercial fisheries was the virtual eradication of right and bowhead whales; archaeologists have estimated that Basque hunting was responsible for a global decline in whales, which began in European waters. Another outcome was the impact on Native Americans. New trade routes were developed to channel the annual influx of European goods. European metal and hardwoods were crafted into knives, drills, engraving tools, and axes. Indian settlements moved nearer to the Basque fisheries to exploit prestige goods, and an Indian entrepreneurial class developed to trade in European products. Probably the most significant result of the commercial fisheries was the importation of European diseases, soon to be spread along the new trade routes into the interior.

CORONADO

STILL LOOKING FOR FABLED CITIES MADE OF GOLD, THE
SPANISH SENT THEIR CONQUISTADORES INTO THE AMERICAN
SOUTHWEST, WHERE, AS ELSEWHERE, THEY WROUGHT HAVOC.

In 1540, Francisco Vázquez de Coronado was selected by New Spain's first viceroy, Antonio de
Mendoza, to lead an expedition to find the fabled Seven Cities of Cibola. Reports of these cities
had been given by Friar Marcos de Niza and Cabeza de Vaca. The Incan and Aztec conquests had
produced vast quantities of gold, so why not this potentially new province? According to myth, it had
been founded by seven refugee bishops, fleeing the Moors in Spain. It was said that they had crossed
the Atlantic in the eighth century to found a new Christian realm.

Coronado collected together some 230 mounted troops, 62 infantry, 800 Mexican Indians, 1,000
African and native slaves, a group of priests, and vast herds of horses, oxen, cows, sheep, pigs, and
mules. They left Compostela, guided by Friar Marcos, while three supply ships followed the coast
and entered the Colorado River. The expedition eventually covered several thousand miles, from the
Gulf of California to south-central Kansas, and from Compostela to the Pueblos at Zuni, Hopi, Acoma,
Tiguez, Taos, and Pecos, in today's Arizona and New Mexico.

First, Coronado's conquistadores reached Hawikuh, a Pueblo that appeared golden in the sunlight,
but in reality was a collection of stone buildings. There, they acquired quantities of corn and beans.
Still hoping to find Cibola, Coronado sent out scouting parties. Pedro de Tovar found the mesa towns of
the Hopi, while García López de Cárdenas reached the Colorado Grand Canyon. Meanwhile, Hernando
de Alvardo discovered the Rio Grande Pueblos inhabited by descendants of the Anasazi. Despite a lack
of gold and jewels, the Pueblos possessed fields and food stocks, which could supply the Spanish over
winter. Coronado moved from Zuni territory to the Tiwa Pueblo town of Alcanfor.

The onset of winter led the Spanish to empty the town for their own quarters, after which they
made demands for food and clothes from all the Tiwa towns. Tiwa resentment occasioned a revolt,

the Tiguex War. Spanish retaliation was harsh, and the towns were burned. Women and children were seized, people enslaved, and men burned at the stake.

In spring 1541, Coronado responded to tales of new cities to the northeast at Quivira. A Pawnee, named Turk by the Spanish, regaled the invaders with stories of gold bells, plates, jugs, and bowls. Coronado crossed the panhandles of Texas and Oklahoma, and entered Kansas. He encountered the vast high plains and the huge herds of buffalo. The expedition followed the Pecos and Brazos Rivers, then headed northward for forty-two days, until they reached Quivira. This Wichita Indian encampment on the Kansas River was a collection of grass huts; there was no gold. Turk was strangled, and the frustrated Spaniards returned to the Tiwa Pueblos for another winter. Totally discouraged, Coronado returned to Mexico City in 1542.

However, Viceroy Mendoza still hoped that the north would be bountiful. Two vessels under Juan Rodriguez Cabrillo sailed along the coast of California, but missed the harbors of San Francisco and Monterey. He did find San Diego Bay, eventually an important Spanish outpost.

The next attempt on the Pueblos was made by Juan de Oñate, who, in 1598, led an expedition of 500, with 7,000 head of livestock, northward along the Rio Grande. He crossed the center of New Mexico and arrived at Okhe Pueblo in the Española Valley. The Indians were ordered out, and Oñate named the town San Juan, choosing it as the capital of the new Spanish colony. Oñate began conquering the surrounding Pueblos, and in 1599, a major conflict occurred at Acoma Pueblo, on a high mesa. The Spaniards forced their way in, but the battle lasted three days and resulted in more than 800 of the 6,000 inhabitants being killed; 500 women and children, and eighty men became indentured for twenty years. In addition, the men were mutilated in the Rio Grande towns, each losing a foot.

A depiction of Francisco Vázquez de Coronado's expedition in the Southwest by the noted American artist Frederick Remington. Like many before him, Coronado endured many hardships only to discover that there were no cities of gold.

Overleaf: Throughout the sixteenth century, Spanish expeditions ranged through the southern half of the North American continent seeking fabled riches. They found none, but had a devastating effect on the Native Americans they encountered.

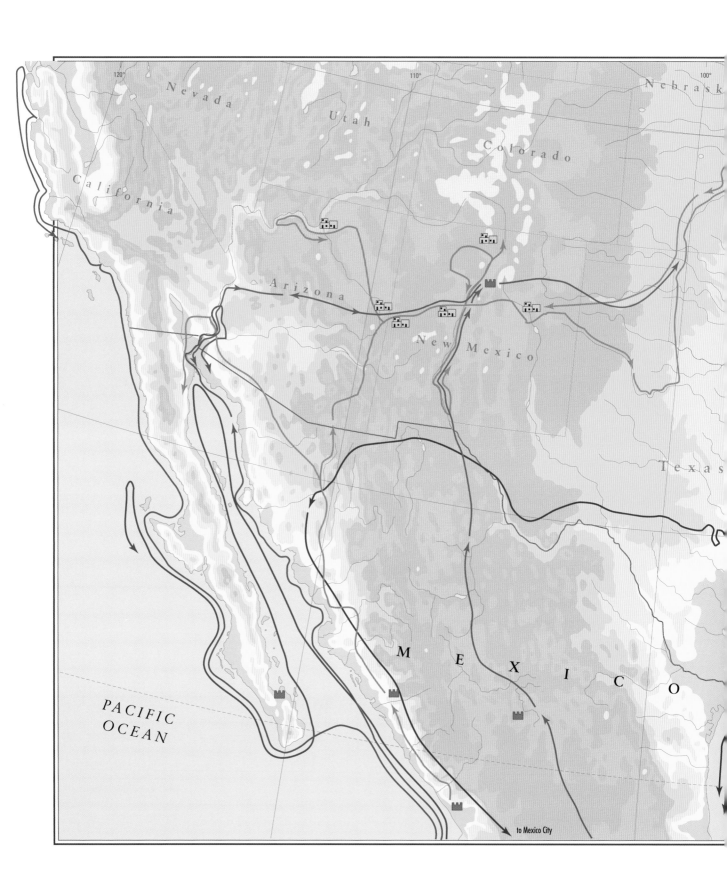

Nevada

Utah

Colorado

Nebrask

California

Arizona

New Mexico

Texas

PACIFIC
OCEAN

M E X I C O

to Mexico City

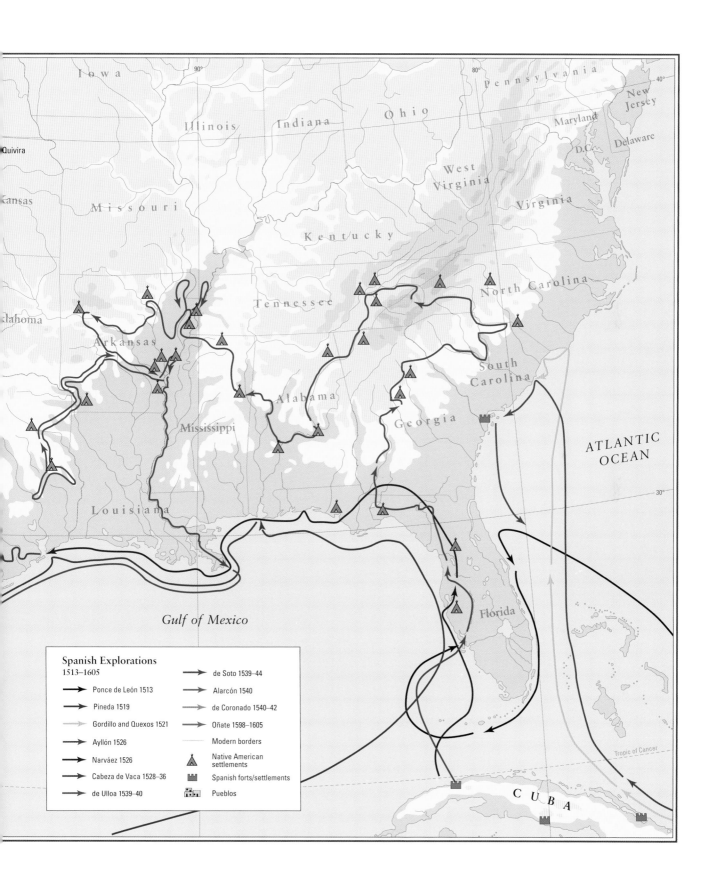

Spanish Explorations
1513–1605

→ Ponce de León 1513

→ Pineda 1519

→ Gordillo and Quexos 1521

→ Ayllón 1526

→ Narváez 1526

→ Cabeza de Vaca 1528–36

→ de Ulloa 1539–40

→ de Soto 1539–44

→ Alarcón 1540

→ de Coronado 1540–42

→ Oñate 1598–1605

　 Modern borders

🔺 Native American settlements

🏰 Spanish forts/settlements

🏛 Pueblos

CARTIER AND CHAMPLAIN

INSPIRED INITIALLY BY IDEAS OF A PASSAGE TO THE ORIENT,
AND THEN BY THE POTENTIAL PROFITS OF THE FUR TRADE, THE
FRENCH SENT EXPLORERS AND COLONISTS TO NORTH AMERICA.

A representation of Jacques Cartier dating from c. 1844 by Théophile Hamel. No portraits painted in his own time are known to exist of the sixteenth-century navigator. Cartier landed on Newfoundland while attempting to discover a Northwest Passage to China and thus inspired French interest in the region.

King Francis I (1494–1547) of France, short of money after waging war in Europe, was interested in finding a Northwest Passage through North America to China in order to trade and repair his finances. Accordingly, in 1534, he sent Jacques Cartier with two ships that made landfall on Newfoundland. They sailed through the Belle Isle Straits into the Gulf of St. Lawrence, and saw Prince Edward Island and New Brunswick. Cartier named Chaleur Bay and landed on the Gaspé Peninsula. In the following year, he explored the St. Lawrence River, meeting Beothuks, Micmacs, Montagnais, and Hurons, wintering near today's Québec. Later, he reached the point where Montréal would stand, then known as Hochelaga. A third voyage with a backer, Sieur de Roberval, and colonists ended in failure in 1543. A severe winter, scurvy among the settlers, squabbling, and hostility from the Iroquois had combined to end the venture.

This abortive attempt at empire building ended official French interest in North America. However, the fishing grounds of the Newfoundland Banks acted as a magnet to fishermen from Rouen, St. Malo, and Dieppe, as well as to the Portuguese and the British. By 1578, 150 French ships were engaged in this trade. The crews traded with the Indians, and the fur business was born, culminating in traders sailing up the St. Lawrence River. French King Henry IV quickly realized the value of Canada and the establishment of a taxable fur-trade monopoly in a royal province, if it could be secured.

In 1603, Samuel de Champlain, with Sieur du Pontgravé, crossed the Atlantic, landing at Tadoussac. Conversations with Indians made Champlain realize that a river and portage route along the Sagueney and Mistassini rivers led to Hudson Bay, while a passage headed south through lakes and rivers south of the Richelieu River (Lake Champlain and the Hudson River). Also, a portage route existed to the Great Lakes along the Ottowa River, across Lake Nipissing, and down the French River. The Indians told him of Lakes Superior, Erie, and Huron, giving the impression that there might be a route to the Pacific.

Champlain was an accomplished geographer and cartographer, and he went on to explore the Bay of Fundy in 1604, and the New England coast as far south as Massachusetts. In 1605, colonists established a settlement at Port Royal, adapted to the environment, and enjoyed friendly relations with the Indians. Québec was founded in 1608 and became a haven for French-Indian trade. Champlain's explorations led to the discovery of Lake Champlain, and he traveled along the inland waterways of southern Ontario and northern New York State. Lakes Huron and Ontario were also investigated.

Relationships with the Native Americans became complex. North of the St. Lawrence were three mutually hostile tribes who sought control of the waterway. The Montagnais roamed the headwaters of the Saguenay, the Algonkin resided in the Ottowa

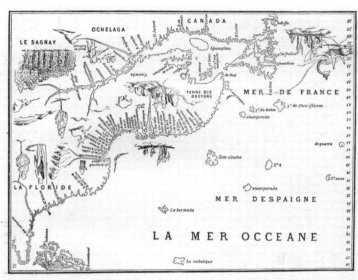

THE "DAUPHIN MAP" OF CANADA, CIRCA 1543, SHOWING CARTIER'S DISCOVERIES

River Valley, and the Huron lived between the Ottowa River and Lake Huron. South of Lake Huron were the five tribes of the Iroquois Confederation. When Europeans first arrived in the St. Lawrence Valley, the Iroquois controlled Lake Ontario and the valley up to Québec, and were expanding eastward. The French opened trade with the Montagnais, and a few years later, the Algonkin and

A contemporary map of the North American Atlantic coast, illustrating Cartier's discoveries on the continent. This map was known as the Dauphin Map.

Samuel de Champlain's arrival off the site of the future city of Québec, from a painting by George Agnew Reid. Champlain explored much of the Northeast of the North American continent, leading the way for the establishment of the colony of New France.

ROANOKE AND JAMESTOWN

LOCKED IN A POWER STRUGGLE WITH THE SPANISH, THE BRITISH SAW COLONIES IN THE "NEW WORLD" AS A MEANS OF COMBATING THEIR EUROPEAN ENEMY.

Opposite: Britain's first North American colony was established on Roanoke Island, off the coast of present-day North Carolina.

Before British colonists attempted to establish a presence in today's North Carolina, the coastal areas were inhabited by a variety of small Indian tribes. Among these were the Algonquian-speaking Poteskeet, Pasquotank, Yeopim, Chowanok, Moratoc, Roanoc, Machapunga, Hatteras, Pamlico, and Secotan. Unfortunately for these Native Americans, there was a sudden British interest in the Americas during Queen Elizabeth I's confrontation with Spain. Courtier Walter Raleigh thought that Spain's power could be destroyed by establishing British colonies in the Americas as bases for actions against Spanish interests. Raw materials could be extracted, markets established, and the New World exploited to finance a European power struggle.

In 1578, Raleigh sailed for America to reconnoiter the coast. This expedition stimulated his desire to found colonies, and in 1584 he sponsored another voyage, which reached Roanoke Island, where the party met the local Secotan Indians. Reports made by Barlowe, the captain of one ship, praised the Secotan's farming, food production, and variety of crops. Queen Elizabeth enthused over the news and knighted Raleigh. A second expedition was dispatched in 1585 to Roanoke Island, where 107 men were left under Ralph Lane to build a fort and explore the region. The expedition had arrived too late to plant crops, however, and food ran short. Lane's attitude toward the Indians became violent as he appropriated their surplus corn. He upset the Secotan and the Chowanoac; then an epidemic raged through the Indian population, and Lane's community was blamed. The Indians planned war, but Lane struck preemptively, killing the Secotan chief, Pemisapan, and slaughtering the settlement of Dasemunkapeac. In 1586, Sir Francis Drake evacuated Lane's colony, but Raleigh sent a third expedition in 1587.

Sir Walter Raleigh, instigator of the Roanoke colony.

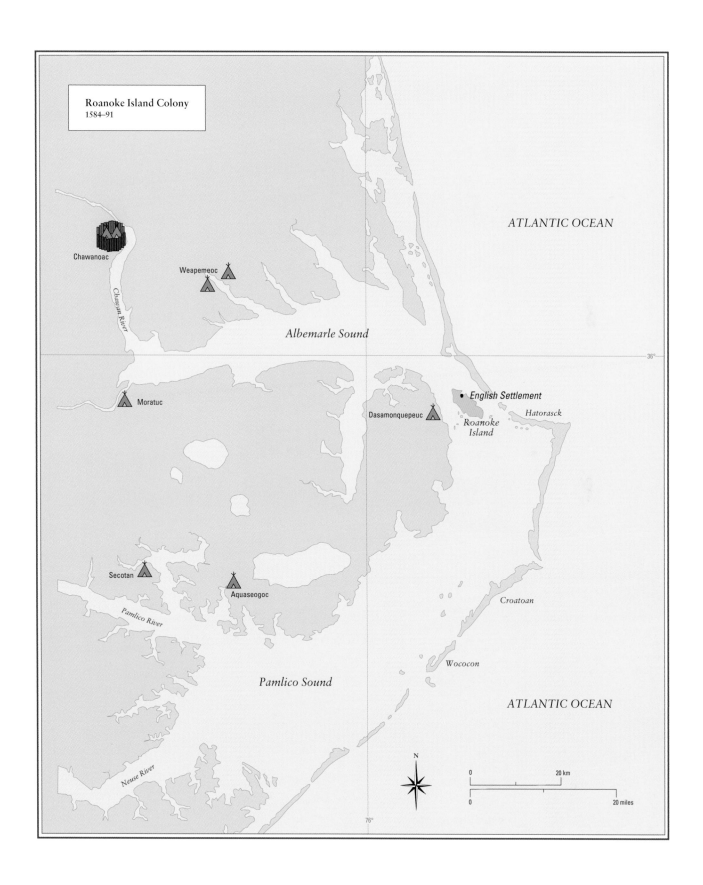

Roanoke Island Colony
1584–91

Chawanoac

Chowan River

Weapemeoc

Albemarle Sound

ATLANTIC OCEAN

36°

Moratuc

Dasamonquepeuc

English Settlement

Hatorasck

Roanoke
Island

Secotan

Aquaseogoc

Pamlico River

Croatoan

Pamlico Sound

Wococon

ATLANTIC OCEAN

Neuse River

N

0   20 km

0   20 miles

76°

A watercolor by John White, leader of the Roanoke colonists, depicting a Secotan village. White's return to Britain to seek help for the settlement saved his life.

INDIAN VILLAGE OF SECOTON (no. 19A, cf. pl. 115)

Raleigh intended that the latest venture would establish a permanent colony of 118 men, women, and children. Again, the settlers arrived too late to plant crops, and the Secotan seemed unfriendly. Governor John White, who had been with Lane, was persuaded to return to England to obtain supplies. He left behind his daughter and granddaughter, Virginia Dare, the first British child to be born in North America. White was prevented from returning to Roanoke until 1590, because England was too busy combating the Spanish Armada to worry about the colony.

On his return, White found the colony deserted, the houses pulled down, and goods scattered about. The only clue to the colonists' fate was the word "CROATAN" carved into a gatepost. Historians have sought to explain where the colonists went, and one day archaeologists may find the answer. Perhaps the colonists sought Croatan Indian help on the

Despite the setback at Roanoke Island, the British persisted in their attempts to establish a colony in North America. The Virginia Company created the settlement of Jamestown on the Chesapeake Bay, and others soon followed in the region.

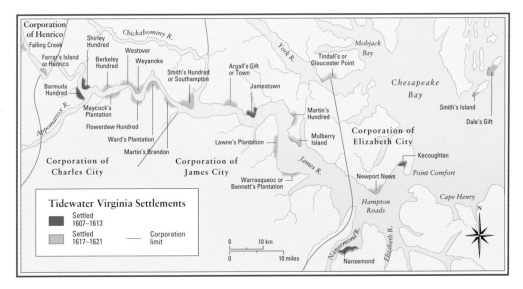

Chesapeake. However, Indians told Captain John Smith that they had been massacred during an Indian war.

A recreation of a Powhatan village at the Jamestown Settlement, a living history center on the coast of Virginia.

Despite the failure of Raleigh's ventures, these early attempts to establish colonies did produce some interesting outcomes. Written reports by Thomas Harriot, a scientist, were published in *A Brief and True Report of the New Found Land of Virginia* (1588). John White produced many watercolors of wildlife and Indians, depicting the latter's clothing, dancing, tattoos, ornaments, ceremonies, cooking styles, and methods of fishing and farming. Noteworthy was his portrait of a woman and baby in Pomeicooc, a Pamlico Sound village.

Raleigh was persistent in his attempts to establish colonies. Although he fell from favor under King James I, the latter was persuaded that further efforts were necessary. Accordingly, the Virginia Company was chartered and authorized to colonize the Americas from latitude 34°N to 45°N, from southern Cape Fear to northern contemporary Bangor, Maine. The company established a colony at Jamestown (1607) on the Chesapeake Bay, where Raleigh had wanted his 1587 colony to be built.

The colonists were regarded with suspicion by Indians, given knowledge of white attacks on the Secotan; the local Powhatan Imperium prepared for trouble. Jamestown was located close to malarial swamps and subject to Indian attack. Even so, the settlement flourished, beginning commercial tobacco production in 1612 and introducing the first African slaves into British North America in 1619.

SPANISH MISSIONS, FROM 1565

FOR THE SPANISH, MISSIONS HAD A TWOFOLD PURPOSE: TO CONVERT "HEATHEN" NATIVE AMERICANS TO CHRISTIANITY, AND TO ACT AS A DEFENSE AGAINST OTHER COLONIAL POWERS.

A hand-colored engraving by Théodor de Bry depicting the French-built Fort Caroline in northern Florida. The fort lasted no more than a year before the Spanish destroyed it.

S pain took real interest in Florida when French Huguenots built Fort Caroline at the mouth of the St. John's River. This potential threat to Spanish shipping was countered by a Spanish attempt to colonize Florida, beginning with the construction of the San Augustine presidio. Missions and garrisons soon dotted the coast, from Tampa Bay to the Carolinas. The first missions were established by Jesuits, but these succumbed to revolts by the Guales and Orista tribes. By 1583, the Franciscans had reopened them and established two mission chains, one along the Atlantic coast, the other spreading westward across the Florida peninsula. Indians were required to pay tribute to the missions in maize, skins, and other goods, and eventually labor too, yet the Spaniards were a small minority. The Franciscans converted large numbers of Guale, Apalachee, and Timucuan Indians, but they began to interfere in Indian domestic politics, and in 1597, the Guale rebelled. Later, the Christian Apalachee revolted, in 1638 and 1647, followed by the Timucuans in 1656.

By 1650, the friars controlled about 26,000 Indians, but the congested mission settlements incubated killer diseases, decimating many coastal tribes. This occurred shortly after the original

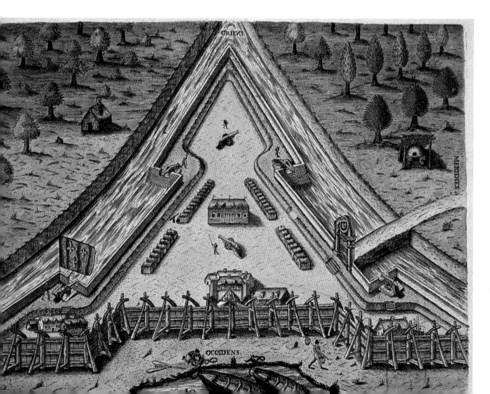

A statue of Juan de Oñate by Reynaldo Rivera at the Oñate Monument Visitors Center, New Mexico. Oñate is honored by some Anglo-, Spanish-, and Mexican-Americans for his explorations of the Southwest, but is vilified by others for his cruelty to the Indians, particularly the Acoma tribe in 1599. Following a skirmish with the tribe during which thirteen Spaniards were killed, his conquistadores murdered 800 of the villagers, enslaved the women and children, and cut off the left foot of every surviving man over the age of twenty-five. In 1998, during New Mexico's celebrations of the 400th anniversary of Oñate's arrival in the region, a group opposed to the statue cut off its right foot, leaving a note saying, "Fair is fair." Although the statue was repaired, some suggested that it should have been left damaged as a symbolic reminder of the foot mutilating incident.

depopulation by disease in the late sixteenth century. The mission system was too weak to resist British slave raids, and by 1710, all missions north of St. Augustine had been destroyed. The Spanish experience left Florida devastated. The Tekesta Indians became extinct, as did the Calusa. The Ais had died out by the 1720s, while the Apalachee were almost annihilated by British and Creek raids.

A second missionary thrust from Mexico was led by Juan de Oñate (1598), accompanied by soldier-settlers, slaves, and Franciscans. Heading from Santa Barbara to San Juan, de Oñate realized that

THE SPREAD OF EPIDEMIC DISEASES

APART FROM DISPOSSESSING NATIVE AMERICANS OF THEIR LAND, EUROPEANS CARRIED WITH THEM DISEASES THAT WOULD DECIMATE LOCAL POPULATIONS.

T he spread of European and African killer diseases in the Americas after 1492 was speedy, wreaking untold damage among the civilizations of Mexico, Peru, and Central America. Trade routes helped diseases and germs to spread inland to regions that had never seen a European. The main illnesses were smallpox, measles, influenza, bubonic plague, diptheria, typhus, cholera, scarlet fever, trachoma, whooping cough, chicken pox, and tropical malaria.

Hispaniola was devastated by the first smallpox outbreak in 1513, and the disease quickly reached the Greater Antilles, then hit the Aztec capital in 1520. Apparently, Florida traded with Cuba, and the disease had arrived before even de Soto started his entrada in 1539. He found numerous abandoned villages choked with vegetation. Apparently, disease had swept the Southeast, and de Soto exacerbated the situation, chiefdoms, customs, and rituals being destroyed. The remnants of the different surviving refugee populations coalesced into federations, such as the Creeks, Choctaw, and Catawba. The population of Florida collapsed under smallpox, measles, and typhus. The Timucuans are thought to have numbered 150,000 before European contact, but by the end of the seventeenth century, 98 percent had died. The Apalachee of northern Florida have been estimated at 25,000–30,000 in the early seventeenth century, but only 8,000 remained at the end of it. Some 250 years after the Spaniards reached Florida, all the original population had vanished. In 1559, influenza swept Europe; two years later, it was an epidemic in the Caribbean and Mesoamerica, before being carried to North America.

In 1585, the Roanoke colony in Virginia transmitted an unknown disease to local villages, killing scores. Even the Pueblo Indians are thought to have suffered smallpox between 1519 and 1524. In 1539, there were 130,000 inhabitants in 150 Pueblos. By 1706, the population had dropped to 6,440 in eighteen Pueblos. De Soto found Arkansas thriving with large towns and cornfields, but when the French arrived in the mid-seventeenth century, the area was empty, with Quapaws, Osage, and Caddoes on the margins.

Survivors of the first smallpox epidemic became immune, but the disease returned in 1562. Whole families were wiped out; sometimes, the young were left with no one to hunt or prepare food. Elders, teachers, and medicine men died, and social bonds were broken as societies were ripped apart. In 1645, a Wampanoag Indian saw a smallpox epidemic tear through Martha's Vineyard. He said, "A long time ago they had wise men which in a grave manner taught the people knowledge, but they are dead and their wisdom is buried with them."

In 1619, the Massachusetts were slaughtered by bubonic plague. In response, the Pilgrims proclaimed that God had killed the natives to free the land

The traditional method used by some Indians to cure diseases such as smallpox was the sweat lodge. The lodge was built near a creek and rocks were heated in a fire nearby. The hot rocks were placed inside the lodge and the sick Indian would enter, having removed all clothing. The covers would be pulled over the lodge to seal in the heat and the Indian would remain inside until completely drenched in sweat. Then he would run to the creek and plunge into the cold water. Not surprisingly, such treatment proved more detrimental than beneficial.

for them. Measles, and possibly smallpox, hit New England and the Great Lakes in 1633. Four years later, another pathogen, probably scarlet fever, hammered the same regions, then smallpox returned in 1639. The swathes of death meant that Indian military power could not combat the westward advance of European colonists. Other dangers were measles in 1658 and 1693; influenza in 1647 and 1675; and diptheria in 1659. Malaria spread through southern North America in the 1690s. Altogether, thirteen known epidemics occurred during the seventeenth century.

Later, smallpox traveled from Texas to New England (1715–21), to the Hudson Bay (1738–39), and to New England again in 1746. Other waves spread to the Great Lakes in 1750–52, 1755–60, and 1762–66; all over North America in 1779–83; to Alaska and Canada in 1785–87; and to the Pueblos in 1788. Measles swept through in 1713–15, and probably across the continent again in 1727–28, followed by the Southwest in 1768–70. Influenza struck in 1761, and diptheria took hold in New England in 1735–36.

Not only did multiple deaths prevent Indians from defending themselves adequately against Europeans, but also disease impacted upon relations between nations. In 1781, smallpox so weakened the Shoshone that by the 1790s, they and their Flathead and Kutenais allies had been pushed out of Montana. In 1778, the Arikara lost 80 percent of their populations and could no longer fight the Sioux. The remnants combined their thirty-two villages into two and retreated north to the Cheyenne River.

Iroquois were obtaining European goods from the St. Lawrence Valley, and that the Susquehannocks were supplying Algonquian groups with iron hatchets, knives, and pieces of iron and brass.

As disease struck, the trade links became more tenuous, so the French stepped in as middlemen traders; to secure good relations, they often married Native American women. The Indians appreciated the benefits of European technology, and became increasingly reliant and dependent upon it. Iron knives and fishhooks were exchanged by the British with the Narragansetts, while the Micmacs wanted metalware from Cartier in Chaleur Bay, especially axes, knives, awls, and trinkets.

More archaeological excavations will be necessary to ascertain the extent of the spread of European goods, but it seems that only small quantities arrived before 1580. Evidence suggests that trade routes spread from Tadoussac along the Ottowa Valley to Lakes Huron and Superior. The St. Lawrence was another route, and goods flowed down to New England. In the late sixteenth century, European goods tended to move from east to west, rather than north to south.

Opposite: A detail from *The Zapotec Civilization* by Diego Rivera, showing Zapotec Indians at work at a number of crafts.

A number of major trading centers were established by the western Indians. The tribes in these areas acted as middlemen, facilitating the exchange of trade goods, which thus were transported throughout the regions they served.

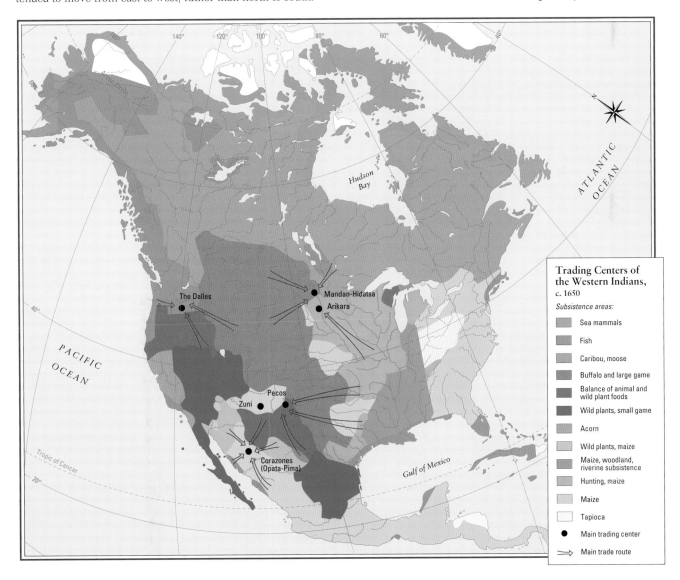

Trading Centers of the Western Indians, c. 1650

Subsistence areas:

- Sea mammals
- Fish
- Caribou, moose
- Buffalo and large game
- Balance of animal and wild plant foods
- Wild plants, small game
- Acorn
- Wild plants, maize
- Maize, woodland, riverine subsistence
- Hunting, maize
- Maize
- Tapioca
- ● Main trading center
- ⇒ Main trade route

THE HORSE

TRANSPORTED TO NORTH AMERICA BY THE SPANISH, THE HORSE WOULD COMPLETELY TRANSFORM THE LIVES OF MANY NATIVE AMERICAN TRIBES, BECOMING A VALUABLE POSSESSION.

Hernán Cortés demonstrates the value of the horse in combat with a Native American.

The Spanish introduced the horse into the Plains, and the animal was traded northward. During the seventeenth and eighteenth centuries, Spanish traders exchanged their goods, horses, and mules for war captives, hides, and skins, especially at Taos, Picos, and Pecos Pueblos, and at Santa Fé. Apache raids ensured that they became the first mounted Indians and, in turn, they sold horses. The 1680 Pueblo Revolt drove the Spanish from New Mexico for several years, and horses left behind were acquired by the Indians. In 1659, Navajos were seen riding horses, and by the 1680s and 1690s, Kiowas and Kiowa-Apaches were selling horses to southern Caddoans, such as the Hasinai villages; the Wichita and Pawnee supplied to the Osage.

In the early eighteenth century, the Comanche raided the Apache and Spanish for horses, trading their booty to the northern Shoshone, on the upper Missouri and during gatherings in the Black Hills. The Shoshone traveled in the Plateau area, following the Green and Colorado rivers; they bartered with the Flatheads and Nez Perce. By the 1740s, Blackfeet and Gros Ventre were mounted, buying their horses from Plateau peoples, the Arapaho, or both. Then, Blackfeet and Gros Ventre sold stock to the western Assiniboines. Simultaneously, the Crow bought from the Shoshone and the Flatheads, then traded in the Mandan and Hidatsa villages, as did other Plains nomads, such as the Kiowa,

A Shoshone man in traditional warrior dress. He wears a war bonnet of eagle feathers and carries a coup stick, while his horse is painted with war symbols.

Looking Glass, a Nez Perce chief. The Nez Perce became major horse traders.

The horse was introduced to the North American continent by the Spanish, and from around 1600 began reaching the hands of the Indians. Some of these had escaped to the wild and been captured, while others were seized during raids. Gradually, the use of the horse by Native Americans spread from tribe to tribe across the Great Plains.

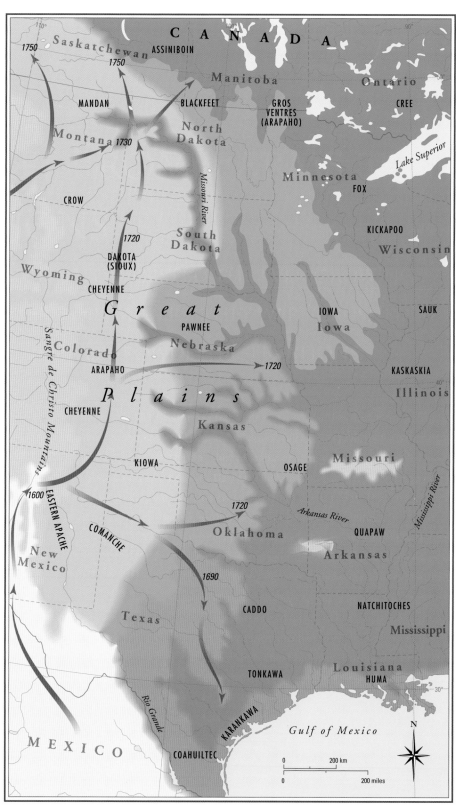

The Great Plains

Vegetation

- Forest and woodland
- Short / tall grass
- Grass and scrubland
- Desert and scrub
- Mountain vegetation
- → Spread of horses, with date of arrival
- CROW Indian nation

Kiowa-Apache, Arapaho, and Cheyenne. They sold in Arikara villages where Assiniboines and Plains Cree exchanged British and French guns for horses, also at the Mandan and Hidatsa settlements. The Arikara villages distributed to the Teton Sioux, who traveled to the James River trade gathering in South Dakota to sell to Yankton, Yanktonnais, and Santee Sioux in the 1750s.

Some Indians became virtual horse merchants, and others horse breeders, such as the Cayuse; the Palouses gave their name to the Appaloosa breed, famous for its spotted coat. Estimates suggest that horses moved north and northwest from Santa Fé at the rate of ten miles (16 kilometers) annually. In addition, herds of wild horses became established in southern Texas and in California after the Spanish settled these areas in 1769. So large were the Californian herds that they became a nuisance to the rancheros.

Horses changed the lives of the Indians. Some previously horticultural bands moved from the Missouri River bluff settlements onto the Plains. Hunting buffalo from horseback transformed Indian food supplies by allowing a surplus to be preserved. This led to a growth in populations. Thus, many sedentary bands left their farms for a nomadic hunting lifestyle.

Apart from being ridden, horses could be used as pack animals and travois pullers, allowing tribes to travel further and faster. Goods could be accumulated, then transported by horse, which was a far easier method than relying on dogs or women for pulling power. Tribes became increasingly mobile in the constant search for fresh horse pastures. Camps were moved frequently, and Indians acquired the skill of burning the ground to encourage early spring growth of grass.

The easier acquisition of food by the hunt liberated young men, who could now engage in horse raiding, since horses had become an economic necessity. Raiding could also lead to the capture of children, who would be adopted, and women for marriage or other liaisons. The personal acquisition of horses could raise a man's status and increase wealth. The more horses owned, the greater the quantity of property that could be carried. Wealthy elites emerged, especially among the Blackfeet and Kiowa.

The Appaloosa horse, with its distinctive spotted coat, came about through the efforts of Palouse breeders in the Pacific Northwest.

Owning many horses could mean that a man could marry several women. Moreover, individuals of low status could improve their social standing by capturing horses, which could be kept or traded with Europeans.

As a consequence, warfare escalated for economic and social reasons, and it changed from pitched battles to small raids relying on surprise. Weapons became shorter to allow mounted combat. Battle achievements were based upon the seizure of an enemy's horse or gun, while casualties could lead to revenge raids. Two tribes that became especially dominant were the Comanche below the Platte River, and the Osage to the east of the Comanche.

A souvenir postcard from the 1907 Jamestown Exposition, depicting Pocahontas, daughter of Powhatan, saving the life of Captain John Smith.

Weetamoo was wife to Wamsutta, who succeeded his father, Massasoit, in 1662, becoming principal chief of the Wampanoag. Weetamoo was a chief in her own right of the Pocasset tribe in the confederacy. When Wamsutta died, she married Quinnapin, the son of Ninigret, chief of the Niantic tribe of the Wampanoag. She retained her status in the Pocasset tribe, despite her new husband already having two other wives. Ninigret's sister, Quaiapan, married the son of a Narragansett tribal chief and headed Queen's North village in Rhode Island. Ninigret had another sister, Awashonks, who was chief of the Sakonnet Wampanoag. Metacomet (Philip) succeeded Wamsutta, and he was married to Weetamoo's sister. Thus, the region was home to several powerful women.

During King Philip's War, Weetamoo supported Metacomet, whereas Awashonks joined the British. Weetamoo commanded 300 warriors, but only thirty survived the fighting. After Philip was killed on August 12, 1676, Weetamoo fled from the British, but drowned in the Taunton River during her flight. Her head and Philip's were displayed on poles in Plymouth to deter any Native American chief who might be considering further resistance against the colony. The British had learned the importance of female power.

Opposite: The British increasingly became the dominant European nation in the East and far North of the North American continent. They dispatched many expeditions to explore the New World.

Elsewhere, the Spanish faced their own difficulties. Renewed missionary activity in Florida, with consequent epidemics, was accompanied by an influx of soldiers, which led to further conflict with the Guales, Timicuans, and Apalachees. Forced labor on plantations owned by soldiers contributed to Apalachee resistance in 1647, and more self-defense by the Apalachee and Timicuans in 1656.

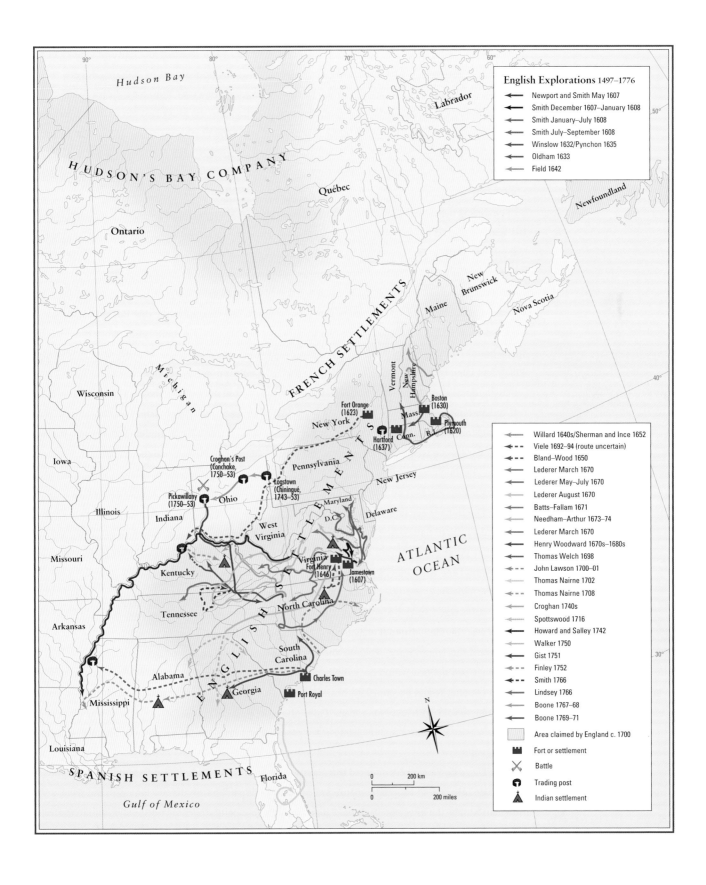

English Explorations 1497–1776

- ← Newport and Smith May 1607
- ← Smith December 1607–January 1608
- ← Smith January–July 1608
- ← Smith July–September 1608
- ← Winslow 1632/Pynchon 1635
- ← Oldham 1633
- ← Field 1642

- ← Willard 1640s/Sherman and Ince 1652
- ← Viele 1692–94 (route uncertain)
- ← Bland–Wood 1650
- ← Lederer March 1670
- ← Lederer May–July 1670
- ← Lederer August 1670
- ← Batts–Fallam 1671
- ← Needham–Arthur 1673–74
- ← Lederer March 1670
- ← Henry Woodward 1670s–1680s
- ← Thomas Welch 1698
- ← John Lawson 1700–01
- ← Thomas Nairne 1702
- ← Thomas Nairne 1708
- ← Croghan 1740s
- ← Spottswood 1716
- ← Howard and Salley 1742
- ← Walker 1750
- ← Gist 1751
- ← Finley 1752
- ← Smith 1766
- ← Lindsey 1766
- ← Boone 1767–68
- ← Boone 1769–71
- ▨ Area claimed by England c. 1700
- ▥ Fort or settlement
- ✕ Battle
- ⬤ Trading post
- ▲ Indian settlement

THE DIVIDED SOUTHEAST

THE SOUTHEAST BECAME A PLACE OF TURMOIL, THE BRITISH, FRENCH, AND SPANISH ALL SEEKING TO GAIN TERRITORY WITH THE AID OF NATIVE AMERICAN ALLIES.

Pierre Le Moyne d'Iberville, founder of the colony of French Louisiana. In 1690, he instigated the construction of Fort Maurepas at Biloxi in a bid to counter British expansion in the Southeast.

Opposite: As Spanish power in the Southeast diminished, the British pushed steadily southward. By 1665, the Charter of Carolina set the southern border of Carolina at 29 degrees North latitude in northern Florida.

Eventually, the Southeast was split under the spheres of influence of Britain, France, and Spain. Britain established a presence in the Carolinas after 1670 by founding Charles Town. The Weapemeoc nation sold its coastal lands and moved away from the European settlers. Erie refugees, known as Westos, became a target for Virginia traders entering the Carolinas, as did the Tuscarora and the Catawba nation. The Westos were adept at hunting for deerskins and capturing slaves by attacking Yuchis, Cherokees, and others; they managed to force the Spanish to close two missions among the Guale in Florida. Traders allied themselves with Shawnee refugees (Savannahs) and slaughtered Westos, driving them from the colony and into confederation with the Creeks.

Many Guales, potential victims of slavers, fled to St. Augustine and Spanish protection, while those remaining in the Carolinas became known as Yamasees. In the late 1680s, Anglo-Creek trade began in earnest. Heavily armed by the British, Yamasees and Creeks attacked Apalachee and Timucuan mission stations for slaves and horses. So badly did they damage the Spanish that their influence north of St. Augustine was severely restricted. The British then began trade with Upper Creeks, who raided the Cherokee and Choctaw for slaves; the Chickasaw also mounted slave raids against the Choctaw and the Illinois on the Mississippi River. Some commerce took place with the Cherokee, but they were less important to the British than the Creek, so the colonists ignored Cherokee complaints about Creek slave raids. By 1700, the region had become so destabilized by slave wars that conflict broke out between the Tuscarora and the Yamasees.

Spanish settlements in Florida were subjected to constant attack, and missions were established in today's Georgia in an attempt to provide a buffer for St. Augustine against encroaching Carolinians. Also, the Spanish employed naval power to prevent the French from entering Pensacola in 1698, and Biloxi in 1699. However, the 26,000 Guale, Apalachee, and Timucua were becoming less loyal to

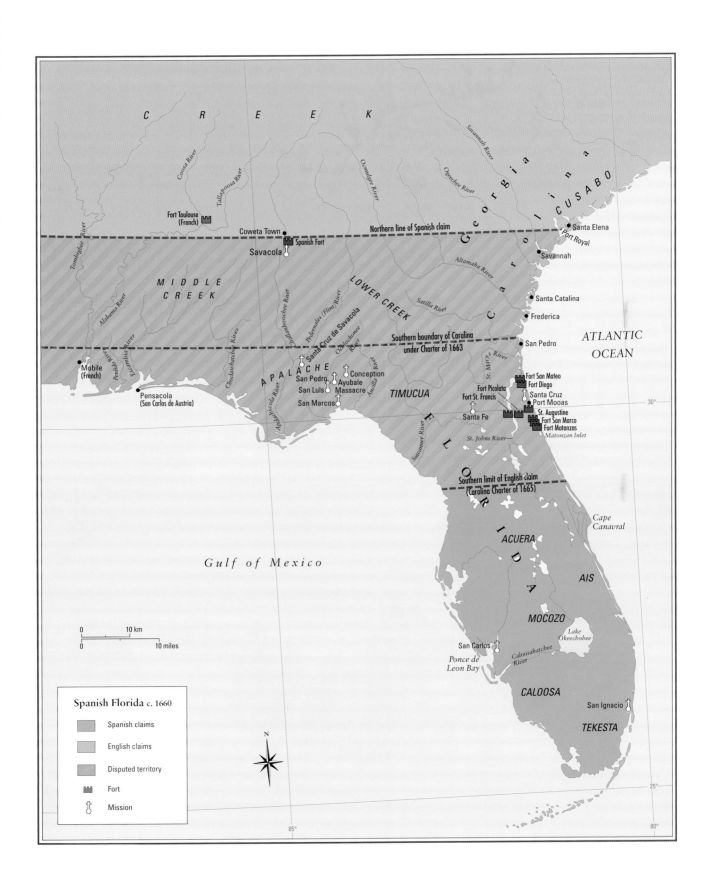

C R E E K

Coosa River
Tallapoosa River
Ocmulgee River
Savannah River
Ogeechee River

Tombigbee River

Fort Toulouse
(French)

Coweta Town
Spanish Fort
Savacola

Northern line of Spanish claim

Georgia

Carolina

CUSABO

Santa Elena
Port Royal

Savannah

MIDDLE
CREEK

Alabama River

Pensacola River

Escambia River

Chattahoochee River

Pedernales (Flint) River

LOWER CREEK

Altamaha River

Satilla River

Santa Catalina

Frederica

Southern boundary of Carolina
under Charter of 1663

San Pedro

ATLANTIC
OCEAN

Apalachicola River

Ochlockonee River

APALACHE

Santa Cruz de Savacola

San Pedro
San Luis
San Marcos

Conception
Ayubale
Massacre

Aucilla River

TIMUCUA

St. Mary's River

Fort Picolata
Fort St. Francis

Santa Fe

Fort San Mateo
Fort Diego
Santa Cruz
Port Mooas
St. Augustine
Fort San Marco
Fort Matanzas
Matanzan Inlet

30°

Mobile
(French)

Pensacola
(San Carlos de Austria)

Suwannee River

F L O R I D A

St. Johns River

Southern limit of English claim
(Carolina Charter of 1665)

Cape
Canavral

ACUERA

AIS

MOCOZO

Lake
Okeechobee

Gulf of Mexico

San Carlos

Ponce de
Leon Bay

Caloosahatchee
River

CALOOSA

San Ignacio

TEKESTA

0   10 km
0   10 miles

N

Spanish Florida c. 1660

Spanish claims

English claims

Disputed territory

Fort

Mission

85°

80°

25°

A contemporary woodcut showing the Dutch negotiating a treaty with the Manahatta band of the Lenape tribe for the purchase of Manhattan Island in 1626. The backdrop is of Fort Amsterdam, which was built on the island in 1625. The town of New Amsterdam grew around the fort and eventually became the City of New York.

was shot, and the Indians began to leave. Undisciplined Dutch militia pursued the Indians, opening fire as the Delaware withdrew to Staten Island and Pavonia. Then they moved to New Jersey, where they destroyed twenty-eight farms, killed fifty Dutch settlers, and took a hundred prisoners.

Eventually, Stuyvesant negotiated the return of seventy hostages. Records fail to mention the remainder, except five children, who were found with the Delaware two years later. Perhaps the Indians felt that hostages would be a surety against Dutch military action, or planned to adopt them. Whatever the case, the Delaware remained peaceful during the remainder of Stuyvesant's administration.

The Esopus Wars were occasioned by Dutch settlers building Wittwyck village and farms along the Rondout and Esopus creeks. Indian-Dutch relations became tense as young warriors became dependent on alcohol from illegal liquor sales. Violence broke out, but Stuyvesant managed to damp it down. The settlers were persuaded to concentrate their numbers for security, and a fort was built at Wittwyck. Bad relations made the settlers attack a group of drunken Indians; some Dutch were killed in retaliation, and the fort was besieged for a short while. Johannes La Montagne, in charge of Fort Orange, employed Mohawks, Mahicans, and Catskill Indians to secure a cease fire. Nevertheless, hostilities continued until Montagne's Indian diplomats were joined by Susquehannas and Delaware, who arranged a peace in 1660.

Opposite: Dutch territorial claims stretched as far west as the Delaware River, where they met those of the British in Maryland. In the middle was the small Scandinavian colony of New Sweden, on the banks of the Delaware. Conflict arose between the Swedes and Dutch, the latter seizing the Swedish colony, although the settlers there were allowed a degree of autonomy.

War broke out again when another village, Nieuwdorp, was built near Wittwyck. The Esopus Indians were incensed and assaulted both villages in 1663. Nieuwdorp was incinerated, but Indians who had infiltrated Wittwyck were driven out. Twenty Dutch were killed and forty-five captured, leaving sixty-nine to defend Wittwyck. The Dutch retaliated, sending troops, led by Martin Crieger, to attack an Esopus village as it was being fortified. The Indians were defeated, thirty being killed or captured, while twenty-three Dutch prisoners were recovered. Peace was secured, but the Esopus were forced to cede more land and compelled to trade at one spot under a flag of truce. New Indian-Dutch disputes would be settled in Dutch courts

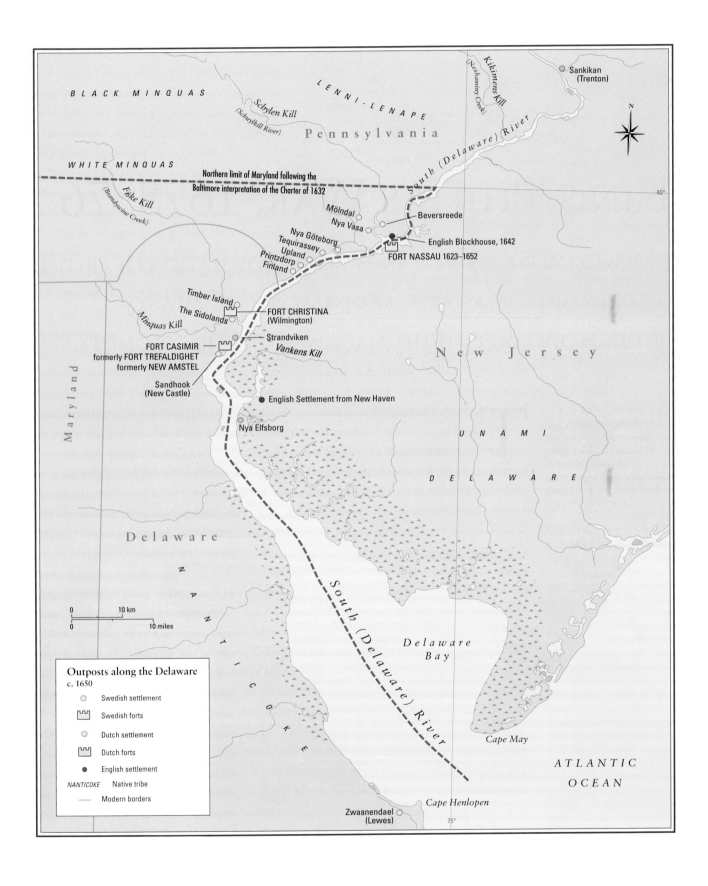

BLACK MINQUAS

LENNI-LENAPE

Schylen Kill
(Schuylkill River)

Kikimens Kill
(Neshaminy Creek)

Sankikan
(Trenton)

Pennsylvania

South (Delaware) River

N

WHITE MINQUAS

Northern limit of Maryland following the
Baltimore interpretation of the Charter of 1632

40°

Fske Kill
(Brandywine Creek)

Mölndal
Nya Vasa

Beversreede

Nya Göteborg
Tequirassey
Upland
Printzdorp
Finland

English Blockhouse, 1642

FORT NASSAU 1623–1652

Timber Island

The Sidolands

FORT CHRISTINA
(Wilmington)

Minquas Kill

New Jersey

FORT CASIMIR
formerly FORT TREFALDIGHET
formerly NEW AMSTEL

Strandviken
Vankens Kill

Sandhook
(New Castle)

English Settlement from New Haven

U N A M I

Nya Elfsborg

D E L A W A R E

Maryland

Delaware

N

A

N

T

I

South (Delaware) River

C

O

K

E

Delaware
Bay

0   10 km
0   10 miles

Cape May

ATLANTIC
OCEAN

Outposts along the Delaware
c. 1650

○ Swedish settlement

⌂ Swedish forts

○ Dutch settlement

⌂ Dutch forts

● English settlement

NANTICOKE Native tribe

— Modern borders

Cape Henlopen

Zwaanendael
(Lewes)

75°

further weakened the Pueblo resolve. Moreover, some Pueblos recognized the benefits accruing from Spanish agricultural methods, and the introduction of cattle, horses, and olive trees.

Eventually, Spanish troops returned, Zia Pueblo being captured in 1689. The new governor, Diego de Vargas, regained Santa Fé in 1692, symbolizing the reconquest of New Mexico. When de Vargas met the leader of all the Pueblos, Luis Tupatu of Picuris Pueblo, he saw irony in a man dressed in skins, wearing a rosary around his neck, and carrying a silver cross, an Agnus Dei, and a cloth depicting Our Lady of Guadeloupe. Henceforth, Spanish rule was more lenient, bringing an end to cultural warfare.

Don Diego de Vargas became governor of New Spain following the recapture of Santa Fé in 1692. His tenure saw a less harsh form of rule.

Opposite: Angered by the Spaniards' failure to protect them from being raided by Utes, Navajos, and Apaches, and by the missionaries' repressive religious regime, the Pueblo peoples united under the shaman Popé and rose up against their European overlords. They drove the Spanish back to Mexico, where they remained for nine years.

Pueblo ruins at Wupatki National Monument.

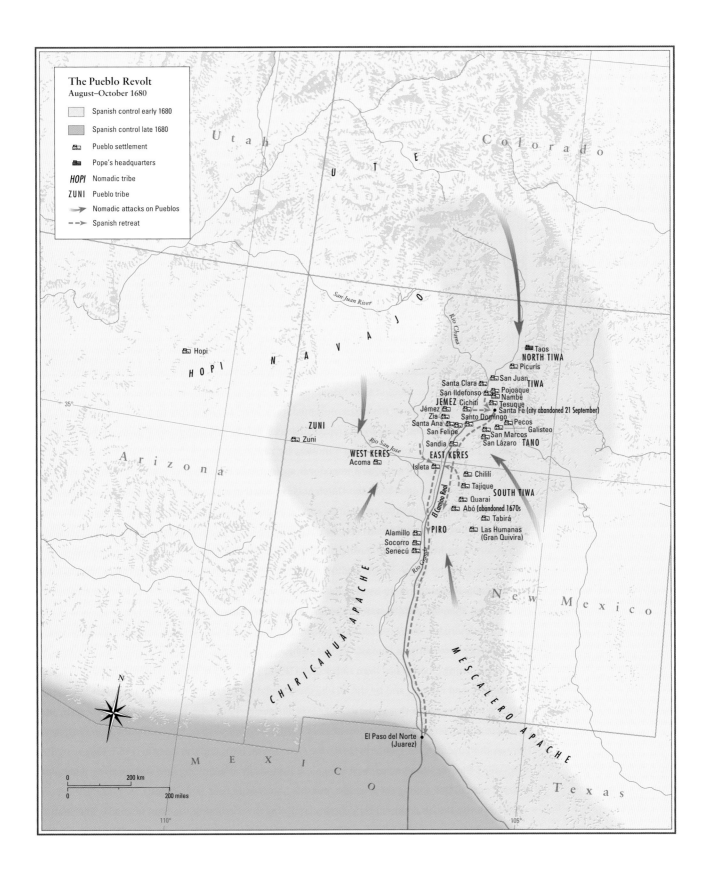

The Pueblo Revolt
August–October 1680

- Spanish control early 1680
- Spanish control late 1680
- 🏠 Pueblo settlement
- 🏠 Pope's headquarters
- *HOPI* Nomadic tribe
- ZUNI Pueblo tribe
- → Nomadic attacks on Pueblos
- --→ Spanish retreat

U T A H

C o l o r a d o

U T E

San Juan River

Río Chama

Hopi

H O P I

N A V A J O

🏠 Taos
NORTH TIWA
🏠 Picurís

🏠 San Juan   TIWA
Santa Clara 🏠
San Ildefonso 🏠 🏠 Pojoaque
🏠 Nambé
JEMEZ 🏠 Cichití
Jémez 🏠   • Tesuque
Zia 🏠   • Santa Fé (city abandoned 21 September)
Santa Ana 🏠 🏠 Santo Domingo
San Felipe   🏠 Pecos
🏠 San Marcos   🏠 Galisteo
Sandia 🏠 🏠 San Lázaro TANO

ZUNI

🏠 Zuni

Río San José

A r i z o n a

WEST KERES
Acoma 🏠

EAST KERES

Isleta 🏠

🏠 Chililí
🏠 Tajique
SOUTH TIWA
🏠 Quarai
Abó (abandoned 1670s)
🏠 Tabirá

Alamillo 🏠
Socorro 🏠   PIRO
Senecú 🏠   🏠 Las Humanas
(Gran Quivira)

El Camino Real

Río Grande

N e w   M e x i c o

C H I R I C A H U A   A P A C H E

M E S C A L E R O   A P A C H E

N

El Paso del Norte
(Juarez) •

M E X I C O

T e x a s

0   200 km
0   200 miles

110°   105°

A contemporary engraving depicting the destruction of the French Fort Frontenac by the British in 1758 during the French and Indian War. The fort occupied a strategic position at the mouth of the Cataraqui River, overlooking the point where the St. Lawrence River leaves Lake Ontario.

Queen Anne's War (1702–13), King George's War (1743–48), and the French and Indian War, also known as the Seven Years' War (1754–61), which finally led to the 1763 Treaty of Paris.

The Comanche were originally Shoshone, but in 1500, they left their homeland near the Great Salt Lake and in present-day Nevada, traveling through the South Pass onto the western part of the northern Plains, where they made a home on the Upper Platte River and in eastern Wyoming. Then they pushed north and east to the Alberta and Saskatchewan plains. The Comanche economy was based upon hunting buffalo on foot, in competition with the Blackfeet, Crow, and Plains Apache. After the 1680 Pueblo Revolt, which forced the Spanish to abandon their New Mexico outposts and leave their horses behind, the Comanche began to acquire these animals from either the Apache or Ute. Since the Comanche were divided into several bands, who seldom cooperated,

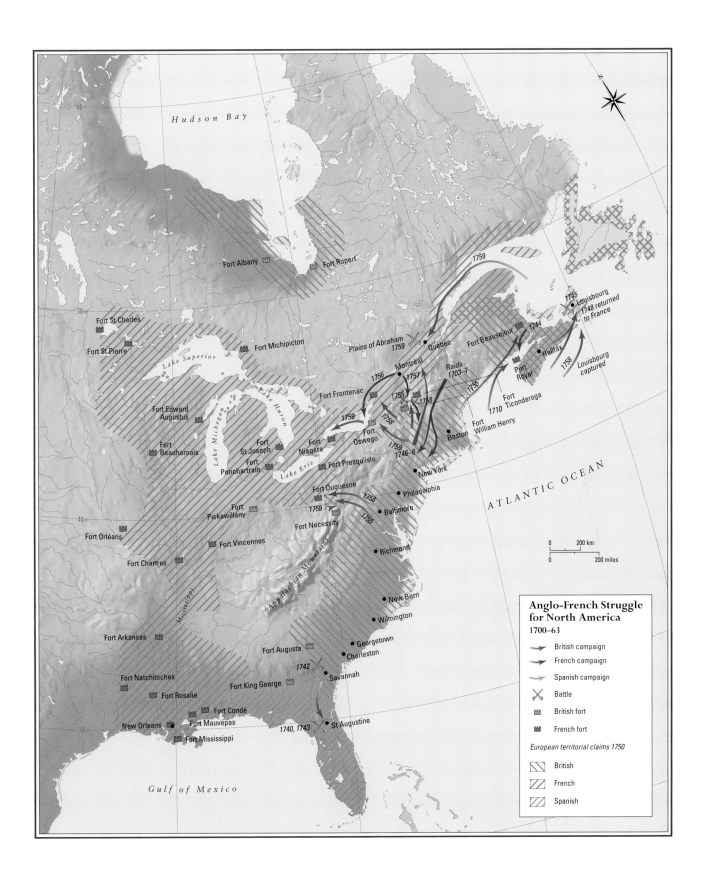

Map labels:
Hudson Bay
Fort Albany
Fort Rupert
Fort St Charles
Fort St Pierre
Fort Michipicton
Lake Superior
Plains of Abraham 1759
Québec
Fort Beauséjour 1744
Louisbourg 1745
1748 returned to France
Montréal
1756 1757
Raids 1703–7
Port Royal
Halifax
Louisbourg captured 1758
1755
1758
1755
Fort Ticonderoga 1710
Fort Frontenac
1759
1758
Fort Edward Augustus
Lake Michigan
Lake Huron
Fort St Joseph
Fort Niagara
Fort Oswego
1759
1746–8
Boston
Fort William Henry
Fort Beauharnais
Fort Ponchartrain
Lake Erie
Fort Presqu'isle
New York
Fort Duquesne
1758
Philadelphia
1755
Fort Pickawillany 1755
Fort Necessity
1755
Baltimore
ATLANTIC OCEAN
Fort Orléans
Fort Vincennes
Richmond
Appalachian Mountains
Fort Chartres
Mississippi
New Bern
Wilmington
Fort Arkansas
Fort Augusta
Georgetown
Charleston
1742
Savannah
Fort Natchitoches
Fort King George
Fort Rosalie
Fort Condé
Fort Mauvepas
New Orleans
Fort Mississippi
1740, 1743
St Augustine
Gulf of Mexico

Legend:
Anglo-French Struggle for North America 1700–63
→ British campaign
→ French campaign
→ Spanish campaign
✕ Battle
⌂ British fort
⌂ French fort
European territorial claims 1750
British
French
Spanish

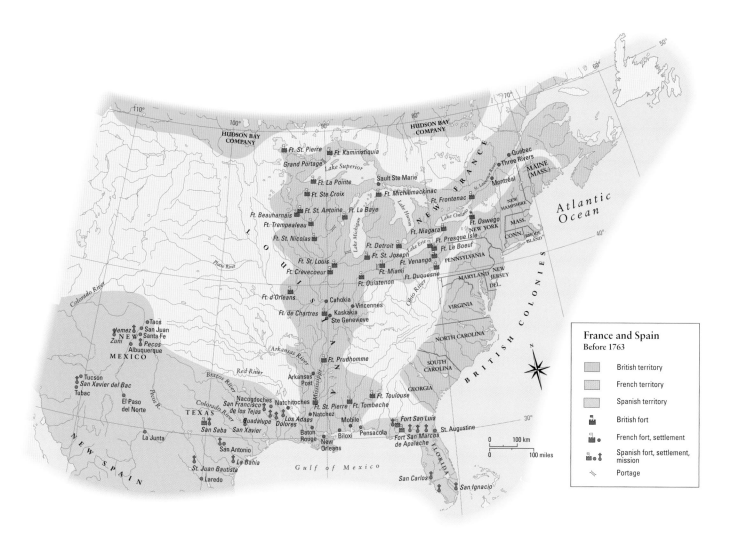

France and Spain
Before 1763

	British territory
	French territory
	Spanish territory
🏰	British fort
🏰 •	French fort, settlement
🏰 • ⚓	Spanish fort, settlement, mission
⚒	Portage

While conflict between Britain and France took place in the Northeast, further south French incursions brought them up against the Spanish, who were well established, particularly in the Southwest.

some would trade with the Apache while others fought them—a chaos that made perfect sense to the Comanche. Subsequently, the tribe migrated south, not to hunt buffalo, which were plentiful in the north, but probably to gain access to the supply of horses in New Mexico. These could be captured and traded to increase tribal wealth. Forming an alliance with the Ute, the Comanche moved from their roaming grounds between the Rocky Mountains and Black Hills, entering the central Plains of eastern Colorado and western Kansas, between the Platte and Arkansas rivers. They displaced the Plains Apache, and by 1706, both the Comanche and Ute were trading in Taos, New Mexico.

The Apache suffered from constant attacks, the Jicarilla and Plains Apache (Lipan and Mescalero) being forced into southern Texas and New Mexico, where they began raiding Spanish settlements. Other Apache bands crossed into Arizona and virtually cut off Santa Fé from El Paso in north Mexico. By 1730, the Comanche controlled the Texas Panhandle, central Texas, and northeastern New Mexico, despite living north of the Arkansas River. Simultaneously, the Ute-Comanche alliance collapsed, the Ute being pushed from the Plains into the western mountains. There, they became allied with the

Spanish and Jicarilla Apache against their common foe, but the Comanche were strong enough to cross the Arkansas, moving into northeastern New Mexico and onto the edges of the Staked Plains of the Texas Panhandle.

The Comanche became notorious horse thieves, supplying former Spanish horses to other tribes, and trading buffalo robes and slaves with New Mexico. French traders penetrated Kansas and moved up the Red River, making contact with the Wichita tribe; they sold guns to the Comanche. In return, they received stolen horses and mules from the Spanish territories. The Comanche became so strong that some bands raided Pecos in 1746, 1750, 1773, and 1775, and Taos in 1760. The Comanche were fighting most tribes of the Central Plains, as well as Spanish expeditions sent against them. Even in 1775, the Yamparika division was fighting the Lakota and Cheyenne near the Black Hills, and attacking the Arikara on the Missouri River. Other tribes were interested in stealing Comanche horses, and war broke out with the Osage and Pawnee in 1746, but the Wichita arranged peace in 1750, which allowed a combined Pawnee-Comanche attack against the Osage in 1751, the latter being defeated. Then the Pawnee moved to the Platte River in Nebraska, but they still mounted raids into Texas and New Mexico to steal Comanche horses; alliances were soon forgotten. The Comanche also fought the Crow, Pueblo, Lakota, Kansa, Navajo, Wichita, Waco, Tonkawa, Sauk, Fox, Creek, Choctaw, Seminole, and Chickasaw.

Elsewhere in Texas, the Spanish felt threatened by French expansion from Louisiana and incursions by their traders from Illinois. Thus, in 1716, a mission-presidio was built at Nacogdoches, soon being followed by additional missions and outposts in eastern Texas. Eventually, this area came under threat from the Plains Apache, pushed south by the Comanche until squeezed into southern Texas along the Rio Grande (1728). When the Apache encountered local tribes, they either wiped them out or assimilated them. Thus were destroyed the Coahuiltec, Cisos, Jano, and Manso nations. These Lipan Apache attacked and traded with the Tonkawa and Caddo tribes of eastern Texas, while still being attacked themselves by the Comanche, who also fought the Spanish. Comanche raids into Texas were only curtailed when the tribe was devastated by a smallpox epidemic between 1780 and 1781.

Warfare in the eastern woodlands differed from the turmoil on the Plains. Whereas an Apache warrior's status would depend upon the food or horses he brought back from a raid, the eastern tribes often took scalps as proof of a warrior's involvement in combat. The Indians were not driven to acquire material possessions, but would seek vengeance. Others would engage in mourning wars, in which the aim was to seize captives who could be adopted and assimilated into the tribe to replace those killed in battle or by disease. Thus, women and children would be prime targets (and allegedly easier to socialize), and the number of captives taken would symbolize one tribe's strength and dominance over another. Adoption after capture was prevalent among Indians in the region between the Atlantic seaboard and Mississippi, from the Iroquois and Huron in the northeast to the Cherokee in the southeast, and among the Great Lakes Ojibwa (Chippewa) and Santee Sioux. However, adoption was not always successful—Huron women were known to commit suicide rather than become Iroquois. On the other hand, white female captives sometimes preferred to stay with their captors rather than return to their own society.

COLONIAL CAPTIVES

THERE WERE MANY INDIAN RAIDS AND PRISONERS CAPTURED ON THE FRONTIERS OF NEW ENGLAND, ESPECIALLY DURING THE COLONIAL WARS BETWEEN FRANCE AND BRITAIN.

Opposite: A monument in honor of Hannah Dustin in Boscawen, New Hampshire. Seized by Indians with another woman and a boy in 1697, Dustin and her fellow prisoners eventually managed to escape by killing and scalping the Indians.

Between 1675 and 1763, some 1,641 white captives were seized in Indian raids and battles. As a rule, the French and their Abenaki allies fought the British with their Iroquois friends. The French allies, from Maine, New Brunswick, and Québec, poured through New England's Iroquois shield to attack settlements in New York, Massachusetts, and New Hampshire.

Indians waged war for many reasons. During the Beaver Wars, the Iroquois fought the Huron, Petun, Neutrals, Erie, and Nipissing to gain control of the fur trade with England. However, there were reasons other than economics and vengeance that prompted war. Taking captives offered the possibility of obtaining a ransom, or a family might adopt a captive to compensate for the loss of one of its members. Women, but more often children, were adopted, since they were easier to socialize and they could maintain tribal numbers; captives were also symbols of victory.

Many captives were ransomed, escaped, or were freed through negotiation. Upon returning to the settlements, many victims published their experiences. Mary Rowlandson's account convinced many that capture was God's punishment for past sins, while others recounted Indian customs, becoming material for anthropological and ethnographical study. Some captives actually preferred the Indian lifestyle, or valued escape from Puritan strictures, even refusing to return to European society. Of these, a few became "white Indians" and fought the colonists.

Mary Rowlandson's account was the first major witness record. It described a raid on Lancaster, Massachusetts, where she was captured in February 1675. Later, she was sold to Quinnapin, a Narragansett chief, but was ransomed in May 1676 at Redemption Rock in Princeton, Massachusetts. Another captive was John Gyles, taken at the age of nine years from Maine in August 1689, during King William's War. He spent six years with Indians, and three years with a Frenchman. In 1698, he was granted his freedom and later wrote an account, published 1736, of his time among the Maliseet Indians along the St. John River Valley.

Map opposite: By 1750, New France surrounded the British colonies along the Atlantic coast. Constant aggression between the two European powers and their Indian allies saw many settlers kidnapped.

A well-known captive is Hannah Dustin, who was seized on March 15, 1697, at Haverhill, Massachusetts, while lying in bed recuperating from the birth of her twelfth child. Taken with Mary Neff, her midwife, and a teenage boy, she was marched some 120 miles (190 kilometers) by two warriors, their wives, seven children, and an older woman. On March 30, they camped on an island at the juncture of the Contoocook and Merrimack rivers, near contemporary Boscawen, New Hampshire. During the night, Dustin, Neff, and the boy killed all but two of the Indians with an axe, scalped them, and returned to Massachusetts. Dustin was granted a £25 scalp bounty; the other two shared a similar sum.

The most memorable captive incident occurred in February 1704, at Deerfield, Massachusetts. Fifty-six settlers were killed and 109 captured, being marched to Canada. Only eighty-eight survived the trek. Eventually, fifty-nine were returned, but the young, mainly those under fourteen years, remained. The Reverend John Williams' daughter, Eunice, married an Indian and refused to return.

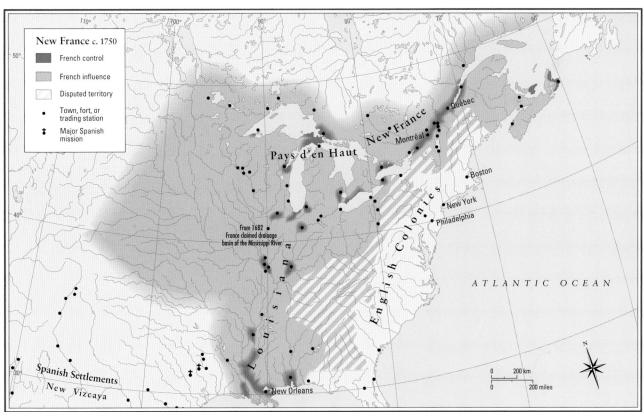

New France c. 1750
- French control
- French influence
- Disputed territory
- • Town, fort, or trading station
- ⚜ Major Spanish mission

Pays d'en Haut

New France

Québec

Montréal

Boston

New York

Philadelphia

English Colonies

ATLANTIC OCEAN

From 1682 France claimed drainage basin of the Mississippi River

Louisiana

Spanish Settlements
New Vizcaya

New Orleans

0   200 km
0   200 miles

N

Apparently, the onslaught against the British colonies had been an attempt by the French to show the Abenakis that they were reliable allies, and to warn the British that war would be fought in New England, not New France.

Mary Jemison, aged fifteen years, was captured in western Pennsylvania in April 1758 by Shawnee warriors. She was taken to the Seneca near the Sciota River, had two Indian husbands, eight children, thirty-nine grandchildren, and fourteen great grandchildren. She suffered with her adoptive tribe during the American Revolution and eventually died aged nintey years. She is claimed by both whites and Iroquois as a folk heroine.

In 1763, after Indians had been defeated at Bushy Run, Colonel Bouquet demanded the return of captives held by the Shawnee and Delaware. Most of them wished to remain with the Indians, however, and some had to be bound before their return, for fear that they would abscond. Some women fled back to Indian villages rather than remain in white society.

A contemporary illustration showing British colonists being taken prisoner by Indians during the French and Indian Wars.

Opposite: Throughout the first half of the eighteenth century, the French and British vied for control of North America. Numerous battles took place, involving Indian allies on both sides. After 1763 almost all the French territory was ceded to Britain or Spain, their sole remaining possession being the tiny islands of St. Pierre et Miquelon, off the coast of southern Newfoundland.

The charge of the Highlanders at the Battle of Bushy Run in 1763, from a painting by C.W. Jeffreys. The action routed a combined force of Delaware, Shawnee, Wyandot, and Mingo warriors.

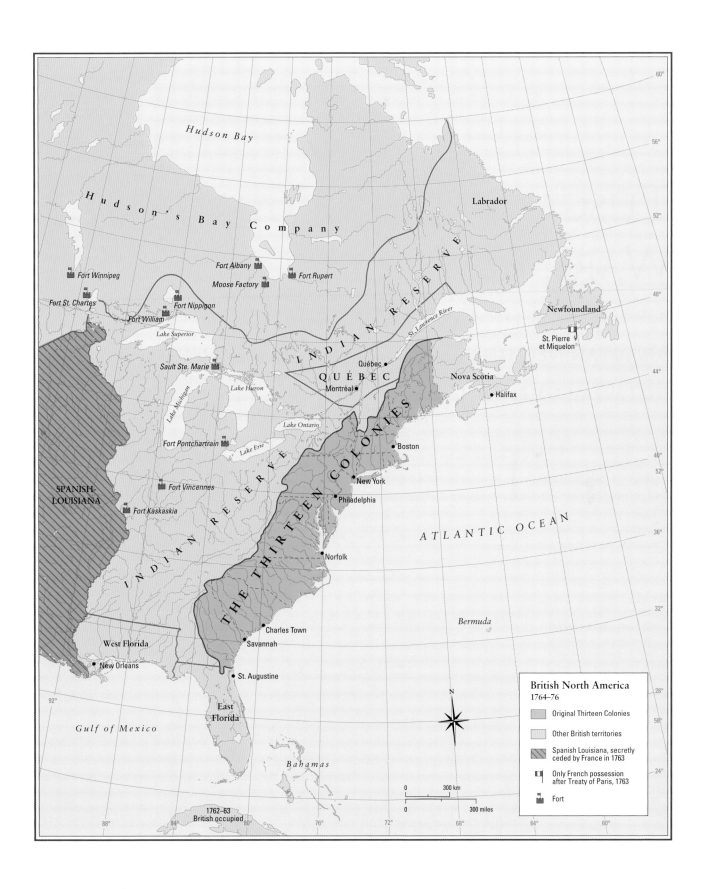

Hudson Bay

Labrador

H u d s o n ' s   B a y   C o m p a n y

Fort Winnipeg

Fort Albany
Moose Factory
Fort Rupert

Newfoundland

Fort St. Charles
Fort Nippigon
Fort William
Lake Superior

St. Lawrence River
I N D I A N   R E S E R V E

St. Pierre
et Miquelon

Sault Ste. Marie

Québec
Q U É B E C
Montréal

Nova Scotia
Halifax

Lake Michigan
Lake Huron
Lake Ontario

Fort Pontchartrain
Lake Erie

Boston

SPANISH-
LOUISIANA

Fort Vincennes

I N D I A N   R E S E R V E

New York
Philadelphia

ATLANTIC OCEAN

Fort Kaskaskia

T H E   T H I R T E E N   C O L O N I E S

Norfolk

Bermuda

West Florida
New Orleans

Charles Town
Savannah
St. Augustine

N

Gulf of Mexico

East
Florida

British North America
1764–76

Original Thirteen Colonies

Other British territories

Spanish Louisiana, secretly
ceded by France in 1763

Only French possession
after Treaty of Paris, 1763

Fort

B a h a m a s

0   300 km

0   300 miles

1762–63
British occupied

THE DESTRUCTION OF THE NATCHEZ, 1729–33

DESCENDANTS OF THE MISSISSIPPIAN MOUND BUILDERS, THE NATCHEZ MAINTAINED A SOCIALLY STRATIFIED SOCIETY, IN WHICH THEIR LEADER, THE GREAT SUN, HAD AUTHORITY OVER LIFE AND DEATH.

In 1542, the Natchez had helped drive de Soto's Spanish troops from the south. They occupied four villages on the first bluffs overlooking the Mississippi. This nation's major European encounter was with the French, who built Fort Rosalie overlooking the major Natchez village.

Initially, French-Natchez relations had been intermittently violent, but eventually the Tattered Serpent, the Great Sun's brother, brought about cordial relations. On his death, however, the French commander of Fort Rosalie, Sieur de Chépart, with the support of Louisiana Governor Étienne Périer de Salvert, began to confront the Natchez. In August 1729, de Chépart demanded that the Natchez leave their main village, which contained their most sacred sites and objects, so that he could establish a tobacco plantation. Such plantations were becoming common in the area, being operated with imported African slave labor.

The Natchez decided to attack all Frenchmen in their lands, persuading the plantation slaves to join them in return for their freedom. On November 29, 1729, the Natchez struck at Fort Rosalie and the French plantations. Approximately 145 men, thirty-six women, and fifty-six children were killed, while 300 African slaves and fifty French women were captured; only twelve Natchez died. Elsewhere, Yazoo allies stormed Fort St. Pierre in their territory. De Chépart was captured, but warriors would not defile their weapons by killing him. Instead, a Stinkard, a member of the lowest Natchez caste, clubbed him to death.

In retaliation, the French sent an expedition, which included 700 Choctaw allies, against the Natchez. On January 27, 1730, the Natchez were attacked, and French women and slaves were recovered, but the Natchez slipped out of their forts at St. Catherine's Creek and eventually reached the Ouachita Indians near contemporary Sicily Island, Louisiana. The French strength was boosted by the arrival of 350 reinforcements from the Company of the Indies and Ministry of Marine. Their commander, the governor's brother, decided to destroy the Natchez by killing or enslaving them.

French forces concentrated on the Red River in early January 1731, assaulting the Natchez forts with cannons and mortars on January 20. After four days, negotiations were opened and some slaves were returned. Around 500 Natchez agreed to surrender and were taken captive, but some Natchez managed to escape. The summer of 1713 saw the construction of a new Natchez village with the Chickasaw, while some 150 Natchez lived in four other villages among the Yazoo, and three on the Mississippi's west side. The Natchez asked neighboring Tunica Indians to treat with the French on their behalf, but fearing a deception, turned on the Tunica with Chickasaw and Koroa allies. Elsewhere, some forty Natchez surrendered, but were all killed after attempting to escape.

Other Natchez, under Flour Chief, attacked, captured, and refortified the French fort of Natchitoches on the Red River. The French retaliated by laying siege for several weeks, being aided by Attakapas, Caddo, and Natchitoches Indians. Many Natchez were killed, but around fifty escaped and waged guerrilla war from the Ouiachita River, attacking the French settlement at Point Coupee during 1732, and also the Chacchiuma Indians. Lack of total success occasioned Périer de Salvert's recall in September 1732, to be replaced by Bienville. During the summer of 1733, Bienville drove the remaining bands of Natchez from their villages on the Yazoo, but a remnant established a refugee village in 1733 with the Chickasaw. Together, war and disease in 1731 virtually wiped out the Natchez. Captives were sold into slavery in Santo Domingo, Haiti. As a tribal entity, the Natchez were destroyed. However, the refugees eventually spread from the Chickasaw to the Creek and Cherokee, where they continued their mystical, sun-oriented religious ceremonies.

A mural from the Natchez Visitor Center, Mississippi, depicting Natchez warriors attacking French troops.

THE CHICKASAW-FRENCH WAR, 1735–40

THE CONFLICT BETWEEN THE FRENCH AND CHICKASAWS DEMONSTRATES HOW AN INDIAN NATION COULD RESIST ONE EUROPEAN POWER BY CONCLUDING A FRIENDSHIP WITH ANOTHER.

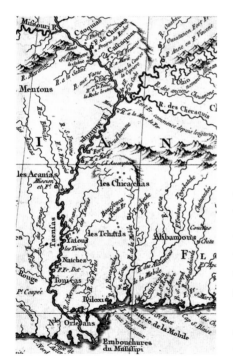

A contemporary map showing the area affected by the Chickasaw Wars of 1720–60. The French campaigns started from Mobile and New Orleans in the south, and Forts Chartres and Vincennes in the north.

The Chickasaw occupied a strategic area centered on Chikasahha, near today's Memphis, Tennessee. Therefore, they could pose a threat to the French domination of the Mississippi by interdicting the route between the French settlements in Illinois, and the southern posts at Mobile and New Orleans. Between the 1690s and 1729, the Chickasaw maintained a balance in their relations with the French and British. In November 1729, however, the Natchez attacked the French forts at Rosalie and St. Pierre, killing or capturing most of the inhabitants. The Chickasaw refused a French request to help punish the Natchez; indeed, fleeing Natchez found sanctuary with the Chickasaw.

Next, the French decided to ally themselves with the Choctaw and hound the Chickasaw, both policies designed to block the British influence in the Mississippi Valley. By 1730, though, some Choctaw had approached the British for support, and this decline in French influence persuaded the French to strike at the Chickasaw. One advantage lay with France's enemy, however, since the Chickasaw had been trained by the British to build fortifications. Nevertheless, the French pressed ahead, planning attacks that employed Choctaw forces to drag them into French affairs.

In 1735, Jean-Baptiste Le Moyne de Bienville, Louisiana's governor, organized an army to assault Chikasahha. In 1736, French and Indian troops advanced up the Tombigbee River to meet forces under d'Artaguette from Illinois. The latter's units attacked Ogoula Tchetoka village, but half of the 137 French soldiers were killed. Bienville fought the Chickasaw at the Battle of Ackia on May 26, 1736. His force comprised 500 troops, settlers, Indians, and armed Africans commanded by free African officers. They were easily defeated, however, and were fortunate that the Choctaw rescued the wounded.

Bienville became determined to thrash the Chickasaw and began organizing troops from Canada, Illinois, and Louisiana; also, he asked for regulars from France. He mobilized 1,200 French soldiers and 2,400 Native American allies in Arkansas, then marched up the Mississippi rather than the Tombigbee River. Lack of geographic knowledge, poor logistics, disease, and delays turned the advance into a shambles, and Bienville was forced to retreat after a provincial council of war. In 1740, he descended the Mississippi just as 100

A section of a map drawn by Edward Crisp, showing the Mississippi River and the disposition of the tribes along it. These include the Chickasaw.

French colonials and 500 Indians, led by Pierre-Joseph Céloron de Blainville, approached Chikasahha. The Chickasaw thought the French force was the vanguard of an entire army. Rather than attack, they sued for peace. Bienville agreed to their terms, but the Choctaw continued to raid the Chickasaw and sell their scalps to the French. Obviously, Bienville was still attempting to weaken the British allies, and he encouraged the Choctaw to avenge French deaths as well as their own.

After the Chickasaw were weakened by a smallpox attack in 1749, the new Louisiana governor, Pierre de Rigaud de Vaudreuil, urged the Choctaw to reengage them. Two forces were dispatched against the Chickasaw in 1752 and 1753. On both occasions, the Chickasaw forts beat off the invaders with enough success not to be involved in the 1754–63 French and Indian War. Nevertheless, the Chickasaw still felt threatened, and on April 5, 1756, one of their leaders addressed the governor of South Carolina: "This is to let you know we are daily cut oft (sic) by our enemies the French and their Indians who seems to be resolved to drive us from this land."

Later, the Chickasaw felt that the 1763 Proclamation Line would protect them, and peace was made with the Choctaw. Support for Britain continued during the American Revolution, the Chickasaw raiding Virginia and the Carolinas. In 1783, Chickasaw representatives signed peace treaties with Virginia at French Licks, and agreed to expel British refugees from their lands, while the Americans promised to keep white settlers out of Chickasaw territory.

TURMOIL ON THE PLAINS

IN VARIOUS WAYS, THE ARRIVAL OF THE EUROPEANS CREATED
MOVEMENT AMONG THE INDIAN NATIONS, WHICH OFTEN
BROUGHT THEM INTO CONFLICT WITH EACH OTHER.

Demographic disruption and dispersion were common in America during the European expansion. De Soto's travels through Arkansas devastated the local population—the land was so depopulated that survivors from Iroquois aggression crossed the Mississippi to hunt. Miami, Delaware, Shawnee, Piankashaw, Peoria, Chickasaw, and Choctaw tribes moved into east Arkansas, confronting settled Caddoes and Quapaw. Further west, along the Line of Semiaridity, lived the "prairie" Indians—the Mandan, Iowa, Kansa, Missouri, Omaha, Osage, Pawnee, Oto, and Ponca. These tribes grew maize and built permanent villages, which provided homes after the annual summer buffalo hunt.

Into this scenario was introduced the horse, originally brought to the continent by the Spanish in the Southwest. This animal set in train a second cycle of migrations as eastern tribes, armed with European guns, pushed the "prairie" Indians onto the Plains. The Cheyenne were encountered by the French on the upper Mississippi in the 1660s, but they migrated from Minnesota to become Plains buffalo hunters, having been expelled by the Lakota. Ojibwa and Cree fought the Teton Lakota, who moved west to begin a nomadic life. Similarly, the Yankton Lakota traveled west from the Red Lake area of Minnesota into North Dakota. The Lakota waged war on the Mandan, Hidatsa, and Arikara, aided by a supply of guns from the Santee Lakota, who lived near British and Canadian traders in Minnesota. The Teton and Yankton Lakota became the dominant power on the Missouri. Their quest for power was helped by an 80-percent reduction in the Arikara population through smallpox. In 1782, the Mandan and Hidatsa were also devastated by epidemics, followed by the Omaha. In North Dakota, the Hidatsa split, one group moving onto the northern Plains and into Yellowstone Valley—they became the Crow tribe. The Shoshone, originally from the Great Basin and the Rocky Mountains, became mounted and also spread onto the Plains, but they were pushed back to the mountains by other tribes.

The Plains Apache, who originated in Canada, had reached the Texas Panhandle by 1515 and split into the Eastern and Western Apache. The former comprised the Mescalero, Jicarilla, Chiricahua, Lipan, and Kiowa; the latter, the Cibecue, Mimbreño, and Coyotero. During the eighteenth century, Kiowa, Comanche, and Wichita horse soldiers, armed with guns, pushed the lance carrying Apache southward into the Spanish border territories of contemporary Arizona and New Mexico.

The Apache tribes generated population movements in the Southwest. In the 1670s, raids by the Apache, Navajo, and Utes, combined with the effects of drought, pushed many Pueblo dwellers to the Rio Grande. When the Pueblos rebelled against the Spanish in 1680, not only did the Europeans flee, but also their Christian Indian followers. The Spanish concentrated their missionary zeal upon the Apache, and eventually mixed marriages detribalized many Indians, who helped New Mexican colonists construct new towns, missions, and forts, such as Albuquerque (1706). A mission was established on the San Sabá tributary of the Colorado River in 1757, but it was destroyed by an Indian alliance led by the Caddoan Hasinai, who thought the Apache might obtain guns there. However, missions were built among the Lipan, on the Nueces River, between 1762 and 1771.

East of the Comanche, the Osage played off the Spanish and French against each other, using French guns to attack Caddoan and Wichita enemies to the southwest, and Pawnee to the northwest. Seizing horses and captives for slavery, the Osage forced the Caddoan down the Red River, while the Pawnee moved back toward the Platte River. The Wichita were pushed south of the Arkansas Valley, and the Osage dominated the area between the Red and Missouri rivers. The small Kansa tribe allied themselves with the Osage for survival. The Osage raided as far as Santa Fé and into Louisiana, while the Lipan Apache reached the Gulf of Mexico in 1796. Such was the turmoil accentuated by the horse and firearms.

A painting by famed American artist George Catlin showing Indians on a winter buffalo hunt on the Plains around the upper Missouri River (c. 1830).

THE CALIFORNIA MISSIONS

FEARING THE INCURSION OF RUSSIAN TRADERS FROM THE NORTH, THE SPANISH SET OUT TO SEIZE THE CALIFORNIA REGION BY ESTABLISHING A STRING OF MISSION COMMUNITIES.

José de Gálvez, Visitor-General of New Spain, sent expeditions northward to counter Russian moves off the Oregon Country.

Opposite: In the late eighteenth century, the Spanish established settlements and missions throughout California.

Spanish colonization in North America made a last "defensive expansion" in the late eighteenth century. Imperial northward movement in Texas had ended in 1763, when the French danger was removed by the cession of Louisiana to Spain. Subsequently, the region became home to 2,000 Spaniards in a dispersed collection of missions, presidios, and villages.

A new perceived threat to Spanish interests was a southward Russian thrust from Alaska by Cossack traders, whose ships were sailing in Oregon Country waters, and who could have threatened Mexico and outflanked possessions in Texas. Thus, the Spanish sought to forestall the Russians by the preemptive seizure of California. Visitor-General of New Spain, José de Gálvez, dispatched two parties from sparsely populated Baja California, one by land, the other by sea. In 1769, two ships reached San Diego Bay from La Paz, being joined later by Gaspar de Portola and the priest Father Serra, who journeyed through 400 miles (640 kilometers) of unexplored desert after leaving Loreto. In July 1769, Portola and 126 survivors of the land party formally took possession of California in the name of Spain. Portola sent a small expedition north to acquire the landlocked harbor of Monterey, where a new settlement became the Californian capital, next to the new mission of San Carlos. Three further missions were established—San Antonio, San Gabriel, and San Luis Obispo. In 1773, sixty-one soldiers and eleven friars maintained five stations and two presidios in California. In 1774, Juan Batista Anza and Father Garcés, with a few servants and muleteers, pioneered an overland route from Tubac to San Gabriel, through the San Jacinto Mountains. In 1775, Anza and Father Pedro led 240 colonists from Sonora to San Francisco harbor. Before long, twenty-one missions dotted the 650 miles (1,050 kilometers) through California between San Diego and Solano,

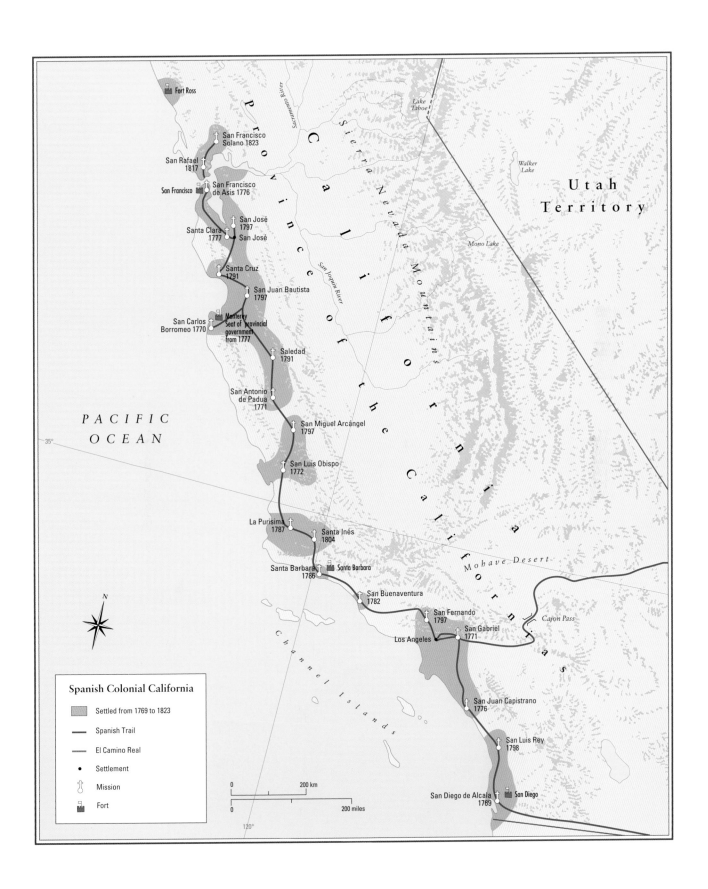

Fort Ross

San Francisco
Solano 1823

San Rafael
1817

San Francisco
San Francisco
de Asis 1776

San José
1797

Santa Clara
1777
San José

Santa Cruz
1791

San Juan Bautista
1797

San Carlos
Borromeo 1770
Monterey
Seat of provincial
government
from 1777

Soledad
1791

San Antonio
de Padua
1771

San Miguel Arcángel
1797

San Luis Obispo
1772

La Purisima
1787
Santa Inés
1804

Santa Barbara
1786
Santa Barbara

San Buenaventura
1782

San Fernando
1797
San Gabriel
1771
Los Angeles

San Juan Capistrano
1776

San Luis Rey
1798

San Diego de Alcala
1769
San Diego

Province of California

Sierra Nevada Mountains

Sacramento River

Lake
Tahoe

Walker
Lake

**U t a h
T e r r i t o r y**

Mono Lake

San Joaquin River

PACIFIC
OCEAN

35°

California

Mohave Desert

Cajon Pass

N

Channel Islands

120°

Spanish Colonial California

	Settled from 1769 to 1823
	Spanish Trail
	El Camino Real
•	Settlement
⚲	Mission
⛫	Fort

0   200 km

0   200 miles

A contemporary illustration of Franciscan missionaries. The Spanish dispensed Christianity to the Indians with the lash and the branding iron.

being served by ports at San Francisco, Monterey, Los Angeles, and San Diego, which were defended by four presidios.

Colonists of mixed Spanish, Indian, and African descent drifted in and helped establish the mission system. Indian neophytes from dozens of tribes congregated in new communities, some 20,000 being converted to Christianity. Cattle herds grew on mission ranches, and Indians trained in new farming methods produced crops in irrigated fields. Hides, tallow, wine, brandy, grain, olive oil, and leather goods were exchanged for manufactured products brought around Cape Horn by American trading vessels, thereby establishing an American interest in the region.

The Spanish regarded the Indians as a valuable economic workforce in the controlled southern and coastal areas. Thus, the imperial presence was sustained by a virtual slave system. No one is entirely certain why Indians joined the missions. Perhaps they enjoyed the rituals, rites, and festivals of the new religious system, assuming that it would coexist with their own traditions. Whatever the reason, the Spanish

Founded in 1772, halfway between present-day Santa Barbara and Monterey, on the Californian coast, Mission San Luis Obispo de Tolosa was one of a chain of Spanish missions that ran throughout California. The mission remains a fully functional Catholic church.

segregated unmarried men and women into separate dormitories at night, using the lash, branding, chains, stocks, and solitary confinement to enforce discipline—"civilization and salvation."

The packed mission communities became breeding grounds for new diseases; between 1769 and 1848, the coastal regions of California witnessed a drop in Native American population of 90 percent. Epidemics such as measles, cholera, and smallpox caused devastation, particularly among the vulnerable young, old, and pregnant women. The Esselen people were the first to become extinct, while the neighboring Salinan suffered great losses, as did the Diegueño in the southernmost region of California. Indian resistance took two forms—escape and violence—as when several hundred Indians made an unsuccessful attack on the San Diego mission in 1775. All this servitude and misery helped provide a home for some 4,000–5,000 Hispanic settlers by 1821.

Even as Spanish California developed, the newly independent United States (1776) became a potential enemy to Hispanics and surviving Indians alike. By 1821, The Spanish empire had crumbled under the impact of the Napoleonic Wars in Spain, the return of Louisiana to France, and the independence of Mexico, which ruled California until 1848.

Mission San Luis Rey de Francia was founded in 1798. It was the eighteenth of the twenty-one missions established by the Spanish in California.

THE SEVEN YEARS' WAR

FROM 1756 TO 1763, ALL OF THE MAJOR EUROPEAN POWERS WERE AT WAR, AND THAT WAR SPREAD TO THEIR COLONIES AROUND THE WORLD, INCLUDING THOSE IN NORTH AMERICA.

After King George's War, the third of four French and Indian Wars, Virginians and Pennsylvanians pushed westward into the Ohio Valley and reached the Mississippi River. In 1749, the Ohio Company was organized and granted half a million acres (200,000 hectares) on the Upper Ohio, where it established a trading center at Cumberland, Maryland. The British claimed Ohio by the Treaty of Lancaster (1744) with the Iroquois, and the Treaty of Logtown (1748) with the Shawnee, Delaware, and Wyandot. The French response was to send a force of Ottowa and Ojibwa warriors, led by Charles Langlade, to attack a British trading post at Pickawillany (1752), where they killed Demoiselle, a Miami chief, and thirteen of his men. Next, the French refurbished some old forts and built new ones: Gaspereau (Nova Scotia), St. Fréderic and Niagara (New York), Toulouse (Alabama), and Presque Isle, Le Boeuf, Venango, and Duquesne (western Pennsylvania). The French planned to construct a complete chain of forts along the Mississippi to link their Canadian and Louisiana territories.

This show of French strength, and the surrender of Fort Necessity (built to mask Fort Duquesne at the fork of the Ohio and Monongahela rivers) by George Washington impressed the Indians. Ottowa, Algonkin, Wyandot, Nipissing, Ojibwa, Potawatomi, Sauk, Shawnee, and Seneca reinforced their dealings with the French. Also, the Delaware, who had been dispossessed by the British and Iroquois, moved into the French camp. On the other side, the British tried to enlist Iroquois support. However, only Chief Hendrick of the Mohawk was willing to be an ally; the remainder of the Confederacy remained neutral.

War formally began in 1755. Major General Braddock decided to attack the French with four columns. One force sailed into the Bay of Fundy, in Acadia, capturing Forts St. John and Beauséjour in June. The second column, led by Braddock, and comprising some 2,500 regulars and provincial militia, advanced on Fort Duquesne. However, the French threw 250 regulars and 600 Indians against the column as it passed through forested country. In the confused fighting, the British were shot down

A late nineteenth-century engraving depicting General Montcalm attempting to stop some of his Indian allies from attacking British soldiers and civilians as they leave Fort William Henry following its surrender to the French in August 1757.

by unseen enemies, and they broke. Washington and his Virginia militia were left to cover the rout. The British force suffered over 800 casualties, whereas the combined French and Indian force had thirty-nine. Braddock died of his wounds, while Washington marched the survivors to Pennsylvania after this disastrous Battle of the Monongahela River.

The third of Braddock's columns, under William Johnson, comprised 3,500 colonials and 300 Indians led by Chief Hendrick. This force advanced from Albany to Crown Point. Johnson's orders were to capture Forts Carillon and St. Fréderic. He was attacked by some 1,600 French, Canadians, and Indians, under the command of Baron Jean-Armand de Dieskau, on September 8, 1755. At Lake George, the French hit a reconnaissance force of 500 Americans and Indians, whose panicky retreat spread confusion among the rest of the column. Colonel Phineas Lyman, of Connecticut, rallied and inspired the Americans and Indians to fight back, and the French retreated after suffering 230 casualties; Johnson lost 262. Johnson then built Fort William Henry, but left his target forts untouched.

The final column, under Massachusetts Governor Shirley, comprised 1,500 men. They marched up the Mohawk Valley to Oswego, intending to attack Niagara, but retreated without attempting anything. Elsewhere, the border regions from Maine to Virginia were raided by Indians, and by mid-1756, they had killed 376 people and captured 276, for the loss of fewer than 100. Many white farmers in Pennsylvania and Virginia abandoned their homes. Attempts to fend off Indian attacks began in 1756. Major Andrew Lewis led 236 Virginia militia to burn Shawnee villages, but his badly organized force deserted him. Delaware from Kittaning village captured Fort Granville, and in retaliation, Lieutenant Armstrong attacked the village and burned it.

In 1756, the French General Montcalm arrived in Canada, as did Loudon to command the British. July saw Captain John Bradstreet, Oswego's commissary, beating off a French and Indian ambush while he was resupplying the settlement. Montcalm harassed British outposts and disrupted Oswego's supply line by seizing Fort Bull and its garrison. Then he assaulted the exposed Oswego and captured four armed ships, seventy cannon, and 1,606 soldiers and sailors, including two regular regiments.

Between June and September 1757, the British mounted an expedition against Louisbourg, but found a French fleet in the harbor and abandoned the attempt after a storm scattered the British fleet. Meanwhile, Montcalm marched into New York State with 6,200 French and 1,200 Indians, laying siege to Fort William Henry. Lieutenant Colonel Munro's 2,100 defenders resisted for a week, but with French artillery within 100 yards (90 meters) of the walls, they were forced to surrender. The British were allowed to march away, having given their parole that they would not fight for eighteen months, but the Indians killed about thirty wounded and seized 529 soldiers to sell to Canadians as forced labor. Montcalm paid for the release of every soldier he could find, but some prisoners were infected with smallpox, which spread among the nations of the Ohio Valley and the Plains.

In 1757, after so many British misfortunes, William Pitt was appointed with the ineffectual Duke of Newcastle to act in coalition and head the British government. The dominant Pitt devised fresh, aggressive plans for the conflict in North America. He encouraged the colonies to raise 21,000 provincial soldiers because he needed to keep regulars in Europe and the Caribbean. Pitt appointed General James Abercrombie as commander-in-chief of British forces; Carillon and Duquesne were Pitt's targets. Abercrombie had 42,000 troops to combat 7,000 French regulars, 12,000 militia, and some 2,000 Indians.

Abercrombie launched an amphibious assault across Lake Champlain against Fort Carillon (later Ticonderoga), but his 15,000-man force was defeated by Montcalm's 3,600, suffering 1,600 casualties. Abercrombie retreated. Next, he dispatched Captain Bradstreet with 3,700 provincial militia and 150 regulars to take Fort Frontenac on Lake Ontario. Bradstreet marched 430 miles, and on August 25, 1758, captured the fort with its 110 troops, nine warships, and seventy-six artillery pieces.

Another major British campaign of 1758 was mounted against Louisbourg. New commander-in-chief Jeffrey Amherst's 14,000 men stormed beaches on Nova Scotia and besieged the fort for six weeks. Governor Augustin de Drucour surrendered on July 25, costing France 3,000 soldiers, 2,600 marines and sailors, and five ships of the line. The final offensive of 1758 was General John Forbes' campaign against Fort Duquesne. All 270 Highlanders and militia of the advanced scouting force were killed or captured. Then, Forbes' main force was attacked by 570 French and Indians, and the British lost all their cattle and packhorses. Forbes was stopped in his tracks, only 40 miles (65 kilometers) from Duquesne. Intelligence persuaded him that the fort was weak, however, so he marched for nine days, only to discover its burnt-out ruins, the French having abandoned it. The British rebuilt it as Fort Pitt.

Elsewhere, Amherst ordered General Prideaux to reoccupy Oswego, then capture Fort Niagara. By early July, Niagara was besieged, and a 2,000-strong French and Indian relief column was driven off by Sir William Johnson's troops, among whom were 900 Mohawks. However, Prideaux died of wounds. Niagara surrendered on July 25, the British taking 600 prisoners, while the French abandoned and burned Fort Toronto before the British arrived. Amherst himself attacked Ticonderoga, capturing its ruins, which had been blown up by the French. Then he advanced to Fort St. Fréderic, which the French had also destroyed, and built Fort Crown Point upon the site. The war then became bogged down, but was enlivened by Major Robert Rogers and his Rangers, who burned the Abenaki village of St. Francis on October 6.

A late campaign against Québec was launched by General Wolfe, who died defeating Montcalm at the

Battle of the Heights of Abraham on September 13, 1759. Montcalm was also killed. Subsequently, the British defeated a French force that attempted to retake Québec. Then British forces were concentrated against Montréal, which was seized, leading to the surrender of all the remaining French garrisons.

The collapse of French Canada coincided with a volcanic outburst of violence in South Carolina. The British had profited from Chickasaw disruption of French trade, aided by some Cherokee and Catawba support. Ill treatment of Indians by the garrison of Fort Prince George caused the Cherokee to attack frontier settlements. Indian aggression ended after a force of 2,500 Highlanders and militia burned fifteen Cherokee towns.

General Montcalm and his French troops celebrate victory over the British at the Battle of Carillon, July 7–8, 1758. They had routed a numerically superior force commanded by General Abercrombie. Painting by Henry Alexander Ogden.

Opposite: Pontiac's War threw
the region south of the Great
Lakes into turmoil. Several
British forts were overrun
by Indians incensed by their
treatment following withdrawal
of the French.

de Villiers, who commanded the French Fort de Chartres on the Mississippi River in Louisiana. He advised Pontiac to make peace. Winter was approaching, quarrels broke out among the tribes, and some bands were negotiating peace with Major Henry Gladwin, Detroit's commander.

Amherst suggested that blankets infected with smallpox should be given to the Indians. Some Shawnee and Delaware received these at Fort Pitt in 1764; the disease spread rapidly and with

A contemporary engraving
showing a British fort being
attacked by Indians during
Pontiac's War. Although the
British eventually regained
control of the region, they
suffered several defeats in the
early stages of the war.

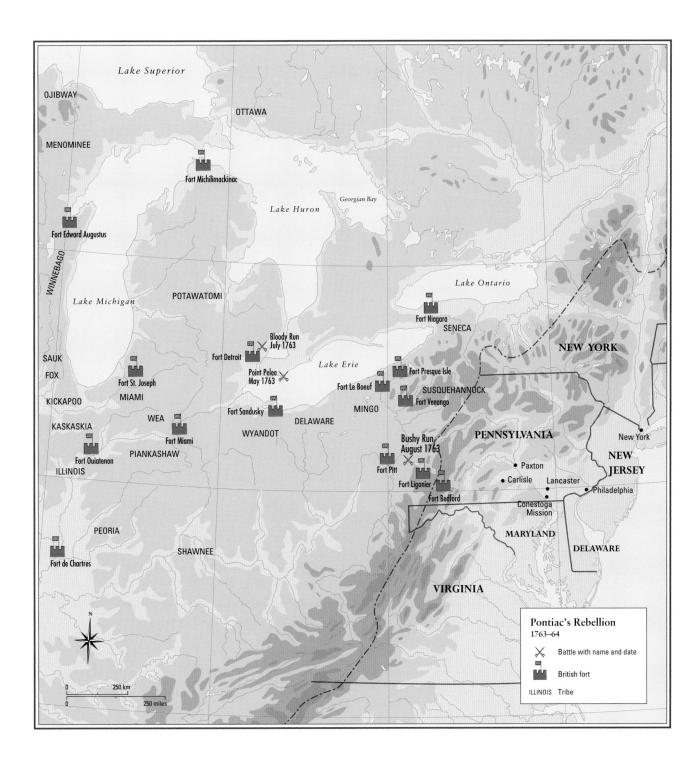

devastating effects, weakening the tribes to such an extent that they were forced to make peace with the British. However, Pontiac did achieve one success. Although the British knew that Indians could be defeated, they realized that the tribes would never submit. Consequently, redress was made with the Proclamation Line of 1763.

THE PROCLAMATION OF 1763

REALIZING THE NEED TO APPEASE THE INDIANS, IN 1763, THE BRITISH ISSUED A PROCLAMATION THAT DETAILED AN INVIOLABLE BOUNDARY LINE BETWEEN THE COLONIES AND INDIAN LAND.

The Proclamation Line of 1763 came about because of the British government's desire to appease the Indians, who resented the incursions of white settlers onto their lands. The line was drawn along the Appalachian watershed, from New York to northern Florida, and colonial settlement was excluded from the interior west of the line. However, the Crown could acquire Indian lands by cession, or could purchase them, but only after a public meeting of the Indians and the governor or commander-in-chief of the colonies. Such a meeting was held with the Creek, Choctaw, Cherokee, and Catawba.

The Indian boundary line finally stretched from the Mississippi, near the mouth of the Yazoo River, eastward across the Gulf coastal plain, around the coastal area of the Florida peninsula, and then north across Georgia and the Carolinas. It progressed westward across Virginia and Kentucky. From the mouth of the Kentucky River, the line followed the Ohio River upstream, crossed Pennsylvania from southwest to northeast, and traversed central New York State to the Mohawk River, near contemporary Rome. From there, it ran north to meet the St. Lawrence River.

In addition, a system of licensing traders was created, and the British administration was responsible for preventing criminals and fugitives from entering Indian land. Superintendents of Indian Affairs in northern and southern areas were to implement these conditions.

The Proclamation was a short-term success. In November 1763, Superintendent John Stuart met most of the southern chiefs at Augusta with governors of the four southern colonies, and boundaries between Indians and settlers were agreed, but not formalized. In spring 1765, Stuart persuaded the Choctaws and Chickasaws to accept British authority and trade. They also agreed to cede land along the coast, and lower Mobile and Tombigbee rivers. These bands helped the British to establish themselves in the Mississippi region to help counteract Pontiac's campaigns in Illinois. In May 1765, the Upper Creek agreed to peace and to regulated trade from Pensacola to Mobile, and to the cession of a ten-mile (16-kilometer) wide parcel of land between the two posts.

In the long term, white demographic growth prompted a flow of settlers, traders, speculators, and hunters onto Indian land, while the colonial authorities had insufficient funds to finance the work of the superintendents, to garrison forts, or to provide gifts for Indian allies. In 1768, Britain's Board of Trade returned control of British-Indian trade to colonial governments, following colonial resistance to further taxation deemed necessary to finance commitments agreed in the Proclamation. The Indians

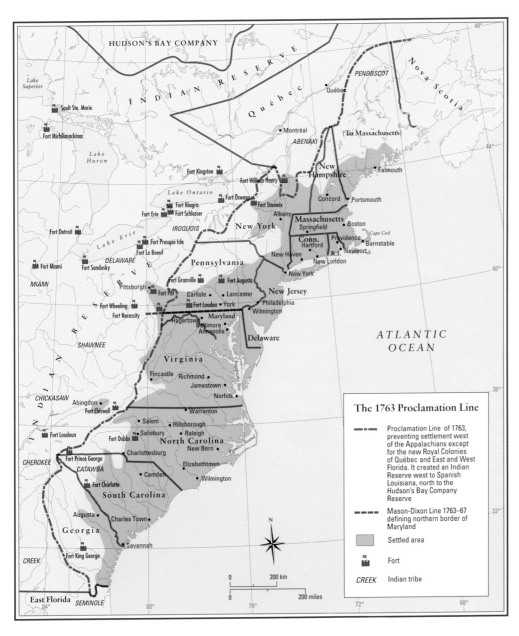

The 1763 Proclamation Line, devised by the British, ran from Nova Scotia to northern Florida and was supposed to provide an inviolable boundary between the colonies and Indian lands. Before long, however, settlers began pushing further westward.

became more resentful. Matters were not helped immediately after Pontiac's resistance came to an end, when Britain was left with forts and garrisons occupying Indian land. White investors were also disgruntled, especially the Virginians, whose ancient charter claimed sea-to-sea rights. They were demanding jurisdiction over much of the Ohio Country. During a treaty conference in 1768, at Fort Stanwix, New York, in response to colonial pressure, northern Indian Superintendent William Johnson induced the Iroquois to cede huge tracts of hunting land on the Ohio, belonging to the Shawnee, Delaware, and Cherokee, territories that the Iroquois had never controlled, nor even occupied. In return, the Confederation was confirmed in its ancestral lands around the Finger Lakes, a situation that would be terminated by the American Revolution.

The Fort Stanwix Treaty, together with other land cessions, instigated a rush of speculators and settlers along the frontiers. By 1774, Virginians were killing Ohio Indians; a Cayuga-Mingo chief, Tachnechdorus (also known as Logan), had all thirteen members of his family murdered at Yellow Creek on the Ohio, 50 miles (80 kilometers) from Fort Pitt and the new settler town of Pittsburg. With Shawnees and Mingos, Logan retaliated, killing several white families and thus unleashing Lord Dunmore's War.

A watercolor depicting a Potawatomi camp at Crooked Creek, just before the tribe was ousted to make way for white settlers.

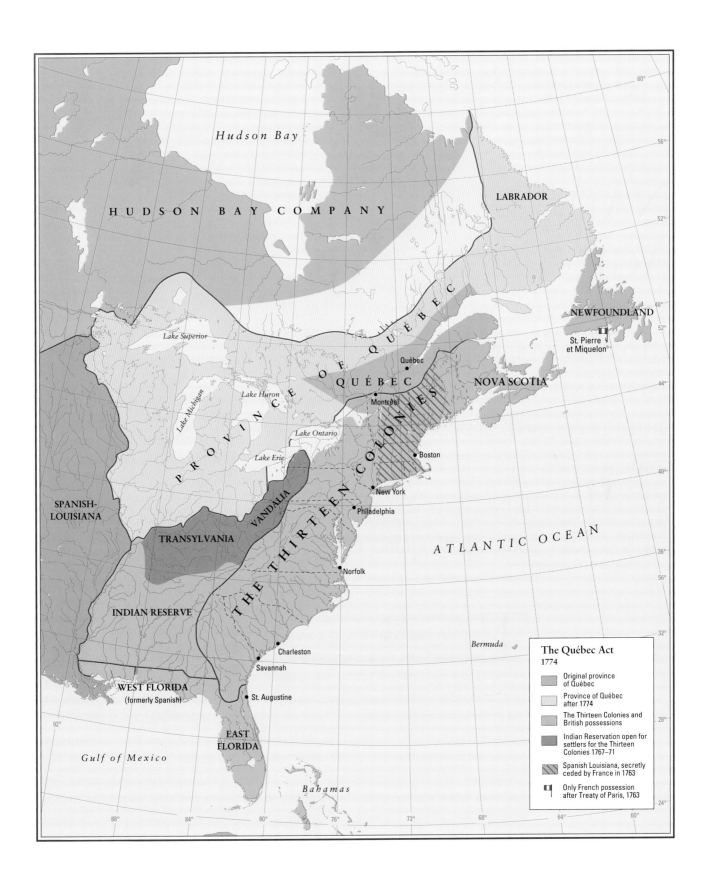

Hudson Bay

HUDSON BAY COMPANY

LABRADOR

Lake Superior

PROVINCE OF QUÉBEC

NEWFOUNDLAND

St. Pierre
et Miquelon

Québec

QUÉBEC

NOVA SCOTIA

Lake Huron

Lake Michigan

Montréal

Lake Ontario

Lake Erie

THE THIRTEEN COLONIES

Boston

SPANISH-
LOUISIANA

VANDALIA

New York

Philadelphia

ATLANTIC OCEAN

TRANSYLVANIA

Norfolk

INDIAN RESERVE

Bermuda

Charleston

Savannah

WEST FLORIDA
(formerly Spanish)

St. Augustine

EAST
FLORIDA

Gulf of Mexico

Bahamas

The Québec Act
1774

- Original province of Québec
- Province of Québec after 1774
- The Thirteen Colonies and British possessions
- Indian Reservation open for settlers for the Thirteen Colonies 1767–71
- Spanish Louisiana, secretly ceded by France in 1763
- Only French possession after Treaty of Paris, 1763

The Shawnee chief Tecumseh, a visionary who dreamed of creating a Native American state in the Great Lakes and Ohio Valley region, sided with the British during the War of 1812, but died during the Battle of the Thames in 1813. His death is recorded in this contemporary lithograph.

Opposite: After the War of Independence, the Mississippi River became the border between the United States and Spanish territory, but before long, American traders and explorers were probing across the great river.

helped lead an American expedition across tribal lands against Detroit. The Delaware turned on the Americans, supporting the pro-British Chief Pipe. Some Delaware sought sanctuary at Fort Pitt, while Pipe moved his people to the upper Sandusky River, leaving Moravian Christian Delaware isolated. In March 1782, ninety Moravian Indians were clubbed to death at Gnadenhutten by American militia. Later, when American Colonel Crawford attacked the Wyandot and Delaware on the Sandusky in June, his force was defeated; Crawford was captured and tortured to death for two hours in retaliation for the Moravian slaughter. *"Crawford died like a hero; never changed his countenance, tho' they scalped him alive, and then laid hot ashes on his head; after which they roasted him by a slow firer."* Captain Caldwell, June 1782.

The killing of Chief Cornstalk inflamed the Shawnee. Previously, in the face of constant American westward expansion, some had joined the Creek, while others had moved west across the Mississippi into Spanish territory. Most Shawnee joined the British after the murder, but Cornstalk's Maquachakes journeyed to the Delaware capital at Coshocton, hoping to retain their neutrality. Later, the Shawnee were thoroughly hammered by Bowman and Clark's expeditions, but many continued to resist until the 1795 Treaty of Greenville. Shawnee anguish caused some to join Tecumseh at the Battle of the Thames (1813) during the War of 1812.

The experiences of the Shawnee and Delaware demonstrate the destruction of traditional Indian society and tribal relationships, while the Americans appeared to be callous, untrustworthy murderers. Thomas Jefferson, Governor of Virginia at the time, saw the conflict with the Shawnee as a war of extermination. Indian society was further shattered when Massachusetts Christian Stockbridge Indians served as Minutemen, while Micmacs, Passamaquoddies, and Penobscots from Maine and Nova Scotia supported the Americans, as did the South Carolina Catawba. After the war, Stockbridge Mahicans returned home to find that their Indian town had been taken over by white neighbors, but they received no recompense. They moved to New York and later Wisconsin. Elsewhere, factionalism split the Iroquois: Mohawks, Onondagas, Cayugas, and Senecas fought Oneidas and Tuscaroras.

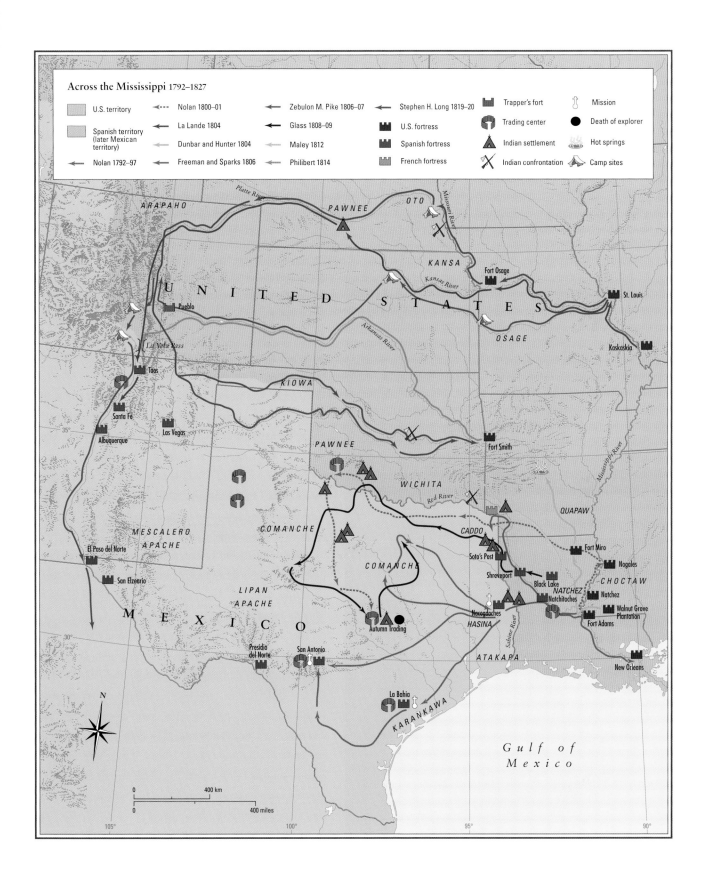

Across the Mississippi 1792–1827

The U.S. Army's "Old Guard" in a historical reenactment to celebrate George Washington's assumption of command of the Continental Army in 1775.

Opposite: Spanish explorers continued to lead expeditions into California and the Southwest toward the end of the eighteenth century and beginning of the nineteenth. France had ceded the Louisiana Territory to Spain at the end of the Seven Years' War in 1762.

one of the worst on record. Starving Iroquois fled to Fort Niagara, imposing a burden on British logistics. Even before Sullivan's invasion, the Iroquois lifeway had been disrupted, since warriors away fighting could neither hunt nor clear fields. Endemic warfare increased the dependency of the Iroquois on their allies for supplies. Sullivan's victories did not prevent some Iroquois from continuing to raid. One of Sullivan's officers said, "*The nests are destroyed but the birds are still on the wing.*"

Chief Brant led raids against the Oneida and Tuscarora in revenge. The Oneida sought sanctuary under American protection near Schenectady, but suffered from the cold, hunger, and inadequate clothing and housing. The Iroquois hegemony over smaller tribes and their united military strength were sundered. After the Treaty of Paris, the British government established reserves in Canada, and many Mohawks followed Brant to the Grand River in Ontario; others went to the Bay of Quinte. Those Iroquois who remained south of the Canadian border saw their reservations shrink, and they became increasingly dependent on the American government. Despair led to alcoholism.

During the war, encroaching settlers led to continual border skirmishes. Even in 1776, Shawnee Cornstalk traveled south from western Pennsylvania to visit the Cherokee, remarking that the old buffalo and deer hunting grounds were inhabited by armed Americans, with forts everywhere. He

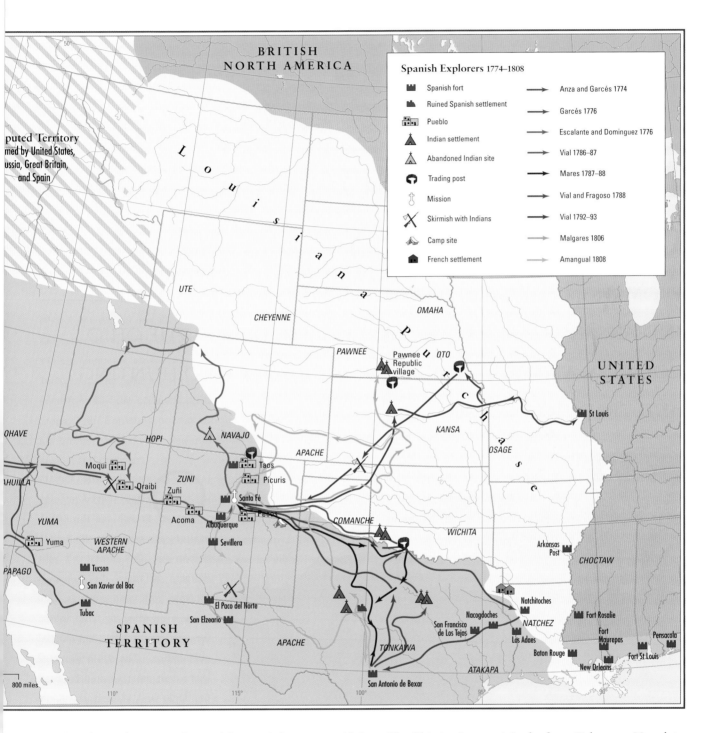

BRITISH
NORTH AMERICA

Spanish Explorers 1774–1808

🏰 Spanish fort   → Anza and Garcés 1774

🏚 Ruined Spanish settlement   → Garcés 1776

🏘 Pueblo   → Escalante and Dominguez 1776

⛺ Indian settlement   → Vial 1786–87

⛺ Abandoned Indian site   → Mares 1787–88

⚭ Trading post   → Vial and Fragoso 1788

♱ Mission   → Vial 1792–93

⚔ Skirmish with Indians   → Malgares 1806

⛺ Camp site   → Amangual 1808

🏠 French settlement

puted Territory
med by United States,
ussia, Great Britain,
and Spain

Louisiana

UTE

CHEYENNE

OMAHA

PAWNEE

Pawnee
Republic
village

OTO

KANSA

OSAGE

UNITED
STATES

St Louis

OHAVE

HOPI

NAVAJO

APACHE

Moqui

Oraibi

ZUNI

Taos

Picuris

AHUILLA

Zuñi

Santa Fé

Acoma

Albuquerque

Pecos

COMANCHE

WICHITA

YUMA

Yuma

WESTERN
APACHE

Sevillera

Arkansas
Post

CHOCTAW

PAPAGO

Tucson

San Xavier del Bac

El Paco del Norte

Natchitoches

Fort Rosalie

Tubac

San Elzeario

SPANISH
TERRITORY

APACHE

San Francisco
de Los Tejas

Nacogdoches

NATCHEZ

Los Adaes

Fort
Maurepas

Pensacola

TONKAWA

Baton Rouge

New Orleans

Fort St Louis

800 miles

San Antonio de Bexar

ATAKAPA

110°   115°   100°   95°   90°

was forced to make a 300-mile (480-kilometer) detour to avoid them. The Ohio territory contained refugee Delawares, Wyandots, Ottowas, Chippewas, Shawnees, Miamis, Potowatomies, and Kickapoos. All were awaiting their fate, since the victorious, independent Americans and the British had ignored the Indians in the Treaty of Paris. All land east of the Mississippi was regarded as conquered territory and owned by the Americans, irrespective of its inhabitants. Indian lands, customs, values, and religions would soon come under siege.

Opposite: Burgoyne's campaign envisioned a thrust southward from Canada to attack Albany, together with a diversionary attack by Colonel St. Leger on Fort Stanwix and then Albany via the Mohawk River valley. A third force, under General Howe, would approach Albany up the Hudson River valley. The last did not materialize, however, and St. Leger was forced to turn back by Benedict Arnold. Burgoyne, meanwhile, had fought his way to Saratoga, but by then was short of supplies and manpower, while American forces were overwhelming. Two major battles took place, the Battle of Freeman's Farm, in which Arnold stopped the British advance, and the Battle of Bemis Heights. In the latter, Arnold drove the British back to their starting positions, precipitating their surrender.

Stanwix. The ruse was foiled when one of the Patriots recognized a former neighbor, now a Tory, and the Americans opened fire upon the force. The fight raged for hours, but the American militia routed the Indians, and the Tories retreated after them.

The losses were high. The Indians probably lost 150, including some Seneca chiefs, which damaged and dismayed that nation, reported later by a white adoptee, Mary Jemison. The Americans suffered between 150 and 200 dead, some fifty wounded, and about 200 captured. St. Leger's Indians, who had suffered so heavily in combat, found that their encampment at Stanwix had been destroyed by a sortie from the fort. They became disgruntled, abandoning St. Leger when they thought Benedict Arnold was advancing with a 623-strong relief column, a rumor that had been planted by Indian spies.

The surrender of General Burgoyne at Saratoga, October 17, 1777. Some 5,800 British troops laid down their arms, the greatest success enjoyed by the Patriots up to that point in the war, and a turning point in the conflict in the North.

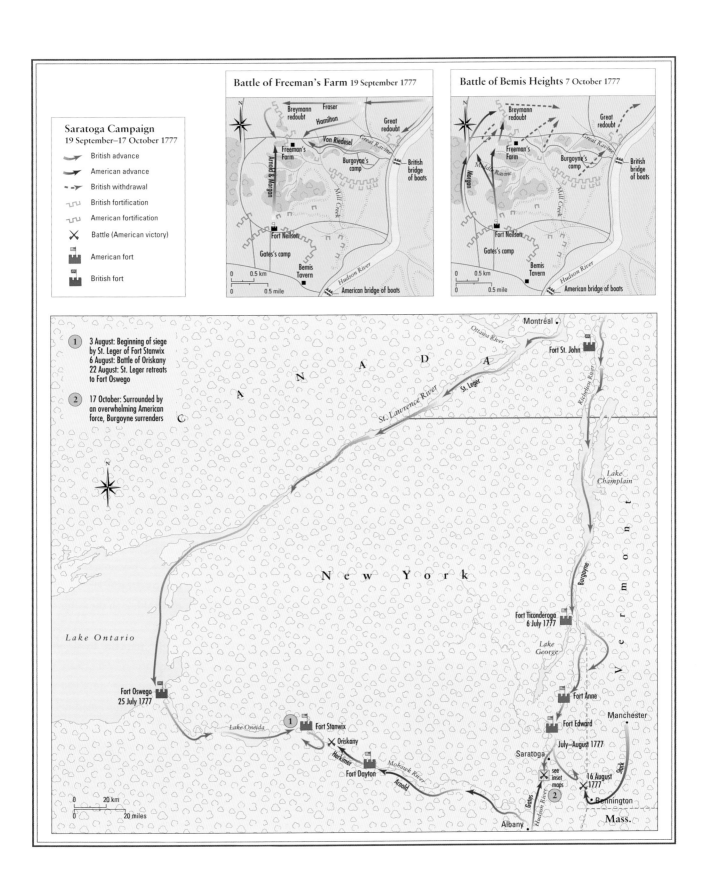

Battle of Freeman's Farm 19 September 1777

Breymann redoubt
Fraser
Hamilton
Great redoubt
Von Riedesel
Freeman's Farm
Arnold & Morgan
Burgoyne's camp
Great Ravine
British bridge of boats
Mill Creek
Fort Neilson
Gates's camp
Bemis Tavern
Hudson River

0 0.5 km
0 0.5 mile

American bridge of boats

Battle of Bemis Heights 7 October 1777

Breymann redoubt
Great redoubt
Freeman's Farm
Middle Ravine
Morgan
Burgoyne's camp
Great Ravine
British bridge of boats
Mill Creek
Fort Neilson
Gates's camp
Bemis Tavern
Hudson River

0 0.5 km
0 0.5 mile

American bridge of boats

Saratoga Campaign
19 September–17 October 1777

British advance
American advance
British withdrawal
British fortification
American fortification
Battle (American victory)
American fort
British fort

① 3 August: Beginning of siege by St. Leger of Fort Stanwix
6 August: Battle of Oriskany
22 August: St. Leger retreats to Fort Oswego

② 17 October: Surrounded by an overwhelming American force, Burgoyne surrenders

C A N A D A

Montréal
Ottawa River
Fort St. John
St. Lawrence River
St. Leger
Richelieu River
Lake Champlain
Burgoyne

N e w   Y o r k

V e r m o n t

Lake Ontario

Fort Ticonderoga 6 July 1777
Lake George

Fort Oswego 25 July 1777
Lake Oneida
① Fort Stanwix
✗ Oriskany
Herkimer
Fort Dayton
Mohawk River
Arnold

Fort Anne
Manchester
Fort Edward
July–August 1777
Saratoga
see inset maps
✗ ②
✗ 1777
Gates
Hudson River
16 August
Stark
Bennington

Albany
Mass.

0 20 km
0 20 miles

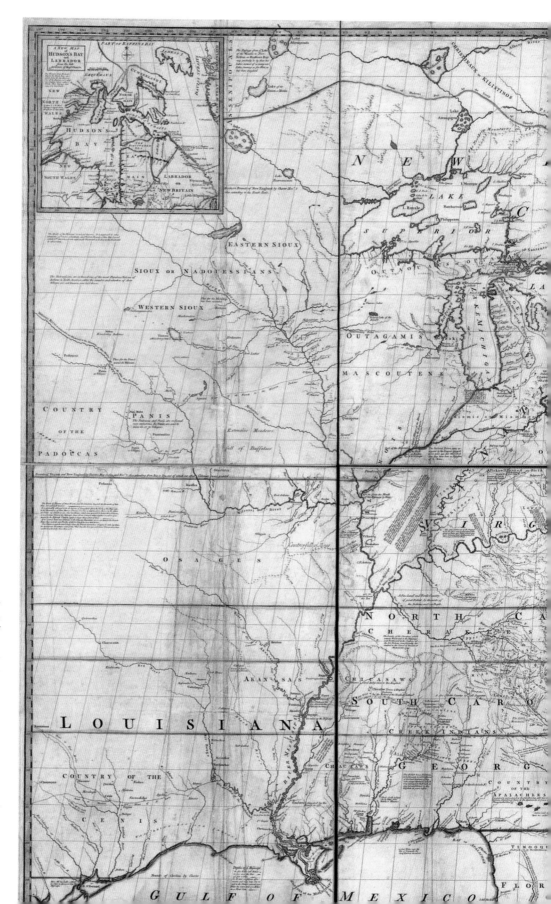

The Mitchell Map. Drawn by John Mitchell, this map is the most comprehensive map of the eastern portion of North America created during the Colonial era. It was used to define the borders of the United States during the negotiations for the Treaty of Paris, and subsequently to resolve border disputes between the United States and Canada, and between individual states. This huge map measures around 6.5 feet (2 meters) wide by 4.5 feet (1.4 meters) high.

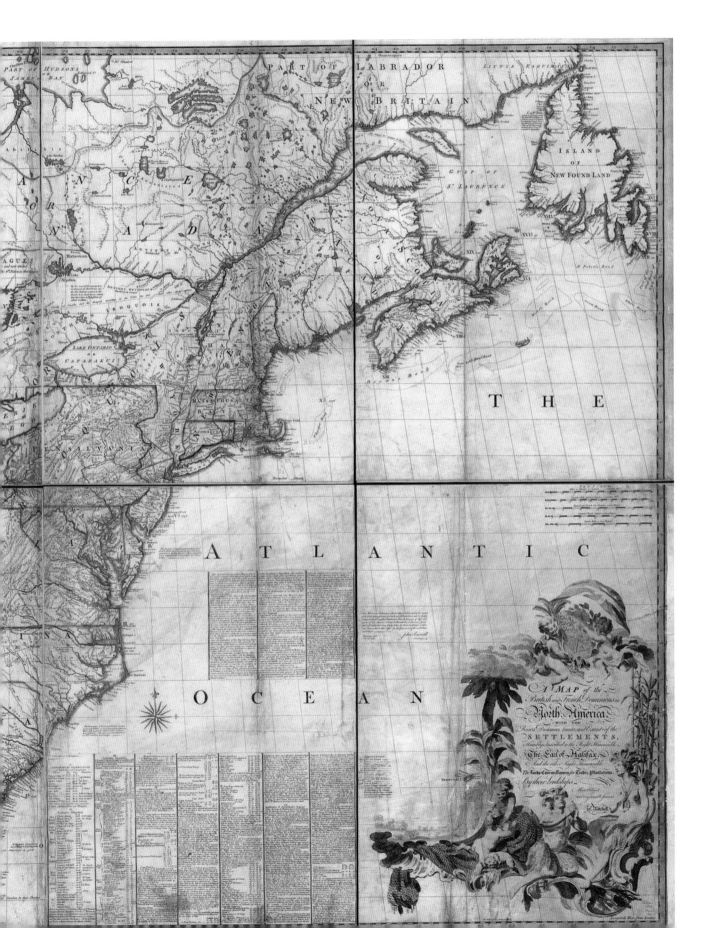

Opposite: Following the Treaty of Paris, many colonists who had remained loyal to Britain continued to live in the United States. A significant number (between 60,000 and 70,000), however, migrated to Canada, Florida, and the West Indies.

After the war, Britain rewarded its Iroquois allies and the members of Butler's Rangers with land grants.

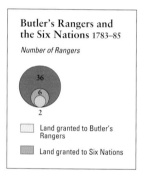

Butler's Rangers and the Six Nations 1783–85

Number of Rangers

36
6
2

Land granted to Butler's Rangers

Land granted to Six Nations

a convention could be held, a constitution adopted, and the area would become a Territory with its own legislature and a non-voting delegate to Congress. When the population of the Territory equaled the free population of the smallest state (about 60,000), it became a State of the Union.

Obviously, the peace treaty and the ordinances envisaged demographic movements into the new lands, and the state had a vested interest in land sales for revenue generation. However, the 1787 ordinance stated that the utmost good faith would be observed toward the Indians, and that their lands and property would never be taken from them. The earlier Royal Proclamation of 1763 forbade colonial settlement west of the Appalachians, while the 1784 Stanwix treaty had established some sort of Indian-American border, albeit constantly disputed.

Irrespective of good intentions, settlers flooded into Indian lands. By 1790, Kentucky had a white population of 74,000, while Tennessee and other frontier regions had 36,000. By 1800, 300,000 people had passed through the Cumberland Gap; avoiding populous Kentucky, many settled in present-day Missouri. Between 1784 and 1789, government officials pressured Indian leaders into land cession treaties, forcing Native Americans into small reservations. The means of acquiring land were decidedly dubious, and most Indians denounced the agreements.

The Iroquois suffered especially, being treated as inferiors and losing much territory to land companies and speculators. Some of their land was granted to war veterans in lieu of cash. Eventually, the Iroquois lost all their lands west of New York and Pennsylvania, as did some of their dependent tribes; instead, they were given small reservations in New York. Alcohol was often used as a bribe, as were threats. Pressure was also applied to the Delaware, Wyandot, Ottowa, Chippewa, Shawnee, and other smaller tribes.

George Washington had been a land speculator, which may have colored his administration's attitude toward Indians. The legal title to Indian land would be held by Indians until it was acquired by the government through fair negotiation or a "just" war, which would terminate the title. Many settlers squatted illegally on non-ceded lands, which provoked the Indians into driving them away. In response, the government would send in military forces to protect the squatters and seize land from the Indians by coercive treaties after the conflict.

Indian culture and identity were under threat from drunkenness and being forced to live on tiny reservations surrounded by a sea of new, hostile settlers. Eventually, these conditions prompted the emergence of visionaries and leaders who sought to reverse the decline, men such as Handsome Lake with his Good Word (gaiwiio), Little Turtle, Tecumseh, and Tenskwatawa.

WOOLWICH
NICHOL
WATERLOO
GUELPH
PUSHLINCH
DUMFRIES
BEVERLY
FLAMBORO'S
ANCASTER
BARTON
GLANFORD
SALTFLEET
PINBROOK

Grand River Tract, purchased by Britain from the Mississauga Indians to make land grants to Mohawks and other of the Six nations who allied with the British fought to prevent American Independence

Land set aside for Butler's Rangers. The Rangers commanded by Col. John Butler were composed of Loyalists from New York and Pennsylvania; their headquarters had been at Niagara

SIX NATIONS

Grand River

Western areas

Lake Ontario

Kingston areas

Butler's Rangers

Lake Erie

NEW YORK

0   15 miles

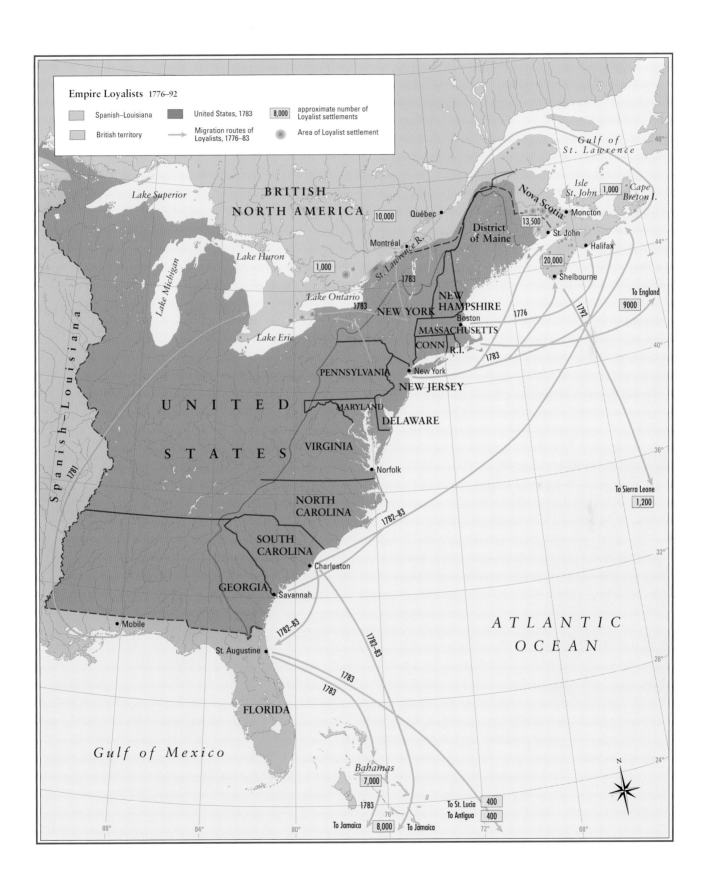

Empire Loyalists 1776–92

Spanish–Louisiana	United States, 1783	8,000 approximate number of Loyalist settlements
British territory	→ Migration routes of Loyalists, 1776–83	Area of Loyalist settlement

Lake Superior

BRITISH
NORTH AMERICA   10,000   Québec

Gulf of
St. Lawrence

Isle
St. John   1,000   Cape
Breton I.

Nova Scotia   13,500   Moncton
Montréal   St. John

Lake Huron

Lake Michigan

St. Lawrence R.

1783

District
of Maine

20,000   Halifax

Shelbourne

1,000

Lake Ontario   1783

Lake Erie

Spanish–Louisiana

1783

NEW
HAMPSHIRE

NEW YORK   Boston   1776

MASSACHUSETTS
CONN
R.I.   1783

1792

To England
9000

PENNSYLVANIA   New York

NEW JERSEY

U N I T E D

MARYLAND

DELAWARE

S T A T E S   VIRGINIA

1781   Norfolk

To Sierra Leone
1,200

NORTH
CAROLINA

1782–83

SOUTH
CAROLINA

1782–83

GEORGIA   Charleston

Savannah

Mobile

1782–83

A T L A N T I C
O C E A N

St. Augustine

1783

1783

FLORIDA

Gulf of Mexico

Bahamas
7,000

1783

To St. Lucia   400

To Antigua   400

N

To Jamaica   8,000   To Jamaica

88°   84°   80°   76°   72°   68°   24°   28°   32°   36°   40°   44°   48°

WAR FOR THE OHIO COUNTRY

ALTHOUGH THE TREATY OF PARIS ENDED THE BRITISH-AMERICAN CONFLICT, TRIBES FORMERLY ALLIED TO THE BRITISH CONTINUED TO RESIST INCURSIONS INTO LANDS NORTH OF THE OHIO RIVER.

Major General Arthur St. Clair mounted two expeditions against the Indians north of the Ohio, but was soundly defeated.

Opposite: Throughout the late eighteenth and early nineteenth centuries, the Indians of the East resisted the westward push, but in the end had to give ground.

After the Treaty of Paris had been signed, Congress had begun land-cession talks with the Indians to clarify ownership. The northern tribes met American officials at Fort Stanwix in 1784, while southern tribes met them at Hopewell, South Carolina, in 1785. The United States took the resultant treaties as evidence that the land belonged to America, and settlers were allowed in; however, the Indians denied the veracity of the treaties. The Shawnee, Miami, Chippewa, and Potawatomi continued to receive encouragement, food, and arms from the British at Detroit and other forts that should have been evacuated.

The Indians attempted to create a confederacy that could make peace, and establish a boundary between them and the Americans. The tribes themselves differed over possible boundaries, but these tensions ceased when two expeditions invaded their lands. George Rogers Clark led 1,000 Kentuckians up the Wabash River, but failed to engage the Indians; his drunken and disorderly force went home. A second Kentuckian raid led to the torching of Shawnee villages on the Miami River, during which Indians were murdered, tortured, and scalped. The construction of Fort Washington (1789) on the north bank of the Ohio in Miami lands, together with American settlements—the origins of Cincinnati—totally enraged the Shawnee and Miami.

Commanded by Little Turtle and Blue Jacket, the tribes struck settlements repeatedly, killing whole families. Indeed, between 1783 and 1790, the Indians killed, wounded, or enslaved 1,500 people. In the meantime, incidents involving Chickasaws and other western tribes painted a picture of a potential pan-Indian war. Major General Arthur St. Clair tried to negotiate peace with the Indians, who insisted that all Americans should withdraw from north of the Ohio.

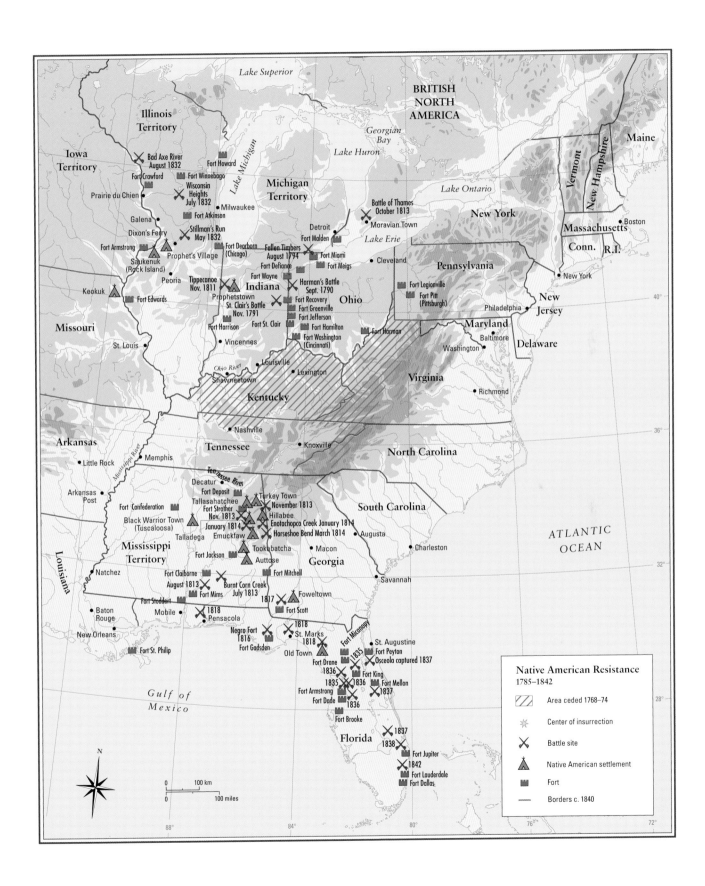

Native American Resistance
1785–1842

- ⬦⬦ Area ceded 1768–74
- ✳ Center of insurrection
- ✕ Battle site
- ▲ Native American settlement
- ⬛ Fort
- — Borders c. 1840

A depiction of Major General Anthony Wayne, creator of the Legion of the United States.

Opposite: With the Treaty of Paris, land to the north of the Ohio River became part of the United States. It was designated the Northwest Territory, but eventually would form the State of Ohio. The first settlement was Marietta, founded by the Ohio Company of Associates in 1788. Two areas, the Western Reserve and Virginia Military District, were used by Connecticut and Virginia to provide land grants to Revolutionary War veterans.

Subsequently, St. Clair mobilized some 1,500 men, comprising regulars and Kentucky and Pennsylvania volunteers, placing them under the command of Brigadier General Josiah Harmer. This force lumbered from Fort Washington through forested country and burned the evacuated Indian town of Kekionga on the Maumee River. Several engagements followed, during which 183 Americans were killed and some militiamen ran away; Harmer withdrew. The exultant Indians continued raiding settlements and Ohio River boats, but also moved their villages down the Maumee to its confluence with the Auglaize River.

After this shambles, St. Clair was ordered to mount a second expedition. In August 1791, he advanced from Fort Washington to Fort Recovery, Ohio, with the entire regular army (600 men) and 1,500 militia, plus 200 camp followers, both women and children. By mid-October, St. Clair had begun construction of Fort Hamilton on the Miami, which was followed by Fort Jefferson, about 5 miles (8 kilometers) south of present-day Greenville, after 300 Kentucky reinforcements arrived. By early November, St. Clair had reached the banks of the Wabash, but had been spotted by Indian scouting parties, among them the young Shawnee warrior Tecumseh. On November 4, Little Turtle and Blue Jacket led a force of warriors from fourteen tribes against the Americans. The latter were crushed, with 623 killed, 258 wounded, and 197 camp followers scalped. Indian losses were twenty-one killed and forty wounded.

Next, Congress ordered Major General Anthony Wayne to build a larger army, which he started in 1792, stamping out drunkenness, malingering, and poor discipline. His command, known as the Legion of the United States and comprising between 3,000 and 4,000 men, advanced from Pittsburgh to Greenville, and then to what is now Toledo, Ohio. Opposing Wayne were some 1,500 Indians. They were located a few miles from the British post of Fort Miami in an area known as Fallen Timbers, because of the many trees that had been toppled by a tornado. The region was full of brush and swamp, and the Indians made effective use of the landscape to harrass the Americans as they passed through. However, there was no American attack for several days, and many Indians gave up waiting and withdrew. When the attack did come, repeated bayonet charges broke the remaining Indians, who fled to Fort Miami, where the gates were shut. Subsequently, the Americans torched the Indian villages and thousands of acres of crops. For 133 casualties, Wayne managed to subdue the local tribes for decades, the conflict being ended by the Treaty of Greenville in 1795.

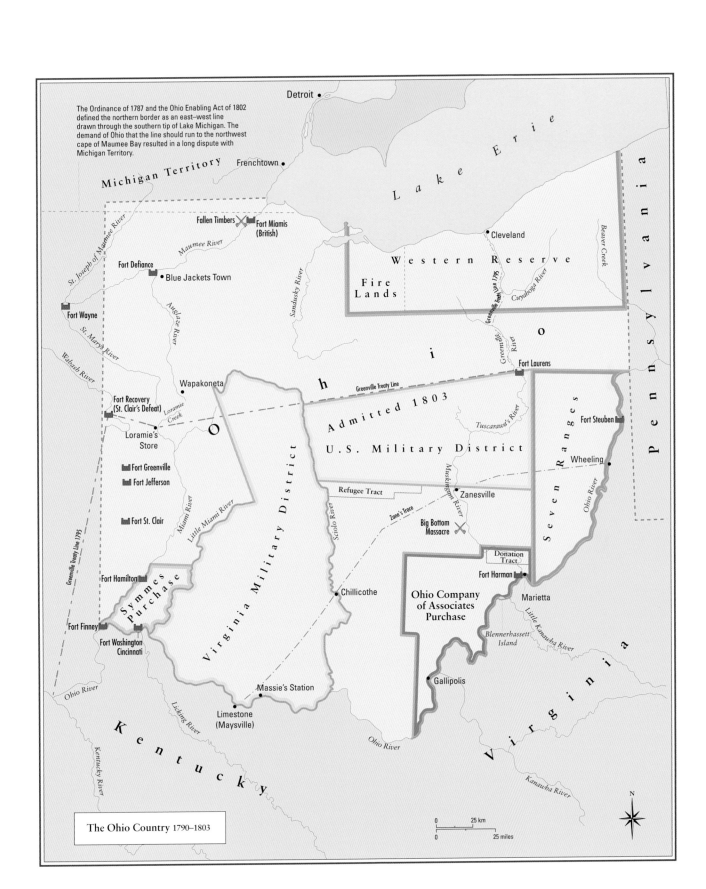

The Ordinance of 1787 and the Ohio Enabling Act of 1802 defined the northern border as an east–west line drawn through the southern tip of Lake Michigan. The demand of Ohio that the line should run to the northwest cape of Maumee Bay resulted in a long dispute with Michigan Territory.

Detroit

Michigan Territory

Frenchtown

Lake Erie

Fallen Timbers ✕ Fort Miamis (British)

Maumee River

Fort Defiance
• Blue Jackets Town

Cleveland

Western Reserve

Fire Lands

Beaver Creek

Greenville Treaty Line 1795

Cuyahoga River

St. Joseph of Maumee River

Fort Wayne

St. Mary's River

Auglaize River

Sandusky River

Pennsylvania

h

i

o

Wabash River

Wapakoneta

Fort Recovery (St. Clair's Defeat)

Loramie Creek

O

Greenville Treaty Line

Admitted 1803

Fort Laurens

U.S. Military District

Tuscarawas River

Fort Steuben

Seven Ranges

Loramie's Store

Fort Greenville

Fort Jefferson

Fort St. Clair

Miami River

Little Miami River

Virginia Military District

Refugee Tract

Muskingum River

Zane's Trace

Zanesville

Wheeling

Ohio River

Greenville Treaty Line 1795

Fort Hamilton

Symmes Purchase

Scioto River

Big Bottom Massacre ✕

Donation Tract

Fort Harman

Ohio Company of Associates Purchase

Marietta

Fort Finney

Fort Washington Cincinnati

Chillicothe

Blennerhassett Island

Little Kanawha River

Ohio River

Massie's Station

Gallipolis

Licking River

Limestone (Maysville)

Ohio River

Virginia

Kentucky

Kentucky River

Kanawha River

N

The Ohio Country 1790–1803

0   25 km
0   25 miles

The Treaty of Greenville, 1795

Major General Wayne's victory at the Battle of Fallen Timbers forced the Northwestern Indians to a peace council lest even more villages and crops be destroyed.

Totally disoriented and broken militarily, bereft of aid from their British supporters, and tormented by raids across the Ohio by Kentucky settlers, the Indians met Major General Wayne at Fort Greenville, Ohio. The meeting, which took place in the summer of 1795, drew in many tribes, including Shawnee, Potawatomi, Kickapoo, Delaware, Ottowa, Wyandot, Ojibwa, and Miami, as well as other smaller tribes. On August 3, a treaty was signed by which the Indian nations ceded 25,000 square miles (65,000 square kilometers) north of the Ohio, more than half of contemporary Ohio. The boundary began opposite the mouth of the Kentucky River, on the north shore of the Ohio, and ran to Fort Recovery, then to Loramie's Creek and Fort Laurens on the Tuscarawas tributary of the Muskingum River, crossing the portage to the Cuyahoga River and along it to Lake Erie. The Indians retained a strip along Lake Erie, a triangle of land in Indiana, and sixteen small patches for trading posts and strategic waterways. In return, Wayne stated that the United States would renounce claims *"to all other Indian lands, northward of the river Ohio, eastward of the Mississippi, and westward and southward of the Great Lakes, and the waters uniting them, according to the boundary line agreed on by the United States and the King of Great Britain."*

The agreement was remarkably precise: *"The Indian tribes who have a right to these lands, are ... to enjoy them, so long as they please, without any molestation from the United States; but when those tribes ... shall be disposed to sell their lands, or any part of them, they are to be sold only to the United States; and until such sale, the United States will protect all the said Indian tribes ... against all citizens of the United States, and against all other white persons who intrude upon the same. And the said Indian tribes again acknowledge themselves to be under the protection of the said United States, and no other power whatsoever."*

The Battle of Fallen Timbers, an illustration from *Harper's* magazine, 1896. The decisive defeat in this battle of the Indians of the Western Lakes Confederacy by "Mad Anthony" Wayne's Legion of the United States forced the tribes to the negotiating table and led to the Treaty of Greenville.

The United States benefited from the peace because the British were compelled to quit the forts south of the Great Lakes, which they had been occupying against the terms of the 1783 Treaty of Paris. However, the British were still allowed to trade with the Indians, according to the terms of the 1795 Jay treaty. Settlers flooded into the Ohio Country, totaling some 45,000 by 1800, and 250,000 by 1812. By that date, roads were passable, small cities abustle, and the countryside covered by cultivated fields.

In 1803, the United States purchased Louisiana from the French, who had recently regained control of the region from Spain. At the same time, President Thomas Jefferson sought to grab as much Indian territory as possible that fronted the Mississippi. Governor Harrison of the Indiana Territory bought large tracts of land, promising future annuities to the Indians. By 1809, the United States had gained title to lands along the Ohio River to the Mississippi, and up that river to the Wisconsin River. Jefferson thought that when hunting lands were purchased, the Indians would become "civilized" and turn to farming instead. Moreover, the acquisition of lands hundreds of miles from the nearest settlement demonstrated the possibility for eventual future white expansion.

Howard Chandler Christy's painting depicting the signing of the Treaty of Greenville.

Although the Treaty of Greenville was signed by almost all of the Indian leadership, many of the young warriors, including Tecumseh, refused to recognize its legality and resisted all incursions upon their lands with violence. Historians have called Tecumseh and similar thinkers Nativist, because of their refusal to reach an accommodation with the white man; as such, they were inclined to bind Native American nations into a pan-Indian force based on prophecy, spiritualism, and combined military might.

The Frontier in 1800

Area of settlement

Fort

BRITISH NORTH AMERICA

Disputed with Britain

To Mass.

Lake Superior

Lake Huron

Lake Ontario

Fort Detroit

Lake Erie

Vermont

N.H.

Portland

Salem

Boston

New York

Albany

Worcester

Mass.

Providence

New Bedford

Conn.

R.I.

Territory Northwest of Ohio River

Pennsylvania

New York

Brooklyn

New Jersey

Lancaster

Philadelphia

Wilmington

Indiana Territory

Cumberland

Baltimore

Maryland

Delaware

Washington

Chillicothe

Cincinnati

Fort Orleans

Staunton

Richmond

St. Louis

Louisville

Lexington

Virginia

Williamsburg

Kentucky

North Carolina

Raleigh

Louisiana

Ceded by Spain to France in secret treaty, 1800
Possession not taken by France until 1803

Tennessee

Charlotte

South Carlonia

Memphis

Augusta

Charleston

ATLANTIC OCEAN

Arkansas Post

Territory South of Ohio River

Georgia

Savannah

Mississippi Territory

Natchitoches

Natchez

Nacogdoches

West Florida

Pensacola

St. Augustine

New Orleans

East Florida

By 1800, the settlements were pushing steadily westward with disastrous consequences for the Indians.

N

Gulf of Mexico

Bahamas

0   400 km

0   400 miles

TECUMSEH

A late-nineteenth-century
depiction of Tecumseh, chief of
the Shawnee.

Opposite: The cession of Indian
lands that would form Michigan,
Indiana, and Illinois prompted
Tecumseh to urge resistance.

TECUMSEH AND THE PROPHET

DISPUTES OVER THE TREATY OF GREENVILLE
AND SUBSEQUENT LAND CESSIONS CAUSED
MUCH INDIAN DISQUIET. FROM THIS
EMERGED TWO CHARACTERS WHO WOULD
INSPIRE RESISTANCE.

In 1803 and 1804, through treaties signed at Vincennes, Indiana, the Kaskaskia had given up a large part of Illinois territory, while the Sauk and Fox had surrendered some 15 million acres (6 million hectares) south of the Wisconsin River. By the end of 1807, the United States had acquired eastern Michigan, southern Indiana, and nearly all of Illinois. This was the work of Governor William Henry Harrison of Indiana Territory.

In response, two Shawnees, Tecumseh and his brother, Tenskwatawa, set out to inspire a united Indian resistance. Tecumseh was unusual in that he had studied American and world history, and literature under the guidance of Rebecca Galloway, a white friend. He began to consider himself as a Native American first and Shawnee second; he believed that the Indian nations should confederate and create their own state in the Great Lakes and Ohio Valley region. He also felt that no Indian individual nor nation had the right to sell land to white people.

Tenskwatawa became known as the Prophet, because he had predicted an eclipse that occurred in 1805, although he might have known about the event anyway. He preached the virtues of old Indian traditions and the need for Native Americans to cast from their lives any vestiges of the white man's world, especially alcohol. The brothers traveled among the tribes spreading their word, and in 1808, they founded the village of Prophetstown at the confluence of the Wabash River and Tippecanoe Creek. Indians from many tribes in the Northeast—Shawnee, Delaware, Wyandot, and Ottawa—

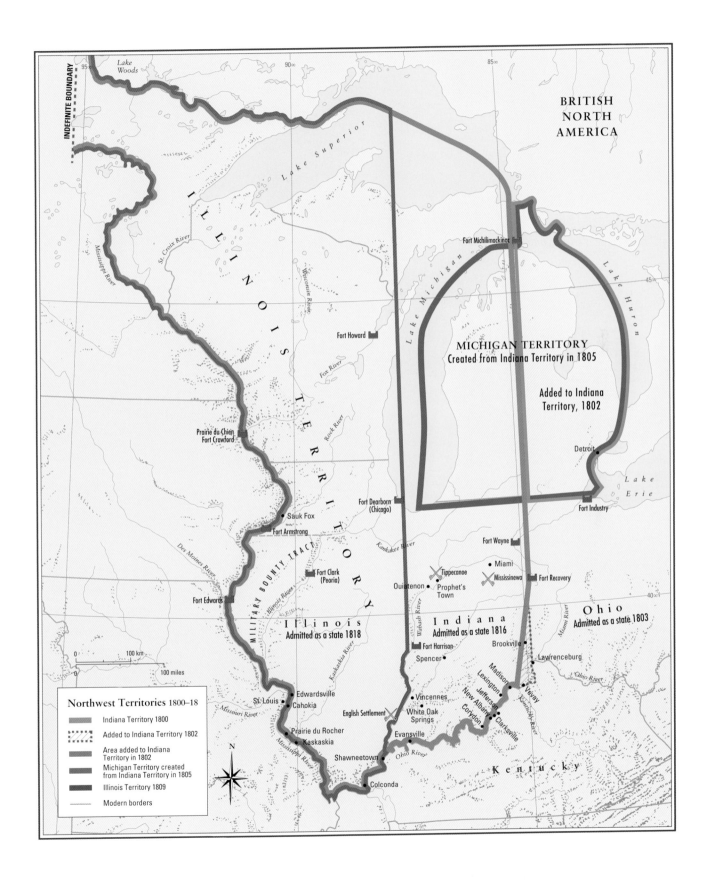

Northwest Territories 1800–18

Indiana Territory 1800

Added to Indiana Territory 1802

Area added to Indiana Territory in 1802

Michigan Territory created from Indiana Territory in 1805

Illinois Territory 1809

Modern borders

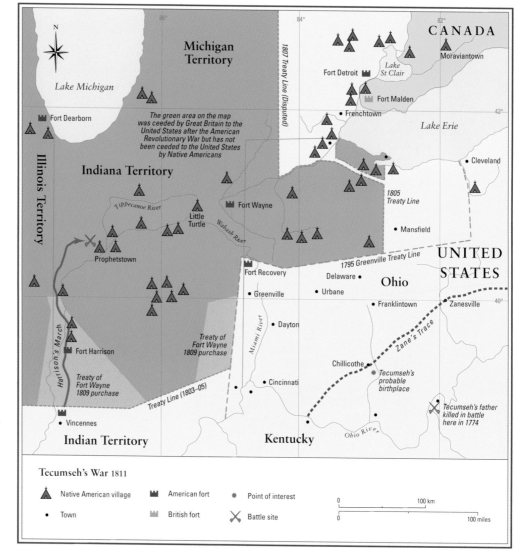

In 1811, encouraged by Tecumseh's absence (he was attempting to subdue the more hot-blooded among his followers), William Henry Harrison, governor of the Indiana Territory, marched on Prophetstown with a 1,000-strong force. Forewarned, the Indians made a preemptive attack on the Americans on the morning of November 7. The resulting Battle of Tippecanoe was a bloody fight, each side losing around 200 killed. It was only ended when Harrison's cavalry managed to drive the Indians from the field.

Tecumseh's War 1811

🏕 Native American village   🏰 American fort   ● Point of interest

● Town   🏰 British fort   ✗ Battle site

journeyed to Prophetstown to listen to the brothers expound their political and religious ideas.

The year 1808 is also significant for the Treaty of Fort Wayne. It was through this treaty that Harrison persuaded the Delaware and Potawatomi to sell 3 million acres (1.2 million hectares) of Indiana land to the United States. Tecumseh told Harrison that no one tribe had title to the land, and that any attempt to occupy it would be resisted. Younger warriors started to pass war belts around the region during 1810–11, and Tecumseh had difficulty in restraining his fighters. In 1811, at a conference in the South, on the Tallapoosa River, he talked with Creek, Cherokee, and Choctaw representatives. He won over the Creeks, but the other tribes were prepared to resist only if their lands were invaded again.

Harrison used Tecumseh's absence to goad the Prophet and his warriors into war. He advanced on Prophetstown with 1,000 regulars and militia, but the Indians left the village and attacked the American camp at dawn on November 7, 1811. The subsequent Battle of Tippecanoe was violent, each side suffering some 190 casualties; only cavalry charges drove the Indians from the battlefield. This indecisive encounter caused the Indians to flee from Prophetstown, which the Americans burned. Subsequently, the Indian survivors launched raids along the frontier during 1812.

The Americans thought that the British in Canada, especially at Fort Malden, were supplying and encouraging the Indians. This belief was one of the factors that led to the War of 1812 between the United States and Great Britain. The American view was that capturing Canada would remove the Indian threat. Tecumseh saw the war as a chance to build an Indian state, and he sided with the British in declaring war upon the United States. Many Indians joined him, and he was ranked a brigadier general in the British Army. Meanwhile, other Indians were continuing their raids against settlers.

Tecumseh aided British Major General Brock in capturing Detroit, and some of his warriors helped take Fort Dearborn, on the site of present-day Chicago. After Brock was killed at the Battle of Queenstown, Tecumseh was forced to cooperate with his successor, General Henry Proctor. The latter was partially responsible for the River Raisin Massacre, when a small party of Kentucky militia, who had surrendered, were slaughtered and scalped by Indians with the British force. Tecumseh, elsewhere at the time, stopped the violence upon his return and berated the British officers for allowing it to happen. Proctor retreated after a force under Commodore Oliver Perry beat the British at the Battle of Put-in-Bay on Lake Erie. Eventually, he stood his ground and was defeated at the Battle of the Thames on October 3, 1813, when Tecumseh was killed—his pan-Indian dream died with him. The Prophet died in obscurity in Canada in 1826.

One of the reasons for the War of 1812 was that the United States believed that Britain was arming Indians, who were attacking American settlers. To prevent this, an invasion of Canada was launched in August 1812, but it was repulsed and the British seized Fort Detroit. A second invasion of the Niagara peninsula was also defeated in October that year. Tecumseh, who saw the war as an opportunity to establish an Indian state, threw in his lot with the British, but was killed in 1813 at the Battle of the Thames. Eventually, the Americans gained naval superiority on the Great Lakes, taking control of Lake Erie and Lake Champlain, but no further invasion of Canada was attempted.

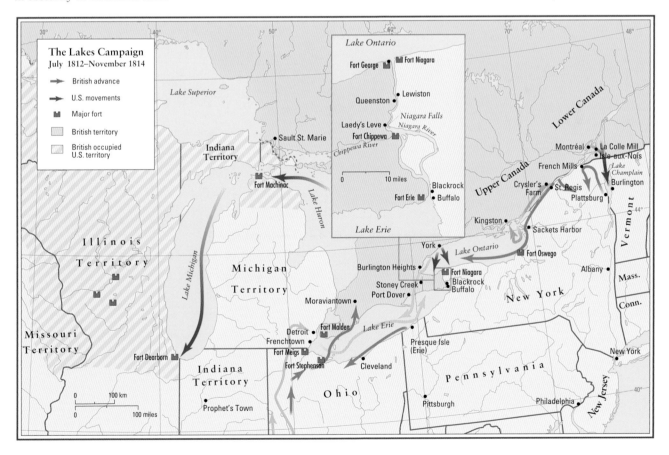

Lewis, Clark, and the Indians

Following the Louisiana Purchase, President Jefferson sent the Corps of Discovery to map the region and make a study of the Indian tribes they met.

Fearful of an aggressive French presence in Louisiana after Napoleon had forced Spain to cede him the region, in 1803, President Jefferson sent James Monroe to France to negotiate the purchase of New Orleans. In Paris, Monroe learned that Napoleon was losing interest in the Americas. The Emperor offered the United States not only New Orleans, but also some 828,000 square miles (2,150,000 square kilometers) of territory, all of Louisiana, for $15 million. This new territorial acquisition ensured Jefferson's reelection as president in 1804.

The American government required maps of the region, and Jefferson persuaded Congress to finance a scientific and cartographic expedition. His private secretary, Meriwether Lewis, William Clark, and some forty-five men were formed into the Corps of Discovery to explore the Missouri River. Jefferson hoped that the river could be used for commerce and communication with the Pacific, and to provide a link with the China trade. He also instructed the men to collect ethnographic information on the various Indian tribes they encountered, and to determine to what extent trade, especially in furs, might be entertained.

In preparation for the task, Lewis studied celestial navigation, botany, and zoology in Philadelphia. The expedition left from St. Louis in May 1804, the party traveling in keelboats along the Missouri. The passage was relatively smooth, and Lewis remarked that the Indians were friendly, generous, and welcoming. The men overwintered near a Mandan village, in present-day North Dakota, and built Fort Mandan. There, Lewis and Clark hired Toussaint Charbonneau as an interpreter, and he was accompanied by his Shoshone wife, Sacagawea (Bird Woman). She proved a useful interpreter and probably made the expedition appear less threatening to the Indians they met.

So far, the corps had overcome all obstacles successfully, feeding itself while collecting botanical and geological specimens, together with data on climate and terrain. In February 1805, however, a brush occurred with a Sioux raiding party. Five members of the expedition were returning to camp with game on sleds when the Sioux attacked, seizing two of three horses, but they were driven off by gunfire.

In the course of exploration, the corps held a council with the Teton Sioux at the site of Fort Pierre, in an attempt to gain their allegiance from Britain. In the spring of 1805, the expedition reached the Falls of the Missouri, and then progressed to its source. Next, Lewis and Clark crossed the Continental Divide in the Rocky Mountains, traveling down the Snake and Columbia rivers to reach the Pacific. They built Fort Clatsop, near a Clatsop village; this tribe belonged to the Chinook.

Winter was spent on the Columbia, and the return began in 1806, the party splitting into two to cover more ground. Lewis's group met and made camp with eight Blackfeet, but the Indians tried to steal their guns and horses. One Indian was stabbed, and Lewis shot another in the stomach. The Indians fled, and the Americans found they had captured four Indian mounts and sundry weaponry. They rode fast for 80 miles (130 kilometers) in case the Indians were joined by a war party.

In September 1806, the Corps of Discovery returned to St. Louis, having covered 8,000 miles (13,000 kilometers) in twenty-eight months. The expedition warned Britain that U.S. power had been projected to the Pacific and enhanced claims to the Oregon territory. Most importantly, Lewis and Clark's collections and diaries added much to the sum of knowledge about the region, its peoples, and a potential peltry trade.

Sacagawea, Shoshone wife of Toussaint Charbonneau, guides members of the Lewis and Clark expedition through the Rocky Mountains. From a painting by Alfred Russell (1904).

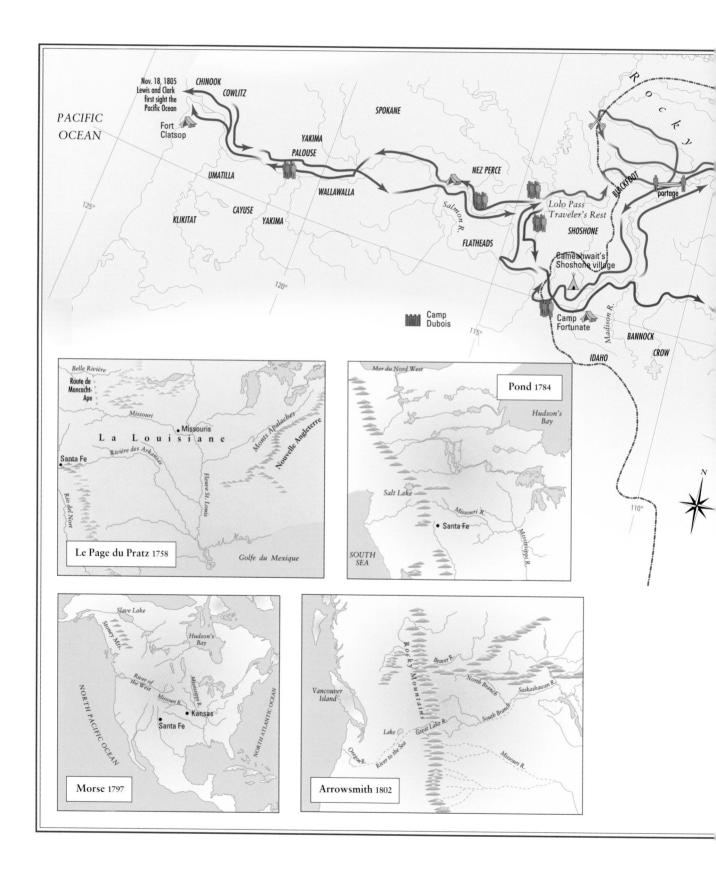

Nov. 18, 1805
Lewis and Clark
first sight the
Pacific Ocean

CHINOOK
COWLITZ

PACIFIC
OCEAN

Fort
Clatsop

YAKIMA
PALOUSE

UMATILLA

WALLAWALLA

KLIKITAT

CAYUSE

YAKIMA

SPOKANE

NEZ PERCE

Salmon R.

FLATHEADS

Lolo Pass
Traveler's Rest

SHOSHONE

Cameahwait's
Shoshone village

ROCKY

BLACKFOOT

portage

Camp
Dubois

Camp
Fortunate

Madison R.

BANNOCK

IDAHO

CROW

Le Page du Pratz 1758

Belle Rivière

Route de
Moncacht-
Ape

Missouri

La Louisiane

Santa Fe

Rivière des Arkansas

Rio del Nort

Monts Apalaches

Nouvelle Angleterre

Fleuve St. Louis

Golfe du Mexique

Pond 1784

Mer du Nord West

Hudson's
Bay

Salt Lake

Missouri R.

• Santa Fe

Mississippi R.

SOUTH
SEA

Morse 1797

Slave Lake

Stoney Mts.

Hudson's
Bay

River of
the West

Missouri R.

Mississippi R.

• Kansas

NORTH PACIFIC OCEAN

Santa Fe

NORTH ATLANTIC OCEAN

Arrowsmith 1802

Vancouver
Island

Rocky Mountains

Beaver R.

North Branch

Saskashawan R.

South Branch

Lake

Great Lake R.

Oregon R.

River to the Sea

Missouri R.

N

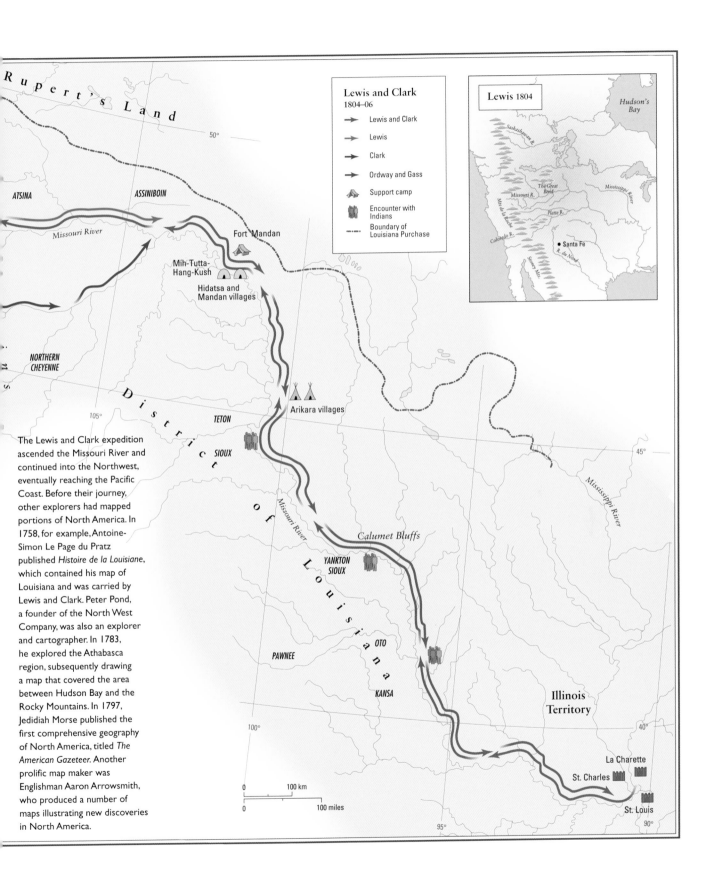

Lewis and Clark
1804–06

→ Lewis and Clark
→ Lewis
→ Clark
→ Ordway and Gass
⛺ Support camp
🧍 Encounter with Indians
–·–·– Boundary of Louisiana Purchase

Lewis 1804

The Lewis and Clark expedition ascended the Missouri River and continued into the Northwest, eventually reaching the Pacific Coast. Before their journey, other explorers had mapped portions of North America. In 1758, for example, Antoine-Simon Le Page du Pratz published *Histoire de la Louisiane*, which contained his map of Louisiana and was carried by Lewis and Clark. Peter Pond, a founder of the North West Company, was also an explorer and cartographer. In 1783, he explored the Athabasca region, subsequently drawing a map that covered the area between Hudson Bay and the Rocky Mountains. In 1797, Jedidiah Morse published the first comprehensive geography of North America, titled *The American Gazeteer*. Another prolific map maker was Englishman Aaron Arrowsmith, who produced a number of maps illustrating new discoveries in North America.

The Opening of the Northwest

The Europeans and, later, Americans found the Pacific Northwest to be a lucrative region for fur trading with local Native American tribes.

Although Russian and Spanish traders had made sporadic forays into the Northwest from 1741, the first major European contact occurred in the spring of 1778, when James Cook arrived in Nootka Sound, off Vancouver Island. Instigated by the Hudson Bay Company, this voyage was made in the hope of finding a Northwest Passage to the Pacific, together with new markets and routes for the company. Cook's crew traded with the Yuquot Indians, acquiring sea otter furs that fetched high prices when the expedition reached Canton in China. News of this fur trade galvanized others, and by the late 1790s, twenty-one vessels were trading in Nootka Sound annually.

In 1792, Captain George Vancouver, a former midshipman on Cook's *Resolution*, arrived and surveyed the American West Coast, from Baja California to Cook Inlet, discovering the insularity of Vancouver Island. At Nootka Sound, he negotiated with Juan Bodega y Quadra for the cession to Britain of all Spanish claims to the Pacific coast north of California. Six weeks after Vancouver left Elcho Harbour in Dean Channel, in the summer of 1793,

Alexander Mackenzie reached the same spot. He had been employed by the North West Company, a rival of the Hudson Bay Company, and had left Fort Chippewa in Athabasca Country in October 1792. Mackenzie had wintered at the confluence of the Peace and Smoky rivers, and reached Elcho Harbor on July 22, 1793. Another notable expedition of the time was that led by Robert Gray, who discovered the mouth of the Columbia River in 1792.

The travels of Vancouver and Mackenzie had a momentous impact, leading to the triangular maritime fur trade. British and, later, Boston vessels sailed to the Northwest to trade goods with the Indians for sea otter pelts, then traveled on to China, where they were exchanged for tea, spices, and silk. This trade had peaked by 1800, however, being overtaken by land-based trade.

A notable trader was the German-American John Jacob Astor, who entered the fur trade in 1786. He formed the American Fur Company in 1808, constructed trading posts along the Missouri and Columbia rivers, and founded the settlement of Fort Astoria, at the mouth of the Columbia River, which became his trade terminus. The fort was taken over by the North West Company during the War of 1812.

The relationship between the early traders and the Indians of the Northwest demonstrates that the latter knew how to drive a hard bargain; they rapidly realized the value of sea otters. Prices were fixed by supply and demand, and competition. Native American requirements had to be met before

Alexander Mackenzie also carried out a major exploration of the Northwest for the North West Company. He left his mark on a rock at Elcho Harbor in 1793. Remarkably, it remains there to this day.

Opposite: A portrait of James Cook by Nathaniel Dance, c. 1775. The British Royal Naval officer helped open up the Northwest to fur traders through his voyage of 1778 in search of the fabled Northwest Passage to Asia.

trade began. Ceremonies were performed and gifts given, and trade took place at the Indians' pace. They exercised great control over the fur trade, which was concentrated at Vancouver Island and the Queen Charlotte Islands. By the 1790s, more traders having entered the business, the Indians were demanding higher prices; they could choose between traders to get the best profit. Initially, payment for furs was made by giving metal tools, but as the number of tools in Indian hands increased, their value dropped; instead, cloth, clothing, and heavy blankets were demanded, and eventually rum, tobacco, molasses, and guns.

The Chinook were important traders, providing a connection for goods to the Dalles trade center. To cement good relations, traders often entered long lasting marriages with Native American women. For example, Fort Simpson trader John Kennedy wed the daughter of Legaic, a Tsimshian leader who controlled trade on the Upper Skeena River.

Trade brought a variety of problems in the early years of European contact, although most relations between traders and Indians were amicable, except in the far north, where Russians virtually enslaved the Aleuts. After the Russians moved to the Alaskan Panhandle, they confronted the more warlike Tlingits, who destroyed Fort New Archangel, Sitka, in 1802, killing twenty Russians and 130 Aleuts, and seizing 3,000 furs. In 1805, Yakutat was destroyed, but antagonism declined after 1820. The only other major attack on Europeans was the 1803 assault at Vancouver Island on a merchant vessel, the *Boston*, which nearly lost its entire crew.

The other major problem was disease; there were smallpox outbreaks in the 1770s and 1801. Venereal disease hit women of childbearing age, affecting fertility rates. Other dangers were malaria, respiratory illnesses, influenza, dysentery, measles,

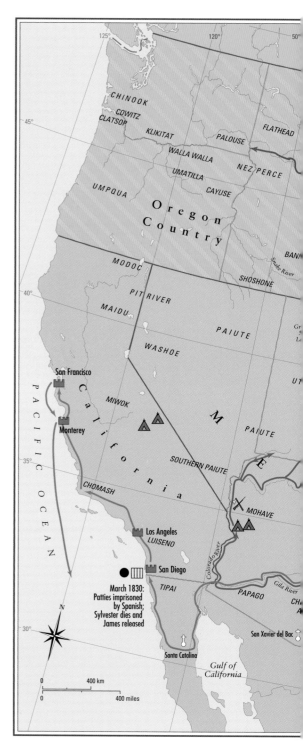

whooping cough, and tuberculosis. Death rates were high, and by 1840, the Chinooks and other Indians on the lower Columbia River had lost 70–80 percent of their population. The evidence for the impact of disease is patchy, however, and in many cases, figures are little more than guesswork.

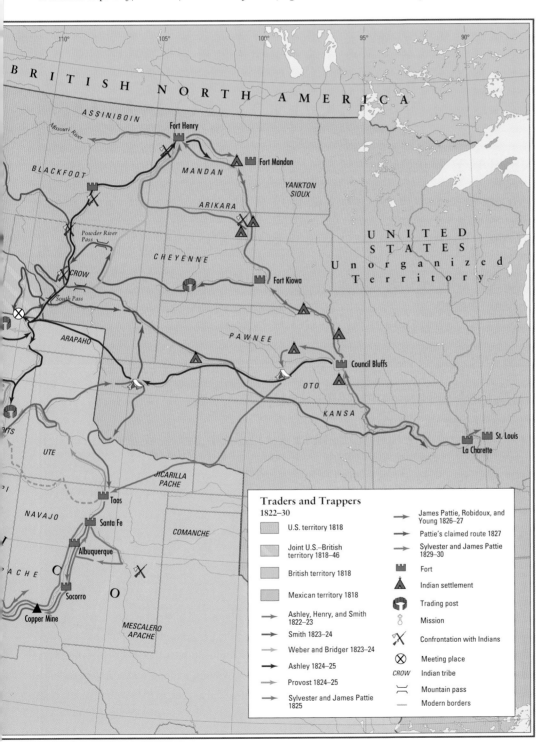

Traders and Trappers
1822–30

- U.S. territory 1818
- Joint U.S.–British territory 1818–46
- British territory 1818
- Mexican territory 1818
- Ashley, Henry, and Smith 1822–23
- Smith 1823–24
- Weber and Bridger 1823–24
- Ashley 1824–25
- Provost 1824–25
- Sylvester and James Pattie 1825
- James Pattie, Robidoux, and Young 1826–27
- Pattie's claimed route 1827
- Sylvester and James Pattie 1829–30
- Fort
- Indian settlement
- Trading post
- Mission
- Confrontation with Indians
- Meeting place
- *CROW* Indian tribe
- Mountain pass
- Modern borders

After Lewis and Clark, many fur trappers and traders entered the Northwest and West during the early nineteenth century. Their wanderings and expeditions created a bank of knowledge about the country that later would help guide settlers into the wilderness, leading to confrontations with the Indians. Among those whose explorations contributed to the opening up of the country was famed mountain man Jedidiah Smith, the first white man to enter California by the overland route and the first to scale the High Sierras among many other accomplishments. William Henry Ashley and his partner, Andrew Henry, set up the Rocky Mountain Fur Company in competition with the Hudson Bay Company, and financed a number of major expeditions, employing, among others, Jim Bridger and John Henry Weber. The first man of European descent to see the Great Salt Lake was Étienne Provost, a French Canadian trapper and trader. Other well-known trappers were Miguel Robidoux, Ewing Young, and Sylvester Pattie and his son, James. The Patties were the first Americans to set foot on Arizona soil.

Indian Lands 1810

■ Indian territory

□ Land occupied by immigrants

0   300 km

0   300 miles

N

The early nineteenth century saw a steady movement westward by American settlers, squeezing the Indians into an ever-smaller area of land.

Opposite: Mississippi Territory came into being in 1798 from land ceded to the United States by Spain through the 1795 Treaty of Madrid. In 1804, the territory was enlarged northward to include land originally claimed by Georgia. Then in 1812, the Mobile district of West Florida was added, the United States claiming that this had been part of the Louisiana Purchase, although this was disputed by Spain until it was occupied by U.S. troops. Eventually, the territory was divided, the eastern portion forming Alabama. The formation of Mississippi Territory, and later Alabama, required substantial land cessions by the Indians, notably the Creek, Chickasaw, and Choctaw nations. They were also subjected to Jackson's removal policy.

In 1812, a band of Creeks under Little Warrior joined Tecumseh in Canada. They were involved in the Raisin River Massacre, then killed two white families at the mouth of the Ohio while returning. The Lower Creek on the lower Chattahoochee and Apalachiola rivers feared white retaliation when the U.S. Government demanded that the murderers be handed over. These moderate Creeks, led by Big Warrior, executed the murderers, which caused the Upper Creek to seek vengeance for Little Warrior. The majority of the Upper Creek towns declared war, taking up their red war clubs, from which they were known as the Red Sticks. They attacked Fort Mims, which was held by mixed-blood Creeks and some white men who had ambushed an ammunition train belonging to the Red Sticks. The defenders were slaughtered, and the incident pushed the United States to intervene in this Creek civil war.

Three U.S. columns advanced on the Red Stick strongholds, two achieving limited success. However, a 2,500-strong Tennessee militia force, led by Andrew Jackson, secured two victories at Tallasahatchee and Talladega. Jackson was reinforced by the 39th U.S. Infantry and, with White Stick Creek and Cherokee allies, advanced on a Red Stick fortification at Horseshoe Bend, on the Tallapoosa River. Battle ensued, during which a certain Ensign Sam Houston was wounded; the Indians lost about 800 dead and wounded, some being drowned in the river. Jackson then enforced the Treaty of Fort Jackson on both Red Stick and White Stick Creeks, gaining a cession of 23 million acres (9.4 million hectares) for the USA, about 60 percent of Alabama and 20 percent of Georgia.

Was this Creek War a forcing ground for Jackson's later removal policy? Certainly, he was concerned with national security in the West. He thought that if white settlers could replace Indians in the Chickasaw and Choctaw regions, the lower Mississippi would be defensible. When he fought the Creek, and the Seminole in the First Seminole War, he was hard on the enemy, but, when commander of the Division of the South, he ordered soldiers to remove white squatters from Cherokee lands. Jackson believed that Native Americans had no concrete title to all the lands they claimed, but were entitled to retain sufficient for their needs. Also, the idea that Indians were sovereign nations, especially when surrounded by U.S. territory, was anathema to him. He thought that these "islands" should be subjected to U.S. laws. He also felt that Indians would adopt the ways of white society and become farmers. After Horseshoe Bend, in April 1814, he pronounced that, *"The weapons of warfare will be exchanged for the utensils of husbandry, and the wilderness which now withers in sterility and seems to mourn the desolation which overspreads it, will blossom as the rose, and become the nursery of the arts."*

Jackson envisaged removal as a means of protecting U.S. civilization, providing land for white settlers, gaining security and buffer lands against foreign invaders, appeasing the Georgia legislature against the federal government, and probably winning votes to boot. He thought that conversion of the Indians to an agricultural way of life could only be achieved if they were not pressured by surrounding white settlements. Thus, removal west of the Mississippi would allow time for them to become

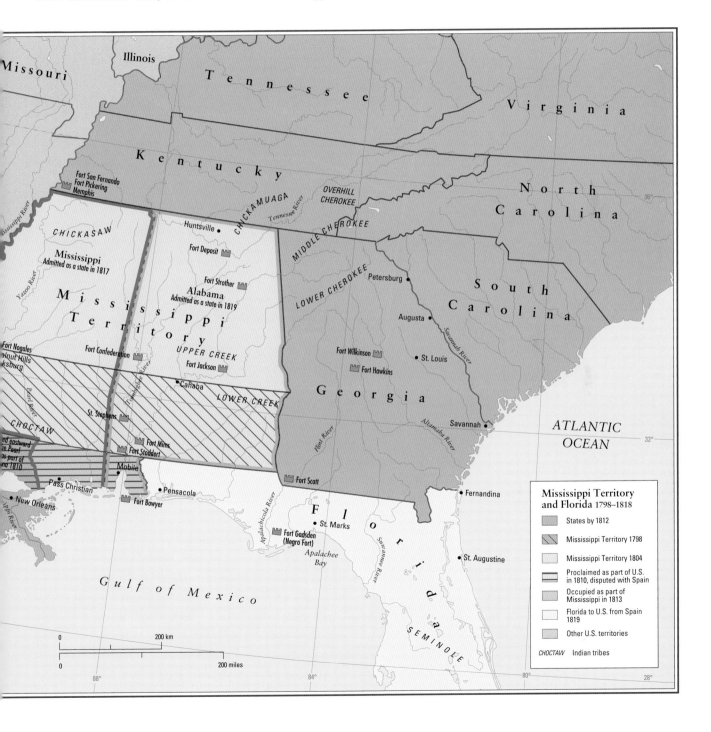

Mississippi Territory and Florida 1798–1818

- States by 1812
- Mississippi Territory 1798
- Mississippi Territory 1804
- Proclaimed as part of U.S. in 1810, disputed with Spain
- Occupied as part of Mississippi in 1813
- Florida to U.S. from Spain 1819
- Other U.S. territories

CHOCTAW Indian tribes

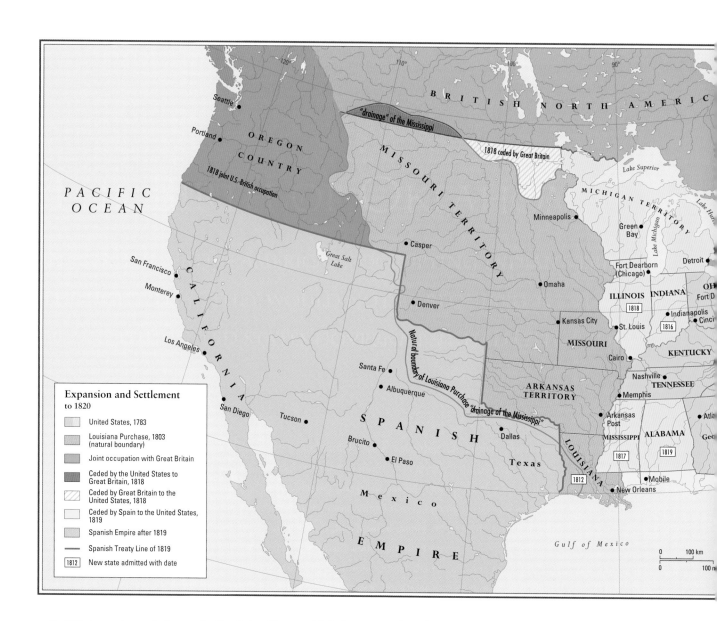

Expansion and Settlement
to 1820

- United States, 1783
- Louisiana Purchase, 1803 (natural boundary)
- Joint occupation with Great Britain
- Ceded by the United States to Great Britain, 1818
- Ceded by Great Britain to the United States, 1818
- Ceded by Spain to the United States, 1819
- Spanish Empire after 1819
- Spanish Treaty Line of 1819
- 1812 New state admitted with date

By 1820, the steady growth of the United States was apparent. Settlers were moving westward, although a substantial portion of the West was in Spanish hands.

agriculturalists. What could Jackson actually achieve in terms of Indian policy? Firstly, he could protect Indian enclaves in the East by treaty agreements and military force. However, the U.S. standing army was too small to achieve this task, and it would be costly. Again, such a policy would allow the Cherokee to be a nation within a nation, and U.S. politics would not let this happen. Secondly, the Indians could be encouraged to assimilate into white society, losing their own culture and identity. However, Indian resilience was too intractable for this to occur. Finally, the Native Americans could have been obliterated and hounded into oblivion by military force, disease, and starvation. Such an extermination policy was actually followed in California, but it was not a policy that Jackson could pursue. Thus, when president, he took over existing removal policies as the only viable alternative to allow survival of culture, to avoid white incursions, and to distance the Indians from federal and state jurisdictions. Removal would rescue Indians from the evils of white civilization, and then they would

"share in the blessings of civilization and be saved from that degradation and destruction to which they were rapidly hastening while they remained in the States..."

Seminole chiefs are captured by U.S. troops in Florida during the First Seminole War (1816–18). The war had been prompted when settlers attacked the Florida Indians, who then retaliated by raiding settlements in Georgia. At the time, Florida was under Spanish control.

The removal policy suffered many problems. Eastern Native Americans found difficulty in adapting to a new, alien, Plains environment in Indian Territory. Ottowa, Shawnee, Potawatomi, Sauk and Fox, Miami, and Kickapoo from the North, and the Five Civilized Tribes from the South, were all used to a sedentary, agricultural lifestyle among the eastern woodlands. Now they faced vast grasslands, which needed different agricultural methods. Furthermore, Native Americans already inhabiting the West were not consulted about this forced invasion of their traditional hunting grounds. The Eastern interlopers, as they were regarded, thought the nomadic Plains Indians to be primitive barbarians. The Osage were furious when the newcomers moved onto their land, while the Kiowa, Wichita, and Comanche claimed that half the lands settled by the Five Civilized Tribes were their own. When the newcomers spread west in search of buffalo, the Kiowa and Comanche attacked them, and federal troops were called in to settle disputes and keep the peace. Clearly, the removal policy had not ended federal involvement in Indian affairs. Also, when the Arapaho and Cheyenne attempted to drive away the Potawatomi, the latter, having been trained by the British during the War of 1812, formed ranks and used volley fire to inflict serious casualties on their attackers, gaining command of the battlefields. Eventually, the mutually-hostile groups kept out of each other's way, the peace being policed by troops from Forts Leavenworth, Gibson, and Towson.

When the Five Civilized Tribes journeyed to Indian Territory, they took their slaves with them. Mixed-blood Indians tended to be the slave owners, but not entirely. Certainly, by 1860, the Cherokee owned 4,600 slaves, the Choctaw 2,344, the Creek 1,532, the Chickasaw 975, and the Seminole 500. The Seminole treated their black "slaves" differently to the other four tribes, however, which led to unexpected trouble. Traditionally, the Seminole did not practice chattel slavery, but called fugitive slaves their "property" to protect them from slave-catchers, whether Chickasaw hunters or white patrollers. The Black Seminoles lived in separate villages in Seminole territory and paid food tribute to the Indians, but also they were allied militarily and fought in the Seminole Wars. When removed to Indian Territory, the Black Seminoles rode in on their own horses and carried their own personal rifles. The Seminole were relocated to Cherokee lands around Fort Gibson, where Creek and Cherokee slave owners feared the influence of free Black Seminoles upon their slave populations. The Black Seminoles settled in the Illinois River bottoms, near Webbers Falls, where the Cherokee slaves socialized with them.

The demand for land from the Indians was continuous, as this map shows. Westward expansion of the United States put unrelenting pressure on Native Americans as the nineteenth century progressed.

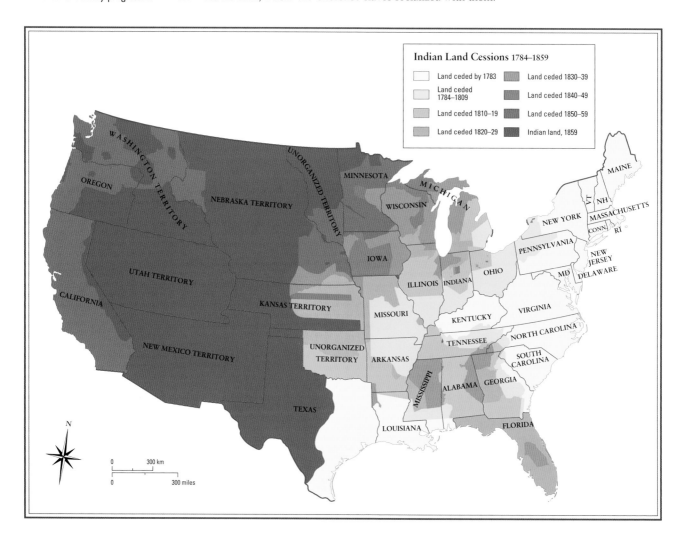

Indian Land Cessions 1784–1859

Land ceded by 1783
Land ceded 1784–1809
Land ceded 1810–19
Land ceded 1820–29
Land ceded 1830–39
Land ceded 1840–49
Land ceded 1850–59
Indian land, 1859

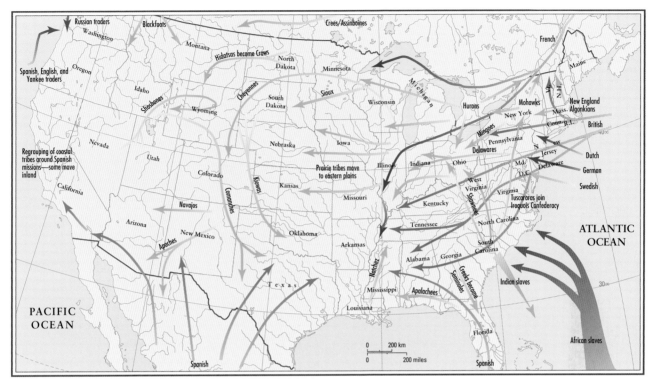

On November 15, 1842, some twenty-five slaves, mainly from a plantation belonging to Joseph Vann, a steamboat owner, locked up their owners and overseers, stole guns, horses, and mules, and set off toward Mexico, where slavery was illegal. Eventually, more than thirty-five men, women, and children were chased by Cherokees and Creeks, who caught up with them near the Canadian River in the Choctaw Nation. A two-day fight began, and two slaves were killed, while twelve were captured. The Cherokees and Creeks went home to summon reinforcements, while the slaves encountered slave-catcher James Edwards with his Delaware companion, Billy Wilson. The slaves killed them and released eight Africans who were being returned to their owner in the Choctaw Nation.

Meanwhile, the Cherokee leader, John Ross, had ordered a well-armed group to chase the slaves. They were discovered north of the Red River, approximately 280 miles (450 kilometers) from Fort Gibson, and surrendered.

The Cherokee attitude toward Black Seminoles became increasingly antagonistic, and by 1843, they were demanding that the group leave the Cherokee Nation. In 1849, some Black Seminoles, under Chief John Horse, left Indian Territory, joining Chief Wildcat and his band; together, they reached Mexico. By 1851, some 300 African slaves had attempted to escape from Indian Territory, heading for Texas or Mexico, while an "underground railroad" route left Washington County, Oklahoma, for Kansas.

Despite the U.S. federal policy that Indian Territory should be inviolate, increasing numbers of miners and settlers were crossing the land en route to Oregon and California. In 1845 alone, some 3,000 people reached Oregon by the overland route. The result was a foregone conclusion.

In the West, missionary doctor Marcus Whitman and his family had settled near Walla Walla, Washington. In 1847, Cayuse Indians were hit by a measles epidemic; shamans blamed the disease on

American Migrations
18th and 19th Centuries

- Native tribes
- Spanish
- British
- French
- Dutch
- German
- Swedish
- Native slaves
- African slaves
- Traders
- Modern borders

The eighteenth and nineteenth centuries saw a steady westward movement of populations in North America. As emigrants poured into the East, the Indians fell back or were pushed back. Eventually, however, the Eastern tribes came into conflict with those in the West, who resented the incursion into their territory.

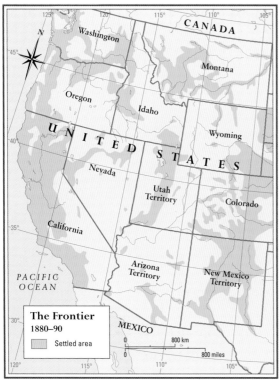

The Frontier
1880–90

Settled area

the doctor and incited the murder of whites. The Whitmans and twelve others were killed, while forty-seven whites were captured, although later released. The Whitman Massacre instigated the events that led to the creation of Oregon Territory in 1848. The Indians were now in a vise, being pressured by settlers on both sides of the continent.

In California, the sudden invasion of white miners devastated some 150,000 local Indians. Having survived Spanish exploitation, now the Indians watched their game being driven away or killed, while the rivers were polluted or rerouted by mine workings. Indian subsistence patterns were destroyed, so they raided mine settlements, stealing cattle and horses. They were decimated by disease, then slaughtered deliberately, until their number had been reduced to below 30,000 by 1870. Marysvllle and Honey Lake townships paid bounties for Indian scalps; Shasta City gave five dollars for each Indian head presented at the city hall. At Roffs Ranch, in 1860, whites killed nine men, then butchered forty women and children, splitting open the latters' heads with hatchets.

A strange occurrence took place in Utah. Democrat President James Buchanan sent an army to eradicate polygamy among the Mormons of Salt Lake City and Utah, and while the federal units advanced west,

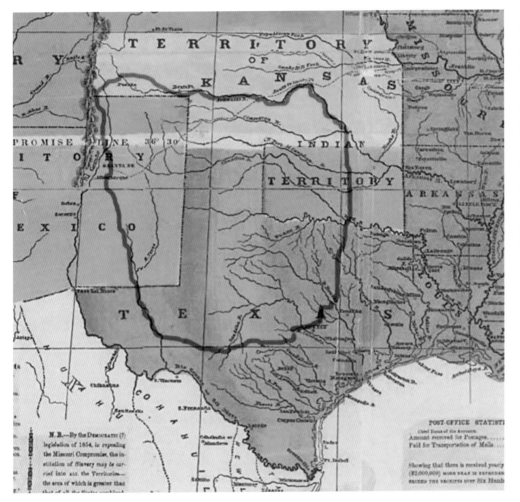

The Comancheria, the historical homeland of the Comanche. This region spanned parts of New Mexico, Texas, Kansas, and Indian Territory (subsequently Oklahoma). For many years, the Comanche maintained their independence, but a peace treaty with the Republic of Texas was thwarted when the Texas legislature refused to guarantee the boundary of the Comancheria. Subsequently, the tribe was decimated by disease through contact with settlers. The remnants were forced to move to a reservation near Fort Sill, Oklahoma, in the 1870s.

the Mormons made an alliance with the Paiutes. Meanwhile, a wagon train, not connected with the federal force, had reached southern Mormon territory at Mountain Meadows on September 7, 1857. About 200 Paiutes attacked, believing that the Missourian train was poisoning the local watering holes. The Indians were driven off, but one escaping Missourian, who sought help for the besieged train, was shot by young Mormons. Their elders realized that if this event was reported by any survivor of the wagon train, the federal troops would punish them. They resolved to wipe out the members of the train and blame the massacre on the Paiutes. On September 11, Mormon John D. Lee approached the wagons under a flag of truce, telling the migrants that if they lay down their arms, he could lead them to safety, and the Indians would not attack. The deceived Missourians followed him, whereupon the Mormons gunned down the men while the Paiutes attacked the women and children. They killed 120 people; Lee murdered all the sick and wounded. Seventeen small children survived and were adopted by Mormon families.

Eventually, the Mormons negotiated peace with President Buchanan. However, their southern Paiute allies were subjected to Navajo and Ute slave raids. They also suffered from white diseases and lost their best lands to their white allies.

Opposite, top: A contemporary engraving depicting the U.S. military expedition sent by President Buchanan to quell the Mormons in Utah.

Opposite: This map shows how white settlement in the West grew rapidly throughout the nineteenth century. This increase put overwhelming pressure on Native Americans.

REMOVALS IN THE MIDWEST

THE GROWING NUMBER OF WHITE SETTLERS, AND THEIR CONSTANT WESTWARD MOVEMENT, PROMPTED THE U.S. GOVERNMENT TO CONSIDER THE IDEA OF A "PERMANENT INDIAN FRONTIER."

John C. Calhoun, Secretary of War under President Monroe, was responsible for drawing up a plan to remove all Indians east of the Mississippi in 1824.

To clear the land for settlement, it was proposed that all Indians should be moved from east of the Mississippi to lands between the 95th and the 101st meridians. A removal plan was formulated in 1824 by John C. Calhoun, President Monroe's Secretary of War, and eastern tribes were "persuaded to accept new western lands." Often, government agents would bribe a corrupt or unthinking chief into signing a removal treaty, which meant an enforced move west.

In reality, the westward migration of Indians from the southern Great Lakes area had begun after the 1780s. In cooperation with Spanish authorities at St. Louis, Delaware, Shawnee, and Cherokee survivors of border warfare in the Ohio territory led a movement into Upper Louisiana. Other Delawares, Kickapoos, and Shawnees entered contemporary Missouri, but when that area became a state in 1821, the white population wanted to expel these Indians. Shawnees from Ohio moved into a 20-mile (32-kilometer) wide strip south of the Kansas River, where they were joined by the Delaware. In the 1830s, Ohio and Illinois also urged the removal of Indian inhabitants. Rapidly, more Kickapoo, Sauk, Fox (Mesquakie), Chippewa, Iowa, Potawatomi, Ottowa, Peoria, and Miami were crowded into reservations just west of the 95th meridian, and a few into western Iowa.

The Potawatomi had numbered some 9,000 and had lived around the base of Lake Michigan and in the Indiana-Michigan border region; they resisted migration. Around 2,000 from northwestern Indiana endured forced removal, while about half of the rest moved to allocated land in western Iowa. The Miami, weakened by the Ohio wars, were slow in leaving their Indiana home by the Wabash River; an 1838 treaty allowed some to remain. The last northwestern tribes to surrender their territories were the Wyandots of Ohio and northwest Michigan, originally Petuns and Hurons retreating from Iroquois expansion. An 1842 treaty removed them, but not to Kansas. Instead, the Wyandots bought a tract from the Delaware at the confluence of the Missouri and Kansas rivers. Eventually, some of the Wyandots were resettled in Wyandot County, Kansas.

The Seneca provide an interesting example of removal. Much of their land had been seized through the 1784 Fort Stanwix treaty and by land speculators, while they lost the remainder on the Genessee River through the 1797 Treaty of Big Tree. Final efforts to remove the Seneca occurred at the 1838 Treaty of Buffalo Creek, by which the four surviving Seneca reservations—Buffalo Creek, Tonawanda, Cattaraugus, and Allegany—were sold, provision being made to relocate the tribe to Kansas. The proceedings were deemed to be corrupt, and the contested treaty was rewritten in 1842. The new terms agreed the sale of Buffalo Creek and

The Seneca Chief Sagoyewatha, also known as Red Jacket for the coat given him by the British during the Revolutionary War, attempted to stop the sale of Seneca land west of the Genesee River by the Treaty of Big Tree in 1797, but without success. The Indians had been supplied with copious quantities of liquor during the treaty talks, while the Seneca women had received plenty of gifts.

Tonawanda, but the Seneca retained Cattaraugus and Allegany. Even so, some Seneca migrated to Kansas, but all bar two returned. The Tonawanda Seneca were not present at the signing of the 1842 treaty and protested. In 1857, another treaty returned most of their reservation, which was purchased with Kansas removal funds. In 1848, the Allegany and Cattaraugus reservations formed the Seneca Nation, which had a written constitution and a democratically elected government.

The Kickapoo were subjected to many removals. Some bands moved to Mexico, while the Prairie band relocated to southwestern Missouri in the 1820s. Treaties of 1832 led to the resettlement of the Prairie and Vermillion bands near Fort Leavenworth in Kansas. However, by the 1860s, many Prairie Kickapoo had moved to Mexico. These southern Kickapoo gained notoriety for raiding American ranches and settlements along the Rio Grande. The U.S. Army attacked them in Mexico, and in 1874, many left Mexico for Oklahoma.

Eventually, it was considered that many northern Indian bands were blocking Missouri River traffic, so they were concentrated gradually in Oklahoma. Even so, many thousands of Indians remained east of the Mississippi.

REMOVALS IN THE SOUTHEAST

THE REMOVAL OF TRIBES FROM THE SOUTHEAST WAS YET ANOTHER SHAMEFUL, BLOODY EPISODE IN THE UNITED STATES' DEALINGS WITH NATIVE AMERICANS.

U.S. Secretary of War John Eaton was charged with implementing President Jackson's removal policy.

On May 28, 1830, President Andrew Jackson signed into law the Indian Removal Act. This bill was aimed primarily at the Chickasaw, Choctaw, Creek, Seminole, and Cherokee nations. Orthodox wisdom has it that Jackson was courting southern voters for the 1832 election, but he was also interested in national security and wanted the borderlands peopled with whites.

The Secretary of War, John Eaton, invited delegates from all tribes to negotiate removal treaties at his home in Franklin, Tennessee. Only the Chickasaw turned up. They agreed that their lands would be surveyed into individual tracts held in free simple title. Each family could then sell their tract of land and use the proceeds to move west. The Chickasaw also won the right to choose their own land. Eventually, in January 1837, the Chickasaw leaders purchased the right to settle among the Choctaw. Some 4,900 people enrolled for removal, marched to Memphis, and crossed the Mississippi with their 1,100 slaves and 4–5,000 horses. The Chickasaw never really relished being engulfed by the Choctaw, and in 1855, the nations separated peacefully, a new independent Chickasaw Nation being created.

The Choctaw were treated similarly. Under the terms of the 1820 Treaty of Doak's Stand, the nation already owned some western land, between the Canadian and Red rivers. Eaton wanted to acquire the Choctaw's eastern landholding of 10,000,000 acres (4,000,000 hectares). Negotiations were bitter, but the newly elected Choctaw Chief Greenwood LeFlore, son of a French father and a mixed-blood Choctaw mother, finalized a deal. In return for ceding the land, the Choctaw wanted annuity payments, finance for the construction of churches and schools, removal expenses, and subsistence for one

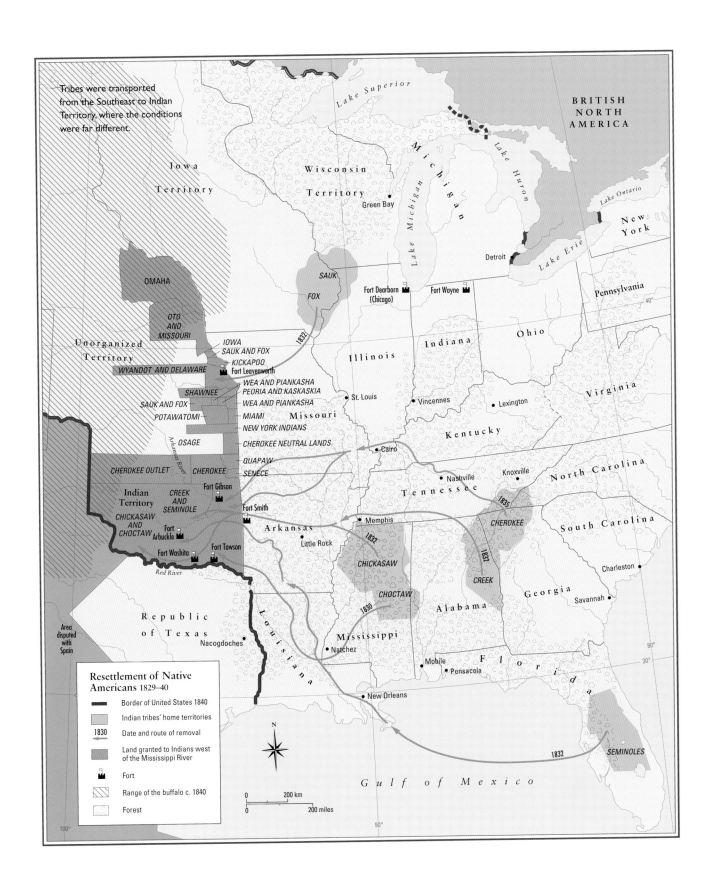

Tribes were transported from the Southeast to Indian Territory, where the conditions were far different.

BRITISH NORTH AMERICA

Iowa Territory

Wisconsin Territory

Green Bay

Michigan

Lake Superior

Lake Huron

Lake Michigan

Lake Erie

Lake Ontario

New York

Pennsylvania

Detroit

OMAHA

OTO AND MISSOURI

Unorganized Territory

WYANDOT AND DELAWARE

SHAWNEE

SAUK AND FOX

POTAWATOMI

OSAGE

CHEROKEE OUTLET

CHEROKEE

Indian Territory

CREEK AND SEMINOLE

Fort Gibson

CHICKASAW AND CHOCTAW

Fort Arbuckle

Fort Washita

Fort Towson

Red River

Republic of Texas

Area disputed with Spain

Nacogdoches

SAUK

FOX

IOWA
SAUK AND FOX
KICKAPOO
Fort Leavenworth

WEA AND PIANKASHA
PEORIA AND KASKASKIA
WEA AND PIANKASHA
MIAMI
NEW YORK INDIANS
CHEROKEE NEUTRAL LANDS
QUAPAW
SENECE

Fort Dearborn (Chicago)

Fort Wayne

Illinois

Indiana

Ohio

St. Louis

Vincennes

Lexington

Missouri

Kentucky

Virginia

Fort Smith

Arkansas

Little Rock

Louisiana

Cairo

Nashville

Knoxville

Memphis

Tennessee

North Carolina

South Carolina

CHEROKEE

CHICKASAW

CHOCTAW

CREEK

Georgia

Charleston

Savannah

Alabama

Mississippi

Natchez

Florida

Mobile

Pensacola

New Orleans

SEMINOLES

Gulf of Mexico

1832
1835
1832
1832
1830

N

Resettlement of Native Americans 1829–40

— Border of United States 1840

   Indian tribes' home territories

1830 Date and route of removal

   Land granted to Indians west of the Mississippi River

🏰 Fort

   Range of the buffalo c. 1840

   Forest

0   200 km
0   200 miles

100°   90°   80°   40°   30°

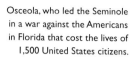

Osceola, who led the Seminole in a war against the Americans in Florida that cost the lives of 1,500 United States citizens.

year. The Treaty of Dancing Rabbit Creek encouraged thousands of Choctaw to travel 550 miles (890 kilometers) to their new home. Most journeyed in the bitter cold winter of 1831–32, and some 2,500 out of 13–14,000 died from exposure and cholera. They settled on the western banks of the Arkansas River without adequate supplies, and in the following spring, floods destroyed their newly planted crops. Around 2,000 Choctaw refused to go and remained in Mississippi, becoming sharecroppers and wage laborers. The descendants of this group remained on tribal owned land in and near Neshola County.

Under the terms of the 1826 Treaty of Washington, the Creek or Muskogee Nation possessed western lands north of the Choctaw, between the Arkansas and Canadian rivers. Initially, substantial numbers of Creeks left Georgia and Alabama, encouraging President Jackson to assume that the remainder would follow. Chief Opothle Yoholo negotiated the adoption of allotment terms, as in the Chickasaw and Choctaw treaties, but individual reserves would be clustered to continue old township relationships. However, land grabbers and squatters evicted Creeks from their allotments before the migration began. In response, young warriors retaliated in a "war," during which they burned a steamboat on the Chattahoochee. The incidents caused the U.S. Army to round up the Creeks and force them to move. Some 14,500 reached the west, their number having been cut by one of the coldest and snowiest winters on record, and by the sinking of a steamship while crossing a river.

The Seminole were more difficult to remove. This nation of migrant Lower Creeks included the remnants of tribes from earlier confrontations with Europeans, such as the Hichite, Apalachee, and Yamasee. Large numbers of African slaves had escaped to the isolation of Florida, and had inter-married, been enslaved, or built their own communities in alliance with the Seminole. Under an 1832 treaty, the nation was allowed to choose its western lands in Oklahoma., but the Seminole land scouts signed an agreement stating that they had found desirable land before discussing it with the nation. Resentful Seminole waged war, led by Osceola, (1836–42), which cost the United States 1,500 lives and $20 million. Some towns moved voluntarily, and by 1842, some 4,000 Seminole and their allies had been relocated to New Orleans, and along the Mississippi and Arkansas rivers as far as the Creek Nation. Approximately 500 remained in Florida, in Big Cyprus swamp and the Everglades. Another war occurred between 1855 and 1858, and 200 more Seminole were dispatched west, but the remainder stayed.

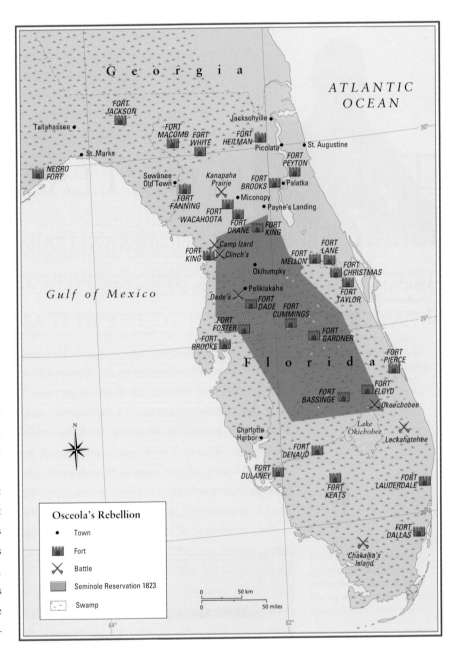

Resentful at being forcibly removed from their lands in Central Florida, the Seminole rebelled, leading to the Second Seminole War with the United States. The war lasted for six years, the resistance movement being led by Osceola.

THE BLACK HAWK WAR

WHEN PEACEFUL PROTEST OVER THE SEIZURE OF HIS LAND FAILED, SAUK CHIEF BLACK HAWK SOUGHT AN ALLIANCE WITH OTHER TRIBES AND DECLARED WAR ON THE AMERICANS.

An 1837 painting of the Sauk war chief Black Hawk by Charles Bird King. The chief suffered humiliation after his defeat.

The Black Hawk War was the last violent Indian episode in the old Northwest Territory. After the War of 1812, southwest Wisconsin and northeast Illinois were opened to white settlement. Black Hawk, a Sauk chief of the allied Sauk (Sac) and Mesquakie (Fox) became increasingly angry at the encroachment of white settlements. In the spring of 1829, he had returned to his village, Saukenuk, after a winter hunt, to find white squatters in some of the Sauk lodges.

Unrest grew, and the U.S. government decided to remove all Indians from Illinois. The General Land Office put up Black Hawk's property for sale. Nevertheless, the chief said that he would return to farm his land after the next winter hunt. In 1832, he returned with 300 warriors and their families, and General Edmund Gaines was given the task of moving the Saukenuk band across the Mississippi. However, Black Hawk vanished across the river, although he returned in June to capitulate. One condition was that he had to submit his authority to Keokuk, a rival chief favored by the Americans.

Black Hawk tried to construct an alliance against the Americans. In this, he was helped by White Cloud, a Winnebago medicine man, who preached conflict with the whites, and sought support for the Sauk Mesquakie from the Winnebago, Potawatomi, and Kickapoo. Black Hawk's force grew to 600 men, and he decided to return to Saukenuk to plant his fields. This peaceful protest was met by Brigadier General Henry Atkinson with over 2,000 men, and supported by Colonel Zachary Taylor, Lieutenant Jefferson Davis, Captain Abraham Lincoln, and Daniel Boone's son, Nat. Black Hawk sent a truce party forward, but some Indians were killed by the Americans. Fighting broke out, Black Hawk's advance guard of forty men repelling 275 militia, who fled 25 miles (40 kilometers) to their camp. This Battle of Stillman's Run encouraged other tribes to raid settlers and miners in southern Wisconsin. As Black Hawk's group moved further into Wisconsin, pursued by U.S. troops, he realized that survival meant crossing to the west bank of the Mississippi.

The Sauk refugees reached the Mississippi at its confluence with the Bad Axe River on August 1, 1832. While they were preparing rafts and canoes, the armed steamboat *Warrior* arrived, whereupon Black Hawk tried to negotiate with its troops under a flag of truce. The Americans opened fire, killing twenty-three warriors. Thwarted in his attempt to cross the river, Black Hawk decided to travel north to Ojibwa territory, but only fifty Indians would join him; the

Chief Keokuk, from an 1834 painting. Keokuk collaborated with the Americans, which brought him into conflict with Black Hawk.

remainder preferred to attempt another crossing. While they were doing this, Atkinson and a force of 1,300 federal troops caught up with them. The Indians tried to surrender, but to no avail. An eight-hour massacre followed, during which the women and children were clubbed to death. Thirty warriors were taken prisoner, while other Sauk and Mesquakie continued the crossing, being shelled by a six-pounder cannon aboard the *Warrior*. Those who made the west bank were attacked by Lakotas, being scalped or enslaved.

Black Hawk moved on to Winnebago territory, but he and White Cloud were interned at Prairie du Chien, near the confluence of the Wisconsin and Mississippi rivers, allegedly for a reward of $100 and twenty horses. Keokuk, the pro-American chief, and other Mesquakie leaders ceded all their Iowa land, the tribes being granted a reservation in Kansas. In 1869, all but Mokohoko's band moved to Oklahoma, but this band eventually joined the Oklahoma reservation in 1886.

Black Hawk was sent to President Jackson, who had him paraded through eastern cities like booty from a war. He died in 1838, but ghoulish thieves robbed his grave and stole his head. Keokuk died a wealthy man in Kansas in 1848, being succeeded by his son, Moses, who remained chief until he died in 1903.

Some Mesquakie wanted to return to Iowa, and in 1856, the Iowa State Legislature approved their plea to remain in the state. The group pooled their money from the sale of horses, annuity payments, and the sale of personal possessions. They purchased 4,000 acres (1,600 hectares) on the banks of the Iowa River, in Tama County, where they remain today, having bought more land since.

INDIAN TERRITORY

THE REMOVAL POLICIES OF THE U.S. GOVERNMENT CRAMMED MANY INDIAN NATIONS INTO A LARGE AREA WEST OF THE MISSISSIPPI, WHICH WAS KNOWN AS INDIAN TERRITORY.

Opposite: The Louisiana Purchase suggested that the Indian nations could be settled beyond the Mississippi.

By 1850, the Indian tribes were being pushed into the Unorganized Territory in the center of the country.

Indian Territory never had a territorial government nor a federally appointed territorial governor. Instead, the Indian nations inhabiting the regions had their own individual governments. Thus, Indian Territory was the Indian inhabited area of the United States, which was not a part of any state or organized territory. Indian Territory was the result of U.S. Indian removal policies. After the 1803 Louisiana Purchase, the notion occurred that the various Indian nations of the eastern United States could be settled west of the Mississippi. Government policies resulted in 1804 legislation that authorized removal treaties with the eastern tribes, preferably on a voluntary basis. Unfortunately for the Indians, white settlers were also moving west of the Mississippi—in 1819 Arkansas Territory was established, and its western border was fixed in 1824, while Missouri had been admitted to the Union in 1821. By 1825, the lands west of Arkansas, Missouri, and Iowa, and east of Mexican sovereignty, became Indian Territory. At its fullest extent, before 1854, it reached the 100th meridian.

In 1830, Congress passed the Indian Removal Act, and in 1834, the Secretary of War established the Bureau of Indian Affairs to implement U.S. policy toward Indians. In March 1849, the Bureau became part of the Department of the Interior, passing Indians from military to civilian control.

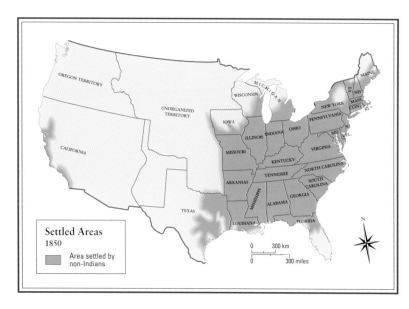

Settled Areas
1850
Area settled by non-Indians

0   300 km
0   300 miles

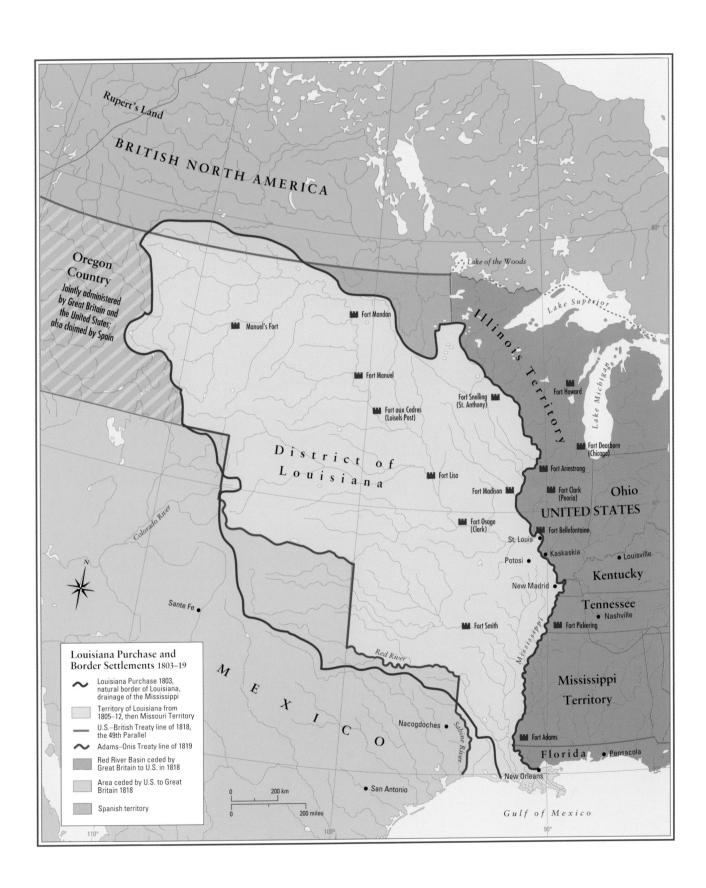

Rupert's Land

BRITISH NORTH AMERICA

Oregon
Country
Jointly administered
by Great Britain and
the United States;
also claimed by Spain

Lake of the Woods

Lake Superior

Illinois Territory

Lake Michigan

🏰 Fort Mandan
🏰 Manuel's Fort

🏰 Fort Manuel

🏰 Fort aux Cedres
(Loisels Post)

🏰 Fort Snelling
(St. Anthony)

🏰 Fort Howard

🏰 Fort Dearborn
(Chicago)

🏰 Fort Lisa

🏰 Fort Armstrong

D i s t r i c t   o f
L o u i s i a n a

🏰 Fort Madison

🏰 Fort Clark
(Peoria)

Ohio

UNITED STATES

🏰 Fort Osage
(Clark)

🏰 Fort Bellefontaine

St. Louis ●
● Kaskaskia

● Louisville

Colorado River

Potosi ●

New Madrid ●

Kentucky

Tennessee
● Nashville

Santa Fe ●

🏰 Fort Smith

🏰 Fort Pickering

Mississippi

Red River

M E X I C O

Mississippi
Territory

**Louisiana Purchase and
Border Settlements** 1803–19

〰 Louisiana Purchase 1803,
natural border of Louisiana,
drainage of the Mississippi

Territory of Louisiana from
1805–12, then Missouri Territory

— U.S.–British Treaty line of 1818,
the 49th Parallel

〰 Adams–Onis Treaty line of 1819

Red River Basin ceded by
Great Britain to U.S. in 1818

Area ceded by U.S. to Great
Britain 1818

Spanish territory

Nacogdoches ●

Sabine River

🏰 Fort Adams

Florida ● Pensacola

0   200 km
0   200 miles

● San Antonio

New Orleans ●

Gulf of Mexico

110°   100°   90°

During the fifteen years after 1830, nearly 100,000 eastern Indians were resettled in a chain of Indian nations and reservations. President Andrew Jackson wanted to go further, however, and argued for a Western Territory Bill, which would have proclaimed Indian Territory as being bordered in the north by the Platte and Missouri rivers, in the south by the Red River, in the east by the states of Arkansas and Missouri, and in the west by the Mexican border. In today's terms, the region included all of Kansas, most of Oklahoma, southern Nebraska, and eastern Colorado. The scheme failed. Into the territory were poured the eastern Great Plains Pawnee, Missouri, Iowa, Omaha, and Oto. These were located near the old northeast tribes, such as the Potawatomi, Miami, Ottowa, Kickapoo, Shawnee, and Sauk and Fox. To their south were the Five Civilized Tribes—the Cherokee, Choctaw, Chickasaw, Creek, and Seminole. Roaming nearby were the western Plains tribes, such as the Comanche, Arapaho, Cheyenne, and Lakota. Conflict arose between the tribes as the newcomers attempted to hunt on the Plains Indians' hunting grounds.

Moreover, Indian Territory soon began to be crossed by white settlers traveling along the Santa Fé, Oregon, and Mormon trails, especially during the period of the California Gold Rush, which began in 1848. Pressure from railroad interests mounted too, as they sought transcontinental routes. Soon, the many small tribes in the north of the territory, being poor and disorganized, were persuaded by federal agents to cede their rights to the land. In 1854, the northern sections of Indian Territory were organized

By 1860, the Unorganized Territory had shrunk considerably because of the steady encroachment of white settlers on Indian land.

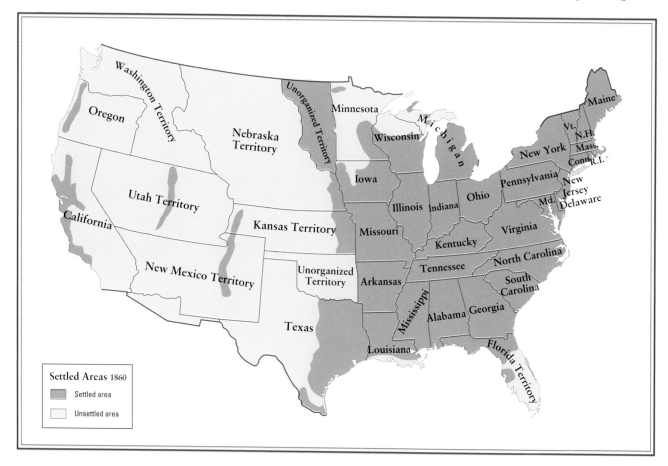

into Kansas and Nebraska Territories. By 1862, the Homestead Act had opened up Indian lands in the territories to white settlers, who were granted 160-acre (65-hectare) plots after living on them for five years. A similar bill, which would have led to the southern portion of Indian Territory being nibbled away, was defeated. So, by this time, the Indian Territory had been reduced to the approximate size of present-day Oklahoma.

Another wave of removals occurred as the U.S. government started clearing the remaining tribes from Texas, Kansas, and Nebraska into the territory. Further shrinkage of the territory occurred in 1866, after the Civil War. Owing to their involvement with the Confederacy, especially through the activities of Cherokee leader Stand Watie, the Five Civilized Tribes were forced to accept reconstruction, which gave the federal government the right to sequester Indian lands. Between 1866 and 1885, new reservations in Indian Territory were given to the Cheyenne, Arapaho, Comanche, Kiowa-Apache, Wichita, Caddo, Potawatomi, Shawnee, Kickapoo, Iowa, Sauk and Fox, Pawnee, Oto, Missouri, Ponca, Tonkawa, Kaw, Osage, Peoria, Wyandot, Eastern Shawnee, Modoc, and Ottawa. By 1885, all the lands available in Indian Territory—except a 2-million-acre (810,000-hectare) region in the center, the Unassigned Lands and the Cherokee Outlet—had been granted to Indian peoples.

During the 1830s and 1840s, Andrew Jackson's removal policy saw the relocation of many thousands of Indians from the East in a series of reservations to the west of Iowa, Missouri, and Arkansas. Before long, however, the old pressure to cede land to white settlers arose again. The establishment of Nebraska and Kansas Territories further west began to squeeze the Indians, who had nowhere else to go.

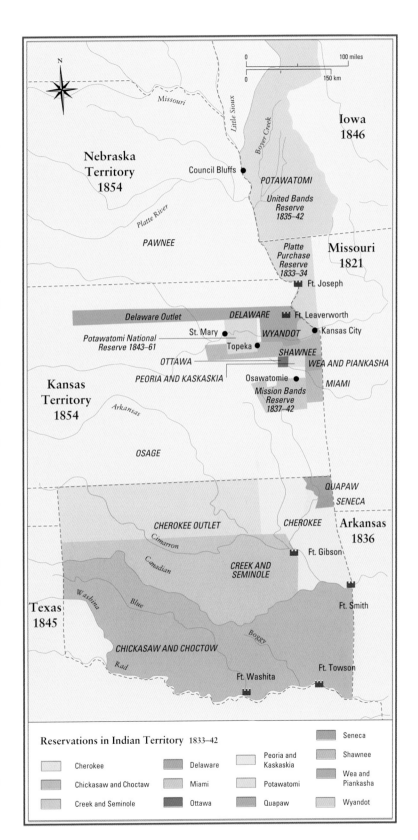

Reservations in Indian Territory 1833–42

- Cherokee
- Chickasaw and Choctaw
- Creek and Seminole
- Delaware
- Miami
- Ottawa
- Peoria and Kaskaskia
- Potawatomi
- Quapaw
- Seneca
- Shawnee
- Wea and Piankasha
- Wyandot

OVERLAND TRAILS AND THE INDIANS

A CONSTANT STREAM OF MIGRANTS, HEADING WEST TO FIND NEW LIVES, FOLLOWED ESTABLISHED TRAILS THROUGH INDIAN TERRITORY, SOMETIMES WITH DISASTROUS RESULTS.

Jim Bridger was a trapper, scout, and guide who traveled throughout the western United States between 1820 and 1840.

Many routes to the West had their starting points at Independence, Missouri, or Omaha, Nebraska. The oldest was the Santa Fé Trail, but more important was the Oregon Trail, with its various branches and cutoffs. The route followed the Platte River to Fort Laramie in present-day Goshen County, Wyoming. From there, it followed the North Platte and Sweetwater rivers to South Pass in the Wind River Range, and on to Fort Bridger, constructed by famed mountain man Jim Bridger. The trail ran through the Bear River valley and north to Fort Hall, in Idaho, then followed the Snake River to Salmon Falls. Fort Boise, a Hudson Bay Company post on the Snake was another stopping point. The route traversed the Grand Ronde River valley and the Blue Mountains, before reaching the Columbia River. A branch left the Oregon Trail at Fort Laramie to become the Bozeman Trail, which ran into Montana and the Yellowstone River country. Another branch left at Fort Hall to form the Mormon Trail into Utah, but the most important branch was the California Trail, from Fort Hall to Sacramento, which fueled the 1849 California Gold Rush.

The first significant wagon train, led by Elijah White, reached Oregon in 1842. Most of the trains stopped at Oregon City, but many others continued south to the bountiful Willamette Valley. The entire journey transported people some 2,020 miles (3,250 kilometers), and arrivals wrote home inspiring others to follow. In 1845, some 3,000 people arrived in Oregon, doubling its population. Migration was an instrument of U.S. government policy, providing an American presence in Oregon to counter any threat from the British or Russians. Oregon fever transferred eastern lifestyles to the Pacific Coast, despite the discomfort of travel and the fear of Indian raids.

Wagon trains encountered huge herds of buffalo west of the Platte River. Sometimes, the trains would wait for hours when herds blocked their way. The migrants hunted the animals for sport, but failed to use the buffalo like the Native Americans, who were astounded at the wasteful, rotting carcasses. One emigrant, Isaac Foster, wrote, *"The valley of the Platte for 200 miles* [320 kilometers]; *dotted with skeletons of buffaloes; such a waste of the creatures God had for man seems wicked, but every emigrant seems to wish to signalise himself by killing a buffalo."* Thus, the migrants contributed to the near extinction of the buffalo and damaged Native American food supplies.

Initially, the Oregon Trail passed through Cheyenne and Pawnee territory, then that of the Shoshone. Expected attacks were infrequent; Native Americans are known to have helped free stuck wagons, rescued drowning migrants, and also rounded up straying cattle. Most meetings with Indians led to the trade of clothes, tobacco, or rifles in exchange for horses or food. However, the Oregon

A hand-colored print depicting an Indian chief forbidding a party of settlers from passing through his land. In the early days of migration, such meetings were rare; in fact, the Indians were often of help to migrant trains experiencing difficulty.

A contemporary image of goldmining in California during the mid-nineteenth century. Gold fever saw thousands flock to the West Coast, where the Indians got in the way.

The Yuma controlled the Yuma crossing of the Colorado River, near the mouth of the Gila River, and could keep the Southern Overland Trail to California closed. The U.S. Army built a fort there in 1850, which was attacked by the Yuma and subsequently abandoned at the end of 1851. In early 1852, the fort was reoccupied and, later that year, used as a base for raids against the Yuma. On one of these, a detachment of twenty-five soldiers entered Baja California, destroying villages and crops, and capturing 150 people.

Ishi, the last surviving member of the Yahi tribe. He walked out of the hills in 1911, but no one could speak his language. He died in 1916.

Ultimately, the Indian population in California was reduced by 90 percent. Fortunately, some people recognized the imminent demise of the Indians, and anthropologists began recording their traditions, helped by survivors, such as the Chumash Fernandi Librado, who had reached the age of 111 years at his death in 1916.

By the late nineteenth century, Indian slave labor was no longer needed, but Indians often worked as domestic servants and fruit growers. The Miwok survived in the lumber, fishing, mining, ranching, and farming industries. The saddest tale is that of Ishi, the last surviving Yahi, who walked out of the hills near Oroville, California, in 1911 to discover that there was no one alive who could speak his language.

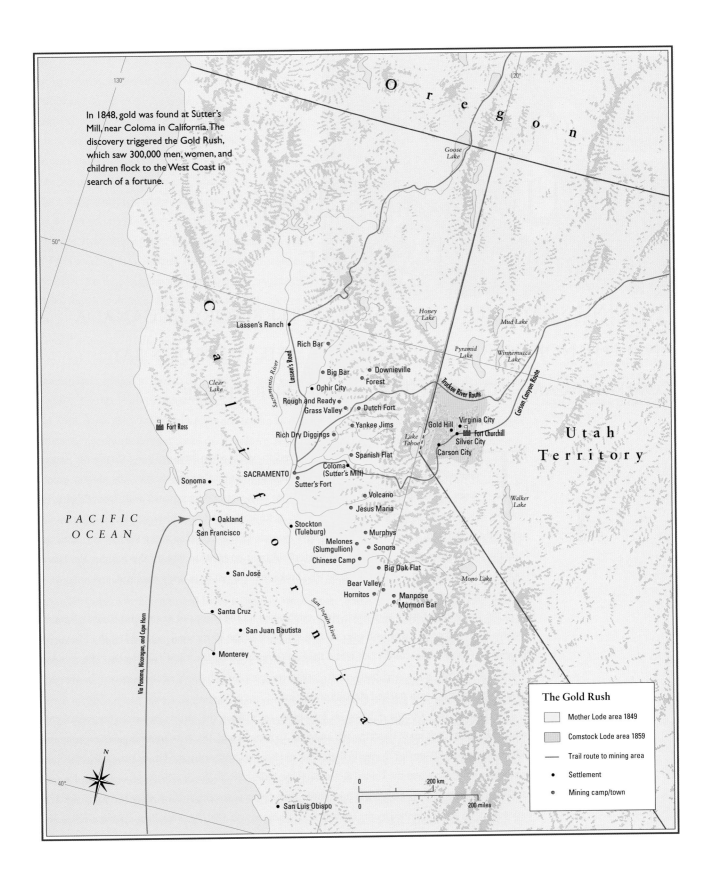

In 1848, gold was found at Sutter's Mill, near Coloma in California. The discovery triggered the Gold Rush, which saw 300,000 men, women, and children flock to the West Coast in search of a fortune.

The Gold Rush

- Mother Lode area 1849
- Comstock Lode area 1859
- Trail route to mining area
- Settlement
- Mining camp/town

THE FUR TRADE

ALTHOUGH THERE WERE MANY WHITE TRAPPERS WHO BENEFITED FROM THE FUR TRADE, IT BROUGHT MUCH WEALTH AND ADVANCEMENT TO NATIVE AMERICAN COMMUNITIES.

Opposite: In the early nineteenth century, Canadian fur trappers and traders carried out many explorations of the Oregon Country and even penetrated further south. Leading figures were Donald Mackenzie (North West Company), Archibald McDonald (Hudson's Bay Company), and Peter Skene Ogden (Hudson's Bay).

The American Fur Company was chartered by Jacob Astor in 1808 to compete with the Hudson's Bay Company and the Canadian North West Company. The venture managed to crush or absorb its rivals in the Great Lakes region, the Missouri River valley, the Rocky Mountains, and Oregon.

Astor sent two expeditions to the Columbia River, one by sea and the other overland. The former established Fort Astoria at the mouth of the Columbia River in April 1811. Meanwhile, the overland party had left St. Louis in March of that year, reaching Astoria in early 1812. When Astoria was seized by the British during the War of 1812, Astor's major competitors were able to entrench themselves in the Pacific Northwest fur trade.

Hundreds of trappers and a thousand or so Indians would turn up at a rendezvous to meet the St. Louis caravan, exchanging furs for goods and alcohol. Business concluded, the trappers and Indians would entertain themselves with horse races, wrestling, shooting matches, and debauchery. This could lead to violent repercussions.

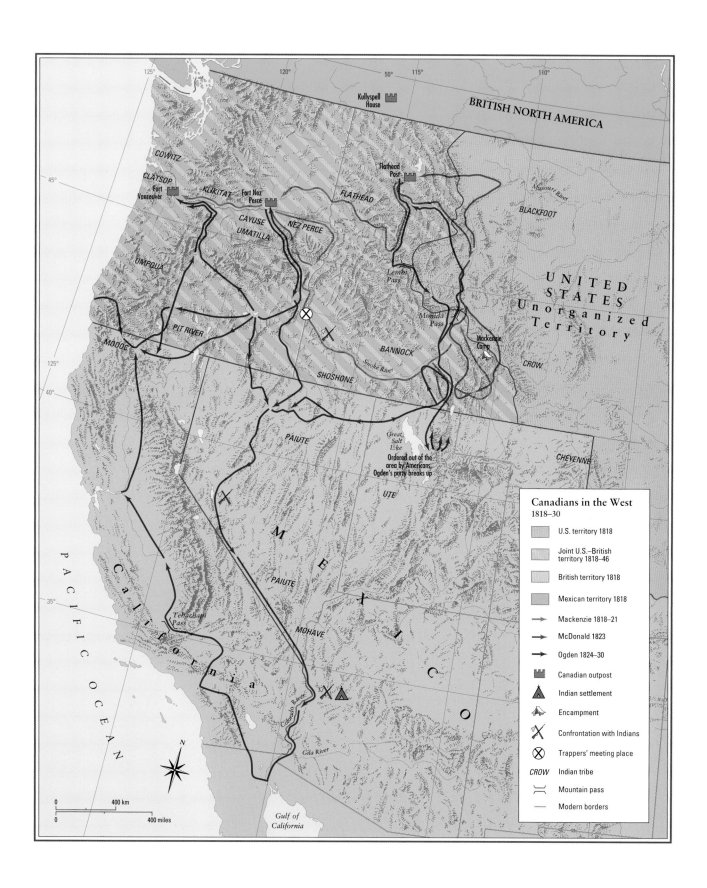

Kullyspell
House

BRITISH NORTH AMERICA

COWITZ

CLATSOP
Fort
Vancouver

KLIKITAT

Fort Nez
Perce

CAYUSE

UMATILLA

NEZ PERCE

FLATHEAD

Flathead
Post

Missouri River

BLACKFOOT

UMPQUA

Lembi
Pass

UNITED
STATES
Unorganized
Territory

PIT RIVER

Monida
Pass

Mackenzie
Camp

MODOC

BANNOCK

Snake River

CROW

SHOSHONE

PAIUTE

Great
Salt
Lake

CHEYENNE

Ordered out of the
area by Americans,
Ogden's party breaks up

M

E

X

UTE

I

PACIFIC OCEAN

C

a

l

i

f

o

r

n

i

a

PAIUTE

C

O

Tehachapi
Pass

MOHAVE

Colorado River

Gila River

N

0   400 km

0   400 miles

Gulf of
California

Canadians in the West
1818–30

- U.S. territory 1818
- Joint U.S.–British territory 1818–46
- British territory 1818
- Mexican territory 1818
- → Mackenzie 1818–21
- → McDonald 1823
- → Ogden 1824–30
- Canadian outpost
- Indian settlement
- Encampment
- Confrontation with Indians
- ⊗ Trappers' meeting place
- *CROW* Indian tribe
- Mountain pass
- Modern borders

A drawing of Jedidiah Smith created by a friend from memory around four years after the mountain man's death. Smith, who traveled more extensively in unknown territory than any other mountain man, blazed many of the trails that helped settlers cross the Rocky Mountains. This tough explorer once survived a run-in with a grizzly bear that left him with a lacerated side, broken ribs, and severe head wounds. He became involved in the Rocky Mountain Fur Company later in life and, in May 1831, was leading a party of traders along the Santa Fé trail when he left them to scout for water. He was never seen again, and it is thought that he was killed by a group of Comanches.

Opposite: This map shows the most significant expeditions carried out by Jedidiah Smith. He once wrote, "*I wanted to be the first to view a country on which the eyes of a white man had never gazed and to follow the course of rivers that run through a new land.*"

The North West and Hudson's Bay companies engaged in a trade war, the latter being victorious in 1821, when the two companies merged. That year, the American Fur Company became prominent again by entering an alliance with Chouteau business interests in St. Louis, thereby gaining a trade monopoly in the Missouri River region and eventually the Rockies.

Before Astor's company penetrated the Northwest in 1827, however, other traders had been busy. In 1824, Peter Skene Ogden, with seventy-five trappers, moved into the Snake River country. This expedition, on behalf of the Hudson's Bay Company, opened up the area to that company for twelve years. Another entrepreneur was William Henry Ashley, from St. Louis. Although his initial trapping expedition was turned back in the Dakotas by hostile Arikara, he went on to target the central Rockies. The region was rich in beaver, and Ashley worked out a novel method of exploiting the area. Normally, Indians and trappers would take their pelts to fortified trading posts, but these angered the Indians, being seen as symbols of white occupation. Also, there were no navigable rivers in the region for transporting furs and merchandise, so Ashley developed the rendezvous system. Trappers would live permanently in the mountains, and in early summer, they would meet at an annual rendevous at a site where game, water, and grazing were plentiful. The mountain men, known for their toughness and survival skills, often married Indian women.

Competition between the Rocky Mountain Fur Company, run by Jim Bridger and Milton Sublette, and small groups from Arkansas and Texas could be accommodated. In 1832, however, the American Fur Company moved into the area. Astor had acquired the Columbia Fur Company in 1827, and in 1831 had established Fort Mackenzie on the Marias River. That year, a steamer had reached Fort Union, built by the company in 1828 at the confluence of the Upper Missouri and Yellowstone rivers, on the edge of Blackfeet territory.

In 1834, the American Fur Company split after Astor's withdrawal. Then the Hudson's Bay Company penetrated the Snake River and gradually monopolized trade. As beaver hats became unfashionable and silk took over, however, beaver pelts began to fetch lower prices. Moreover, many rivers had been trapped out. The mountain men declined in numbers and were forced to seek other occupations, such as guiding expeditions and wagon trains.

The fur trade was extremely important for Native Americans, since it allowed them to join the consumer revolution of the eighteenth century. The introduction of European goods changed the manner in which Native Americans achieved subsistence, while profits bought luxury goods beyond the requirements of subsistence. Hudson's Bay Company records show such luxuries as lace, baize, duffel, flannel, gartering, beads, combs, looking glasses, rings, shirts, and vermillion.

Native Americans along the Northwestern Pacific Coast certainly benefited from the fur trade, although wealth did not reach all tribes. The Chinook around Fort Astoria became middlemen between coastal trade and the interior. Native Americans were canny, tough-minded negotiators, who manipulated competition between white traders.

Newly acquired wealth encouraged art to flourish, along with ceremonial life. Metal

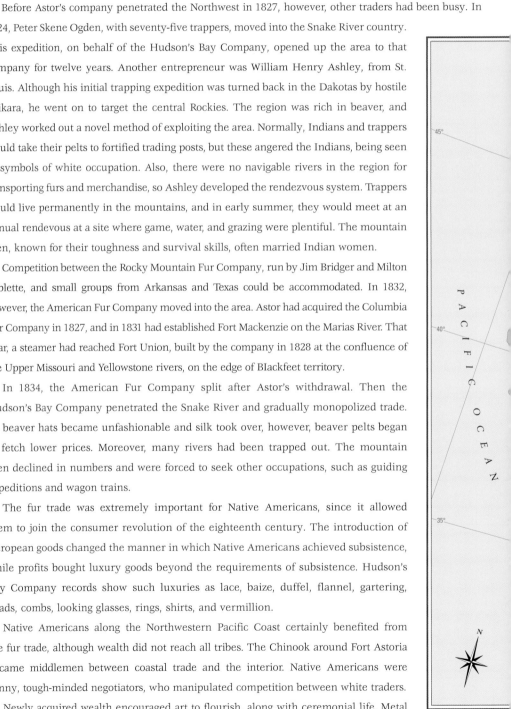

tools facilitated woodcarving, and Haida totem poles increased in number and innovative design. Haida carvers made curios, which they sold to seamen as a precursor to a tourist trade. The Tlingits grew potatoes and sold them to Russian settlers, as well as exporting them, thus developing an alternative income, like the Haida, to compensate for the eventual decline in the fur trade. Thus, Native Americans entered the capitalist system, seeing and responding to economic change.

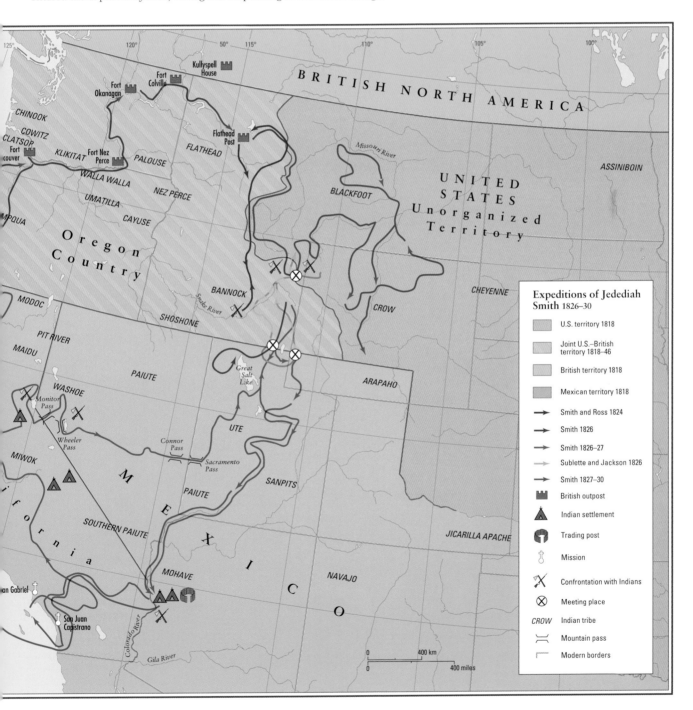

THE APACHE WARS

THE MEXICAN CESSION OF SOUTHWESTERN LANDS TO THE UNITED STATES LED TO CONFLICT WITH THE APACHE, WHICH SPREAD ON BOTH SIDES OF THE BORDER.

General George Crook, named by the Apache Nantan Lupan (Gray Wolf), employed Apache scouts to hunt down their own tribe. In the field, he favored mule trains for carrying supplies rather than wagons, allowing his troops to traverse rough country with relative ease.

The Apache bands, who had arrived in the Southwest about AD 850, developed a reputation as nomadic raiders, targeting Spaniards, Mexicans, Pueblo Indians, and, later, Americans. After checking Spanish-Mexican advances northward, they confronted American troops when the United States acquired their homelands from Mexico in 1848. After this date, while attempting to assess U.S. power, the Apache attacked Mexicans south of the border and, occasionally, travelers on the Santa Fé Trail and southern Butterfield Stage route.

In 1854, the Gadsden Treaty led to the cession of Arizona and New Mexico from Mexico to the United States, which led to further U.S. encroachment into the Southwest. An incident in 1861 inflamed relations between the Apache and the United States. Cochise of the Chiricahua Apache had been accused (incorrectly) of stealing a rancher's children and cattle. Unaware of this, he agreed to meet Lieutenant Bascom of Fort Buchanan, near present-day Sonoita, Arizona. Cochise and members of his family were arrested, but he escaped and began raiding along the Butterfield route, being joined by White Mountain Apache and Mimbrenos, led by Mangas Coloradas, Cochise's father-in-law. In retaliation, Bascom seized more hostages, hanging all the males, among them Cochise's brother. In revenge, the Apache killed 150 Americans and Mexicans over the following two months; thirty-five years of unrest followed.

To secure peace, General Joseph West, commander of the Department of New Mexico's southern region, invited Mangas Coloradas to negotiations at Pinos Altos in January 1863. When he arrived, he was imprisoned, then shot dead while allegedly escaping. Elsewhere, General James Carleton sent Kit Carson against Mescalero Apaches who were raiding the Butterfield Stage route near El Paso,

Texas. Carson's forces wore down the Apache and forced them onto a reservation at Bosque Redondo, in southeastern New Mexico.

Ten years later, the Apache erupted again. At Camp Grant, north of Tucson, Eskiminzin's Aravaipa (Western) Apache had made camp and surrendered their weapons. Fearful Tucson citizens organized a vigilante force that attacked the Aravaipa on April 30, 1871; 90–150 innocents, mainly women and children, were slaughtered. President Grant was so angered that he sent a peace commission to Arizona, and a reservation system was established for the Apache, with four agencies in Arizona and one in New Mexico. The Chiricahua came in under Cochise, remaining peacefully at Apache Pass until his death in 1874.

Other Apaches continued raiding, however, while drawing reservation agency rations. To end their depredations, the U.S. Army pursued the Tonto Basin Campaign in central Arizona, near the Mogollon Rim. General George Crook engaged the Apaches at Salt River Canyon (December 28, 1872), and their friends, the Yavapais, at the Battle of Skull Cave and Turret Peak in March 1873. Some 6,000 exhausted Apaches and Yavapais surrendered and entered the reservations. In 1875, however, all Apaches west of the Rio Grande were ordered to the San Carlos Reservation in Arizona.

Two warriors resisted reservation life. Victorio led Mimbreno Apaches in a war that lasted from 1877 to 1880; Geronimo led Chiricahuas and others in a final stand between 1881 and 1886. From San Carlos, Victorio led 300 men into the mountains, and in September 1879, he killed eight buffalo soldiers (African-Americans in the U.S. Army). Joined by Mimbrenos, his group ranged from Mexico to Texas, through New Mexico, and back to Arizona. They were hunted by American and Mexican troops on their respective sides of the border. Eventually, Victorio was cornered by Mexican forces in the fall of 1880 at the Battle of Tres Castillos, in northeastern Chihuahua, where he and half his warriors died. Most of the survivors were captured.

Geronimo had wanted to remain at Apache Pass, but was interned at San Carlos. After an Apache mystic, Nakaidoklini, was killed at Cibecue Creek in August 1881, Geronimo and another Apache chief, Chato, together with seventy-four men, quit the reservation, attacked its police chief, and persuaded Mimbrenos to join them. Elsewhere, on July 17, 1882, White Mountain Apaches fought the U.S. Army at the Battle of the Big Dry Wash, on the Mogollon Rim. In May 1883, General Crook led troops into the Sierra Madre and wore down Apache resistance. Warriors trickled back onto the reservation, among them Geronimo, but he broke loose again, was returned, and then escaped with twenty-four Apaches and Nachise, Cochise's son. Some 5,000 U.S. troops were mobilized, and finally Geronimo was captured at Skeleton Canyon, in the Peloncillo Mountains, on September 4, 1886. The Apache were relocated to San Carlos, but the Chiricahua were offered a home with the Comanche and Kiowa in Indian Territory. Geronimo died from pneumonia, a prisoner-of-war at Fort Sill, Oklahoma, in 1909.

Geronimo, probably the most famous of the Apache leaders. He broke out from the reservation with Chiricahua and Mibreno warriors in 1881, and over the next five years led a bloody resistance to the Army's attempts to return them.

NORTHWESTERN WARS

AT FIRST PEACEFUL TOWARD SETTLERS IN THE NORTHWEST, LOCAL TRIBES WENT TO WAR WHEN DECEIVED OVER LAND DEALS AND ATTACKED BY CIVILIAN MILITIA.

Isaac Stevens, the first governor of Washington Territory, promised several tribes that they could stay put for two years if they ceded most of their land, but he had lied. During the Civil War, he served as a Major General in the Union Army and was killed at the Battle of Chantilly in 1862.

Native Americans in the Northwest had been peaceful ever since white settlers had entered the Columbia Basin, although the presence of the latter had caused the depletion of salmon stocks, a staple Indian food. In 1853, Lieutenant George McClellan arrived at Fort Vancouver to explore the Cascades for a pass for the Northern Pacific Railroad. To facilitate the railroad's construction, and in the hope of opening up the region for further white settlement, Governor Isaac Stevens of Washington Territory held a conference with local Indians in the Walla Walla Valley, between May and June 1855. Stevens wanted the Nez Perce, Cayuse, Umatilla, Walla Walla, and Yakama to hand over most of their lands in exchange for reservations, homes, schools, horses, cattle, and annuities. Most tribal leaders signed because they were promised that they could stay put for two years. The Yakama were asked to give up 29,000 square miles (75,000 square kilometers) in return for 1.2 million acres (490,000 hectares). Stevens had lied, however, and settlers were allowed to enter the region before the two years were up.

As settlers moved in and miners headed to the Colville mines, Kamiakin of the Yakama readied for war, persuading the Puget Sound tribes to act likewise. Several prospectors were killed, as was A.J. Bolon, a respected Indian agent; he had been investigating the murders, but the Indians thought that he was about to call in the Army. Other tribes also rose in rebellion, among them the Takelma and Tututni (Rogue Indians), and the Coeur d'Alene (Schitsu' Umish). On October 6, 1855, a U.S. Army detachment under Major Granville Haller, from Fort Dalles, was on patrol in the Cascades, but was beaten back by 500 Yakama, suffering twenty-two dead and wounded. A November expedition also achieved nothing, but a group of volunteer militia from Oregon City, under Colonel James Kelly, killed the chief of the Walla Walla, thereby bringing them, the Umatilla, and Cayuse into the war. Raid and counterraid ensued, and innocent settlers and peaceful Indians died, while the Army failed to protect anyone. By the summer of 1856, the Indians had scattered, but in July, 300 of them were defeated in the Grande Ronde Valley, forty warriors being killed and a village burned, at a cost of seven white casualties. The responsibility for policing the region was given to Colonel George Wright of the regular U.S. Army, and the volunteers pulled out. Although the Indians honored the treaties, the region was dominated by two new forts, Simcoe and Walla Walla.

Elsewhere, war erupted on the Rogue River, in southern Oregon. Captain Andrew Jackson Smith of Fort Lane took in some peaceful Indians, but before they were joined by their women and children, some volunteer militia attacked their camp, killing twenty-three. In revenge, the Indians slaughtered twenty-seven innocent settlers. In the spring of 1856, Smith was on patrol with eighty soldiers when he was assailed by Rogues. He held out until rescued by reinforcements under Captain Augur. The combined U.S. force suffered thirty-one casualties. A month later, the Rogues surrendered and were herded onto the coastal Siletz Reservation, but their leader, Old John, was imprisoned at Fort Alcatraz.

The Yakamas were not prepared to be full reservation Indians like the Rogues, and some militants killed settlers and Colville miners, while Kamiakin sought alliances with the Palouse, Coeur d'Alene, and Spokane against the whites. In 1858, the Army decided to intervene, and Lieutenant Colonel Edward J. Steptoe, from Fort Walla Walla, moved against the hostile Indians in what became known as the Coeur d'Alene or Spokane War. Steptoe was leading a force of 164 men and Nez Perce scouts, equipped with two howitzers, when they encountered 1,200 mounted Indians of the alliance. He was formally warned off and he retreated, but the Indians fell upon his rearguard. Steptoe defended Steptoe Butte throughout May 17, 1858, but retreated during darkness. Later, Colonel Wright confronted the Indians at the Battle of Four Lakes (September 1, 1858). His howitzers drove the Indians from their cover among the trees, then his troops' new rifled muskets, which had increased range, tore into them. Finally, the Indians were charged by dragoons and they fled, leaving behind sixty dead, while more were wounded; the Americans were unscathed.

On September 5, 1858, Wright again encountered war parties on the Spokane Plain. His 680 men faced around 1,000 Indians from several tribes, using artillery, the new rifles, and dragoon charges to scatter them. Wright demanded unconditional surrender from the beaten tribes, and the ringleaders were hanged. In addition, 900 Palouse ponies were shot to immobilize the tribe; Indian cattle and grain were also destroyed. Subsequently, forts were built at Boise and Colville to protect settlers and subdue the tribes.

This painting by John Mix Stanley, dating from the 1870s, shows an Indian war band traveling through a pass in the Rocky Mountains.

CONQUEST, 1865–1900

"AT SAN CARLOS ARE THE APACHES, WHO ARE REGARDED AS THE MOST VICIOUS OF THE INDIANS WITH WHO WE HAVE TO DEAL ... I HAVE WITHIN THE LAST TWELVE MONTHS TAKEN FROM THAT RESERVATION ABOUT TWO HUNDRED [CHILDREN]. THEY ARE TODAY WELL FED AND PROPERLY CLOTHED, ARE HAPPY AND CONTENTED, AND MAKING GOOD PROGRESS. DID I DO RIGHT?"

THOMAS JEFFERSON MORGAN,
COMMISSIONER OF INDIAN AFFAIRS, 1889.

The 1860s and 1870s saw an increase in conflict between white Americans and nomadic Native Americans. Whether against the Comanche and Apache of the Southwest, or the Sioux in the North, the U.S. Army faced a difficult task in confronting fast moving guerrilla horsemen. The 1851 Fort Laramie treaty and the 1867 Medicine Lodge Creek Treaty attempted to fix boundaries and reservations, but a major problem was convincing Native Americans to honor treaty provisions and remain on reservations while settlers and miners made incursions into Indian lands. Events like the 1864 Sand Creek Massacre served to harden Indian resolve to resist white hypocrisy, especially after the Cheyenne and Arapaho were forced to concede lands agreed by the Fort Laramie treaty in 1861. The Red Cloud War and the 1874 campaign against the Southern Cheyenne, Kiowa, and Comanche exacerbated tensions. The failure of the U.S. government to prevent miners from entering the Black Hills, sacred to the Sioux, brought matters to a head in 1876, when Custer's command was annihilated in the valley of the Little Bighorn. The subsequent Great Sioux War saw the Sioux and Cheyenne bands being systematically defeated and forced back onto the reservations. In the South, the

Indian Wars
1860–90

Land seccessions:

Ceded before 1850

Ceded before 1850–70

Ceded before 1871–90

Never formerly ceded

NAVAJO Indian tribe

✕ Indian battles with dates (west of Mississippi)

Railroads in the West
1869–93

〜 Railroads

① Central Pacific Railroads-Union Pacific Railroads 1869

② Northern Pacific Railroads 1883

③ Atchison, Topeka and Santa Fe Railroads 1883

④ Southern Pacific Railroads 1883

⑤ Great Northern Railroads 1893

0   200 km

0   200 miles

Apache were defeated by 1886. Thus, the American military conquest of the West was complete and, according to Hollywood, that goal had been achieved exclusively by white cavalrymen.

In reality, the defeat of the Native Americans had been brought about through internecine strife between tribes, the substantial employment of African-American (buffalo) soldiers by the U.S. Army, and the slaughter of the buffalo, a major life resource of the Plains Indians. However, the last was partially caused by the Indians themselves, who never matched the patronising and mythological

During the second half of the nineteenth century, the West was engulfed in several Indian Wars as Native Americans fought to keep their way of life. The flood of settlers, aided by the railroads, however, would change their lives forever.

A corporal of the 9th Cavalry, one of the all-African-American regiments raised by Congress after the American Civil War and known to the Indians as "buffalo soldiers." These regiments, both cavalry and infantry, played a major part in subduing Native American resistance during the late nineteenth century.

image of the "ecological Indian" applied to them by European observers.

The U.S. Army's activities on the Great Plains became enmeshed in inter-tribal conflicts. In Montana, Teton Sioux contested buffalo hunting grounds with Crow, Blackfeet, Gros Ventre, and Assiniboine groups. These tribes considered the Teton to be more dangerous than the United States, and Crow warriors began scouting for the Army against the Sioux in the hope that their last hunting grounds would be preserved. In 1868, the Crow ceded most of their land and were given a reservation on the remainder. The Gros Ventre comprised one third of the Blackfeet confederacy, and were pressured by Teton, Yankton, Yanktonais, and Santee Sioux flooding into Montana to hunt buffalo. They needed U.S. and Crow allies to survive.

This state of tribal movement coincided with U.S. military actions in the area. The Army realized the merits of Native American scouts, who served in nearly every area of western conflict. Scouts were given a uniform and repeating rifle, but they supplied their own mounts. These Indian soldiers would find and reconnoiter enemy trails, then ascertain the enemy's tribal name and numbers. The Army needed the Indians to keep pace with their mobile enemies, to aid concealment, and to help execute surprise attacks. In many ways, the Army was forced to adopt its scouts' methods, tactics, and use of terrain. Sometimes, when patrols were attacked, rescue occurred at the hands of Indian scouts.

Native Americans joined or helped the Army for many reasons. Pamnee, Arikara, and Hidatsa bands needed Army assistance against the Sioux during the 1860s and 1870s. Osage scouts aided the Army against the Cheyenne, who competed with them for buffalo on the Arkansas. Elsewhere, Pavmee, Caddo, and Wichita sought help against tribes like the Comanche, who persistently raided for horses. Scouting had other advantages. Food and ammunition were of personal benefit to the Indian soldier, but families left on reservations were fed, too. Also, any enemy horses and property captured could be retained. The monthly pay of $13 was an absolute necessity for some Indian families.

Scouts were essential in locating Comanche and Kiowa bands who attacked buffalo hunters. During the 1870s, winter campaigns destroyed their camps and provisions, driving the hungry Indians back to their reservations. By that time, the Arapaho had been reduced to fewer than 1,000 souls, and in this weakened state were dependent upon reservation supplies. When war broke out over white incursions into the Black Hills, the Northern Arapaho abandoned their Cheyenne and Sioux allies, and some became Army scouts in 1876 and 1877. As a reward, they negotiated a permanent settlement on the large Shoshone reservation in Wyoming—an irony, since the tribes were traditional enemies. After the Little Bighorn battle, the Northern Cheyenne were hit hard by Army attacks on their winter camps. One group surrendered at Fort Keogh in Montana, some enlisting as scouts.

Particularly effective were the Seminole Scouts. Of mixed Indian and African-American slave parentage, these thirty men were employed by the Army in Florida, then moved west in 1870, when the Army needed more scouts in that region. They operated for nine years, fought in twelve major engagements, and finally fled to Mexico to escape racial discrimination and in anger against the government's refusal to grant them land as promised.

African-American troops also played a vital part in conquering the West. Two regiments of African-

American cavalry were formed, the 9th and 10th, as were two infantry regiments, the 24th and 25th. The 9th Cavalry first saw service in Texas in June 1867. It was ordered to protect stage and mail routes, build and maintain forts, and police the area from the Staked Plains to Brownsville. Its enemies were Mexican revolutionaries, and Comanche, Cheyenne, Kiowa, and Apache raiders. By 1876, the 9th had been transferred to New Mexico, where it fought the Apache led by Nana, Victorio, and Geronimo. In 1881, the regiment moved to various forts in Kansas and Indian Territory, and was charged with evicting illegal white settlers from Indian lands. During 1885, the regiment operated from Forts Robinson and Niobrara in Nebraska, and Fort Duchesne, Utah. The 9th's last action on the frontier was the 1891 Ghost Dance Campaign, although it was not involved in the massacre at Wounded Knee.

The 10th Cavalry, formed at Fort Leavenworth in 1866, moved to Fort Riley, Kansas, and for the next eight years was stationed at various forts throughout Kansas and Indian Territory. The regiment guarded work parties on the Kansas and Pacific Railroad, strung telegraph lines, and built much of Fort

The African-American regiments acquitted themselves well in a number of battles during the Indian Wars.

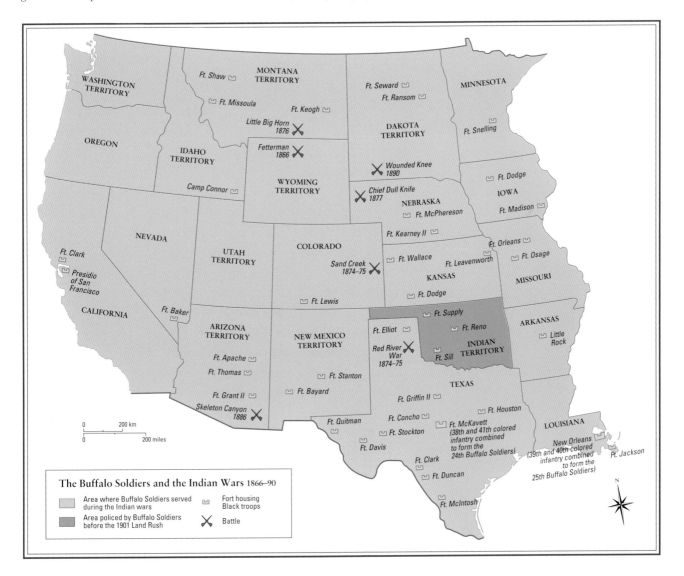

The Buffalo Soldiers and the Indian Wars 1866–90

Area where Buffalo Soldiers served during the Indian wars

Area policed by Buffalo Soldiers before the 1901 Land Rush

Fort housing Black troops

Battle

x2574-07

Oglala warriors, from the Pine Ridge Indian Reservation in South Dakota, stage the planning of a raid for photographer Edward S. Curtis. The picture appeared in the third volume of Curtis's work, *The North American Indian* (1908).

Sill. During the winter of 1867/68, the 10th joined General Sherman's campaign against the Comanche, Cheyenne, and Arapaho, and was instrumental in driving the Cheyenne toward Custer, whose 7th Cavalry gained a decisive victory over them on the Washita, near Fort Cobb. In 1875, the 10th moved to Fort Concho in west Texas, where it scouted nearly 35,000 square miles (90,000 square kilometers) of unmapped terrain, built 300 miles (500 kilometers) of road, and strung 200 miles (300 kilometers) of telegraph line. During 1879–80, the 10th campaigned against Victorio and his Chiricahua Apache band. They had broken out of their New Mexico reservation and raided settlements on their way to Mexico. The 10th engaged the Apaches at Tinaja de las Palmas, a waterhole south of Sierra Blanca, and at Rattlesnake Springs, north of Van Horn. Victorio was prevented from returning to New Mexico and was forced back into Mexico, where he and many of his men were killed by Mexican soldiers on October 14, 1880, at the Battle of Tres Castillos. In 1885, the regiment was transferred to Arizona, where it became involved in campaigns against the Apaches under Geronimo.

The 24th Infantry Regiment occupied posts in the Southwest, fought Indians, built roads, guarded stage stations, and strung telegraph lines. In addition, it guarded waterholes, escorted supply wagons, survey parties and mail coaches, and scouted the region. The 25th had been organized in Louisiana in 1868, but after 1870, its units were scattered among many posts in west Texas. Those at Fort Davis protected nearby stage stations, and built and operated a lumber camp and saw mill. Off-post activities included constructing new roads through Wild Rose Pass and Musquiz Canyon, guarding government lumber trains, and protecting U.S. citizens at Presidio del Norte from Mexican bandits. In 1880, the regiment was transferred to the Dakotas, Minnesota, and Montana; some units took part in the Pine Ridge Campaign of 1890–91.

The conquest of the West was not achieved purely by the Army and Indian auxiliaries, but mainly by the destruction of the Indians' primary food source, the buffalo, which historians claim began in 1867, when the Union Pacific Railroad was built. The vast numbers of buffalo (estimated at approximately 13,000,000) provided the Plains Indians with food, and skins for tepees, robes, and other clothing. Glue could be made from boiled horns, bones, and hooves, and paunches could be formed into buckets, while the guts could be made into bow strings. In 1846, before white hunters moved onto the Plains, Southern Cheyenne Chief Yellow Wolf observed that the buffalo were decreasing. At that time, increasing numbers of tribes were moving onto the Plains, and pressure on the herds was growing. Occasional droughts cut the grazing capacity, while competition from Indian horses and cattle belonging to settlers exacerbated the situation. Bovine diseases also struck down buffalo. Indian hunting methods could be wasteful, too, such as when vast numbers of animals were driven over a cliff and not all were butchered. Furthermore, Indians realized that there was a European market for buffalo robes and began killing for trade reasons.

However, the severest damage occurred when commercial buffalo hunting began in 1870. The hunters and European sportsmen began killing the animals in large numbers. The Army, in concert with the hunters, set out to destroy the buffalo to make way for railroads, ranchers, and settlers. Destruction of their natural food source would break Native American resistance by causing starvation and dependence on reservation agency food supplies. Although the end of the buffalo-robe trade occurred in the 1870s, it gave way to a demand in the eastern United States for hides that could be made into leather and machinery belts for factories. By 1878, the southern herd had been exterminated, and by 1883, the buffalo had become almost extinct on the Northern Plains. By 1903, the number had declined to thirty-four. One hunter claimed that if he could shoot a hundred buffalo a day, he would earn $6,000 a month. The construction of railroads meant that buffalo meat and hides could be shipped rapidly to eastern markets, making the trade even more attractive.

The winter campaign was an effective method of destroying Indian food supplies. After the Battle of the Little Bighorn, troops hit Dull Knife's Northern Cheyenne village on the Powder River in Wyoming. Two hundred tepees were burned, tons of buffalo meat destroyed, and 1,000 buffalo robes and 750 ponies seized. Such campaigns led to the death of many Indians through starvation, among them more than a quarter of the Blackfeet in 1883.

The destruction of the buffalo turned the Indians into starving dependents. Crow woman Pretty Shield said, "*We believed for a long time that the buffalo would again come to us; but they did not. We grew hungry and sick and afraid, all in one. Not believing their own eyes our hunters rode very far looking for buffalo, so far away that even if they had found a herd we could not have reached it in half a moon.*" Crow Chief Plenty Coups was even sadder: "*When the buffalo went away the hearts of my people fell to the ground, and they could not lift them up again. After this nothing happened. There was little singing anymore.*"

The westward movement of Indians from the East, displaced by white settlers, brought the tribes into conflict with Native Americans on the Plains. The Assiniboine, for example, were faced with competition for buffalo from the Ojibwa. This increased pressure on the Plains Indians' primary food source contributed to the animal's near extinction.

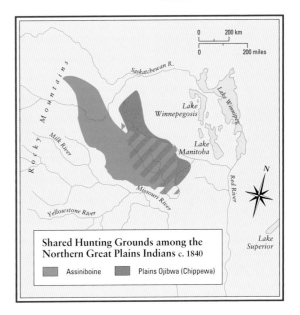

Shared Hunting Grounds among the Northern Great Plains Indians c. 1840

Assiniboine Plains Ojibwa (Chippewa)

Red Cloud's War, 1866–68

ANGERED BY REPORTS OF MASSACRES, THE SIOUX WAGED WAR
AGAINST THE BOZEMAN TRAIL AND THE FORTS BUILT TO
PROTECT IT, EVENTUALLY FORCING THEIR CLOSURE.

Red Cloud led the Sioux in a guerrilla campaign against the forts along the Bozeman Trail, which provided a route to the mining settlements of Montana. Despite the Army's superior firepower, the Indians still managed to virtually close the trail.

Mackenzie's 1865 Powder River expedition, the Chivington Massacre, and tales of the recent Cheyenne-Arapaho War had angered the Sioux. Moreover, the defeated Minnesota Sioux, who had found sanctuary among the Plains Indians, were demanding revenge. Other Indians were fearful of the American advance into Montana, since, by 1865, thriving mining settlements existed at Virginia City, Bozeman, and Helena. The government planned to build a road, the Bozeman Trail, from Fort Laramie to Bozeman so that the miners could be better supplied.

The proposed trail would cut through hunting grounds in the foothills of the Bighorn Mountains, and the Sioux became more apprehensive when three Army outposts were constructed: Fort Reno on the Powder River; Fort Philip Kearny, south of Sheridan, Wyoming; and, Fort C.F. Smith, at the junction of the Bighorn and the Powder River road. The Sioux hindered the building of Fort Philip Kearny by sniping at sentries, and ambushing hay and wood cutting parties; when shelled by howitzers, they retreated, only to return at night to shoot at sentries. Wagon trains were harassed, and the forts were virtually under siege. Led by Red Cloud, the Sioux were waging a successful guerrilla campaign. He was joined by Arapahoes under Black Bear; Hunkpapa Sioux led by Sitting Bull and Gall; Oglalas with Crazy Horse; and Miniconjous commanded by Hump.

On December 21, 1866, the Indians struck hard. Crazy Horse and Hump led two small parties of warriors against a wood train. Captain William Fetterman led a mixed force of cavalry and infantry from the fort to rescue the wood train, but the eighty-one-man detachment was ambushed, and all died. Fetterman and another officer, Captain Brown, probably committed suicide to avoid torture. The bodies of the Americans were mutilated, and even a pet dog was killed. However, the wood train made it back to the fort.

The weather worsened, with appalling snowy conditions, and before Red Cloud could attack the fort itself, infantry reinforcements arrived from Fort Laramie, 235 miles (380 kilometers) to the south. These had been summoned following an epic four-day ride through blizzards by a miner named John Phillips.

Red Cloud had hoped to prevent all traffic to and between the forts, but the garrison at Fort Philip Kearny, under Colonel Henry Carrington, had been rearmed with breech-loading Springfield rifles. Although single-shot, they could be reloaded much quicker and were more effective than the previous muzzle-loaders. On August 1 and 2, 1867, the Indians

A contemporary illustration depicting the Fetterman Fight close to Fort Philip Kearny on December 21, 1866. A clever ambush by the Sioux led to a detachment of eighty-one men, under Captain William Fetterman, being wiped out.

attacked again. Thirty civilian hay cutters plus nineteen guards were working 2 miles (3 kilometers) from Fort C.F. Smith. When attacked by 500 Cheyennes, the Americans sheltered in a log corral and stopped the Indians in their tracks with the new rifles. The Indians set the grass on fire to use the smoke for cover, and although this failed, they did manage to retrieve their wounded. Subsequently, this battle became known as the Hayfield Fight.

Next day, Red Cloud, Crazy Horse, and another Sioux chief, American Horse, led a force against Fort Philip Kearny. They stampeded the mule and horse herds, then attacked a wood cutting party. The Americans withdrew to a makeshift fortification assembled from fourteen wagon beds. The thirty-two-man party, led by Major J.W. Powell, fought 500 Sioux. Six Americans died and two were wounded, while Red Cloud's force lost an estimated sixty dead, with 120 wounded.

Fetterman's defeat and the virtual closure of the Bozeman Trail made it clear that the besieged soldiers could not protect travelers. This forced the U.S. government to face the fact that its Indian policy was failing. One reason was that two of its institutions were employing contradictory policies. The Department of the Interior's Indian Office appeased the nations with gifts, reservations, and annuities, while the War Department attacked them whenever they broke any white rules. Moreover, settlers and miners, under federal protection, were constantly encroaching on Indian lands. The Army was attacked for the Chivington Massacre, and Congress created a Peace Commission of four civilians and three generals. Their purpose was to end Red Cloud's War and remove the causes for conflict. A prevailing view was that the Indians should be isolated and reeducated as sedentary farmers to help their transition into the white world. Treaties were necessary to contain the 54,000 Plains Indians and 86,000 southern Indians. The 1867 Medicine Lodge Creek Treaty gave the Cheyenne and Arapaho a reservation in Indian Territory; the Comanche, Kiowa, and Kiowa-Apache were treated similarly. However, the Sioux had to wait another year for a treaty, which was signed at Fort Laramie.

THE NAVAJO WAR AND THE LONG WALK

BEATEN INTO SUBMISSION BY KIT CARSON, THE NAVAJO WERE FORCED TO WALK 300 MILES (480 KILOMETERS) TO THE HELL OF THE BOSQUE REDONDO RESERVATION.

Manuelito of the Navajo. When the Indian leader refused to move his people to Bosque Redondo in 1864, he provoked the wrath of Colonel Kit Carson, who led a force of volunteers against the Navajo homeland. Manuelito held out until 1866, but eventually all his people were sent on the Long Walk.

The Navajo, or Diné (the People), arrived in the Southwest about AD 1050, occupying lands between the Rio Grande, San Juan, and Colorado rivers. This area, known as Dinéteh, placed the Navajo close to the Pueblo peoples, from whom they learned agriculture and architecture. They acquired sheep through raiding, and their flocks soon multiplied. They also acquired slaves in the same manner. During the 1846–48 Mexican War, U.S. troops entered the area and threatened punishment if the Navajo continued their slave raiding habits.

Treaties with the Americans were broken several times, and tensions increased because the Navajo continued raiding. The Americans built Fort Defiance near Canyon Bonito, in present-day northeast Arizona, and pastureland at the mouth of the canyon became disputed territory. The Navajo wanted the land for sheep grazing, but the Army needed it as horse pasture. Soldiers shot Navajo animals, and on April 30, 1860, Navajo warriors, led by Manuelito and Barboncito, attacked the fort, coming close to capturing it. The Americans responded by sending a force under Colonel Edward Canby into the Chuska Mountains to pursue the Navajo. Skirmishes took place, but a truce was agreed in January 1861, since the fleeing Navajo needed to tend their sheep and fields, and obtain food.

During the American Civil War, the U.S. government wanted to keep the Arizona and New Mexico territories within the Union, and to maintain transport links with California. To achieve this, Mescalero Apache and Navajo raids had to be prevented. A five-month campaign by Colonel Kit Carson placed the Mescalero on a reservation at Bosque Redondo, an arid, barren area near Fort Sumner on the Pecos River.

When Manuelito refused to move his people, Carson turned on the Navajo. His New Mexican volunteers together with some Utes, devastated Dinéteh, destroying fields and peach orchards, and seizing livestock. Then Carson moved against the Navajos' sacred stronghold in the Canyon de Chelly. He blocked one end and sent in troops at the other. The Navajo were flushed from their hiding places, and by the summer of 1864, Carson had sent 8,000 of them on the Long Walk to Bosque Redondo. A further 4,000, under Manuelito, fled west, but eventually surrendered at Fort Wingate on September 1, 1866. The Long Walk was a journey of some 300 miles (480 kilometers), and people were shot if they complained.

Bosque Redondo was a hideous place, and the Army had made inadequate arrangements for the Indians sent there. Disease and a lack of food, blankets, and good shelter killed many. Drought conditions and poor agricultural land made the reservation useless. Disputes with hostile Mescalero Apaches were a further problem, as was homesickness and general misery. A delegation was permitted to visit Washington in 1868 to ask the government to allow the Navajo to return to Dinéteh. General Sheridan was shocked by conditions at Bosque Redondo and approved a return to the homeland, provided the Navajo remained peaceful; if they did not, they would be sent to Oklahoma Indian Territory. This undertaking was enshrined in an 1868 treaty.

The Navajo reestablished themselves as farmers and herders, as well as turning to new economic ventures; they became famous as weavers and silversmiths, and are well known for sand painting. They grew more prosperous after they were given sheep by the U.S. government. The railroad arrived in the region in 1880, and the Navajo began to trade maize, wool, mutton, hides, livestock, and crafts in return for food and manufactured products. Eventually, leases were negotiated with them to exploit the oil, gas, timber, coal, and uranium found on their reservation.

Kit Carson, trapper, guide, Indian agent, and soldier. When the American Civil War began, Carson joined the New Mexico Volunteer Infantry, which was part of the Union Army. He was given the task of subduing the Apache and Navajo to prevent their raiding.

The Long Walk, an arduous trek through the harsh desert lands to the hell of Bosque Redondo.

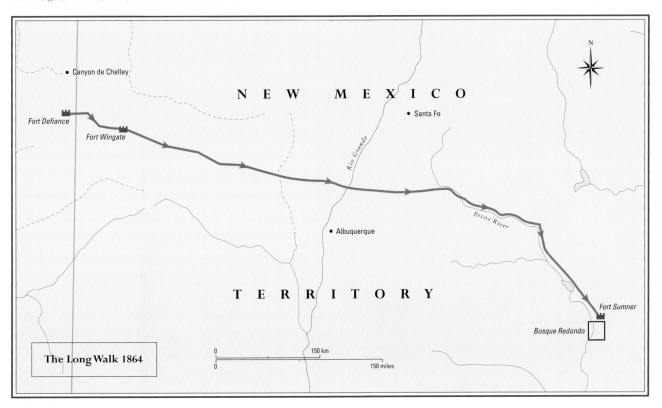

The Long Walk 1864

OTHER NATIVE AMERICANS IN THE CIVIL WAR

MANY NATIVE AMERICANS FROM OUTSIDE INDIAN TERRITORY SERVED IN BOTH CONFEDERATE AND UNION FORCES DURING THE AMERICAN CIVIL WAR, AND FOR A VARIETY OF REASONS.

Native Americans were present at the Second Battle of Bull Run and the Battle of Antietam in 1862; at Chattanooga in 1863; at the Wilderness, Spotsylvania, and Cold Harbor in 1864; in Union attacks on Petersburg in 1864 and 1865; and during Sherman's Carolina campaign toward the end of the war. While some 20,000 Indians were actively involved in the war, other tribes waged their own campaigns against the Union and whites generally. During the war years, Cochise was at large; the Great Sioux Uprising occurred in Minnesota; the Navajo were being chased by Kit Carson; and the Sand Creek Massacre was overseen by Chivington.

Indians possessed contrasting allegiances, and a wide range of motives persuaded them to join the white man's war. Ottowa and Ojibwa from Michigan served the Union as sharpshooters, in the hope that they would be rewarded with a larger, consolidated land base. Company K of the First Michigan Sharpshooters became a famous Indian unit, which fought in adverse conditions from Spotsylvania to the Crater at Petersburg and the Appotomax. Fewer than two-thirds of their original number were mustered out of service at the war's end.

One aspect of the Civil War in southern New England was the characterization of Native Americans as colored, thereby writing them out of history in the U.S. Colored Infantry. The surviving Pequots and Mohegans from the early colonial wars were deprived both economically and politically. Some had found work on whaling ships, but that industry was declining, and the military offered some economic salvation. By 1864, the state of Connecticut was offering a $600 bounty to any recruit who signed up.

The most famous Native American in the Union forces was Brigadier General Ely S. Parker, a Seneca, who became General Grant's adjutant. Later, he became the first Native American to serve as the United States Commissioner of Indian Affairs (1869–71). Parker had been born Hasanoanda at Indian Falls, New York, on what was then the Tonawanda Reservation. He became a translator to the Seneca chiefs in their dealings with the government, then sought a law career, but was prevented from taking the bar exam because he was an Indian. Then he studied engineering and became a civil engineer. After an abortive attempt to raise a regiment of Iroquois for the Union, he joined the Union Army following Grant's intervention. He was commissioned a captain in 1863.

Other Senecas from the Tonawanda band supported the Union because they regarded the Federal government as an ally against those whites who wanted to acquire their lands in western New York State.

There were other reasons for joining the Union. The Kansas Delaware had fought for the United States before in many campaigns, yet they had been pushed progressively westward. They thought that fighting for the Union cause might result in a settled homeland. Eventually, the Delaware were allowed to buy land from the Cherokee, and 985 Delaware registered themselves as citizens of the Cherokee Nation. The Pamunkey tribe, the last of the old Powhatan Empire, served as river pilots for George B. McClellan's Army of the Potomac in 1862. One Pamunkey, Terrill Bradley of Chickahominy ancestry, became a land guide, then a spy for Allan Pinkerton's Secret Service, and finally a pilot on the USS *Schockon*, where he was wounded in action.

Ely Samuel Parker was a Seneca who rose to the rank of brigadier general in the Union forces. An aide to General Ulysses S. Grant, he wrote the final draft of the Confederate surrender terms at Appomattox.

In North Carolina, the Lumbee Indians were classed as non-white and were not allowed to fight for the South. Instead, many were sent into virtual slavery at Fort Fisher on the North Carolina coast, being employed to build fortifications. Their lot was starvation and disease. Many escaped, while other Lumbees hid in the swamps to avoid conscription. When William Tecumseh Sherman marched from Savannah to Goldsboro in fifty days, he was aided by Lumbee swamp guerrillas, who attacked Confederate Home Guard white-supremacist units. After the war, between 1865 and 1874, one guerrilla band, the Lowries, continued their campaign against racists. In contrast, the tiny Catawba tribe sent nineteen men to serve the Confederacy; reputedly, only three made it back home in one piece. Another notable Native American contribution to the Civil War was the North Carolina Thomas Legion, based on the Eastern band of the Cherokee. Employed for local defense, it saw varied service and surrendered one month after Lee.

Other tribes earned respect during the summer of 1863 at Vicksburg, where Indians of the 14th Wisconsin Sharpshooters silenced cannonfire by sniping at Confederate gun crews. A year later, Seneca of the 14th New York Heavy Artillery captured snipers at Spotsylvania. Oneida in the 14th Wisconsin were noteworthy hunters, who made squirrel soup as a break from normal rations.

Whle African-Americans were emancipated at the end of the war, Native Americans remained "domestic dependent nations," and their communities had to contend with amputees and cases of shell shock among returning warriors. Indians had a dubious status. The 1868 Fourteenth Amendment excluded "Indians not taxed" from the number of people in each state, which was used to apportion the number of congressmen.

LITTLE BIGHORN

BLOODIED BY THE BATTLE OF THE ROSEBUD, THE ARMY
ATTACKED THE SIOUX AND THEIR ALLIES AT THEIR ENCAMPMENT
ON THE LITTLE BIGHORN RIVER, LEADING TO THE MOST FAMOUS
ACTION OF THE INDIAN WARS.

George Armstrong Custer,
headstrong leader of the U.S.
Army's 7th Cavalry.

After the Rosebud battle, the Native Americans gathered by the Little Bighorn River. Northern Cheyenne and various Lakota divisions (Brulé, Oglala, Yankton, Santee, Miniconjou, Sans Arc, and Hunkpapa) were encamped and numbered some 15,000, among them 4,000 warriors. Major chiefs included Sitting Bull, Crazy Horse, Gall, Hump, and Two Moons. Four days after the Battle of the Rosebud, Terry's and Gibbon's columns met on the Yellowstone River. A scouting party under Major Marcus Reno found the general location of the Indian camp, and Terry dispatched Custer's 7th Cavalry to cut them off from the south, while the rest of the force moved in from the north. Terry wanted Custer to attack and drive the Indians toward Gibbon's infantry, who would pin down the warriors. Thus, the Lakota and Cheyenne would be bottled up in the Little Bighorn Valley.

Custer moved off with between 600 and 700 cavalry, but refused the offer of four troops from the 2nd Cavalry and a Gatling-gun platoon. None of the Americans knew the size of the Indian concentration, or that some warriors were armed with Winchester repeating rifles—the soldiers were equipped with single-shot Springfield carbines. The Indians were prepared to stand and die, which meant that Custer's method of dashing in, as he had done at Black Kettle's camp on the Washita, would not work this time.

At around noon on June 25, 1876, Custer divided his command. Captain Frederick Benteen was sent with three companies to scout on his left; three hours later, he found the upper end of the Indian camp. Next, Custer sent Reno with three companies to cross the river and charge the camp between the river and Shoulderblade Creek, on the extreme left of the 7th Cavalry's thrust. Custer personally led four companies into a fold in the ground where he could not see the size of the camp.

Reno began the battle at 3pm, his force advancing against the southern end of the camp, where it met a counteradvance by the Hunkpapa, who wanted to gain time for their women and children to escape. Reno's 112 men were vastly outnumbered, and with no support from Benteen or Custer, they retreated into a cottonwood grove. Finding his force being infiltrated, Reno retreated further, digging in on a bluff across the river, but he left some men among the trees. Many of these were lost as they tried to withdraw. In forty-five minutes, Reno had lost half his command as casualties or missing.

Meanwhile, Custer charged the first northern village, but was counterattacked by Northern

Gall, a Hunkpapa Lakota, who fought with utter determination at the Battle of Little Big Horn armed only with a hatchet, driven by the desire to avenge the loss of two of his wives and three of his children killed by the U.S. army.

During the Bighorn campaign, the U.S. Army sent three converging columns against the Cheyenne and Sioux, leading to battles at the Powder River (Reynolds), Rosebud Creek (Crook), and the Little Bighorn (Custer), but all three saw intense Indian opposition.

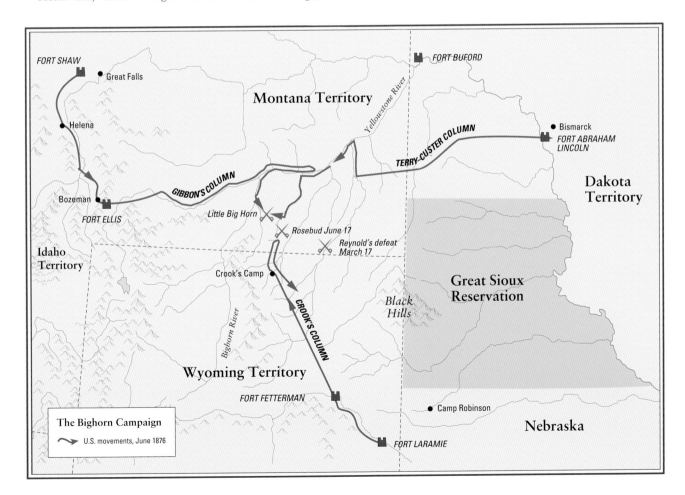

FORT SHAW

● Great Falls

Montana Territory

FORT BUFORD

Yellowstone River

● Helena

TERRY-CUSTER COLUMN

● Bismarck
FORT ABRAHAM
LINCOLN

Bozeman ●

GIBBON'S COLUMN

**Dakota
Territory**

FORT ELLIS

Little Big Horn

Rosebud June 17

Reynold's defeat
March 17

**Idaho
Territory**

Crook's Camp ●

Bighorn River

**Great Sioux
Reservation**

*Black
Hills*

CROOK'S COLUMN

Wyoming Territory

FORT FETTERMAN

● Camp Robinson

Nebraska

The Bighorn Campaign
➤ U.S. movements, June 1876

FORT LARAMIE

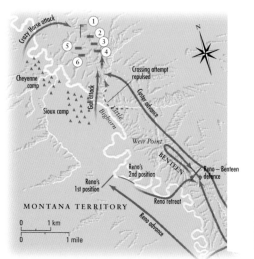

Captain Frederick Benteen
survived the battle to become a
colonel of the 7th Cavalry.

Battle of Little Bighorn
Phases 1 and 2
25 June 1876

1. Col. CUSTER
2. Company F. YATES
3. Company I. KEOGH
4. Company L. CALHOUN
5. Company C. T.W. CUSTER
6. Company E. SMITH
7. Indians under CRAZY HORSE
8. Indians under GALL

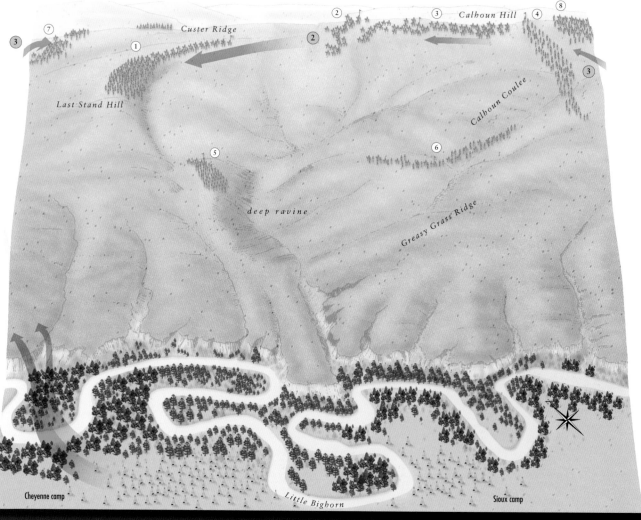

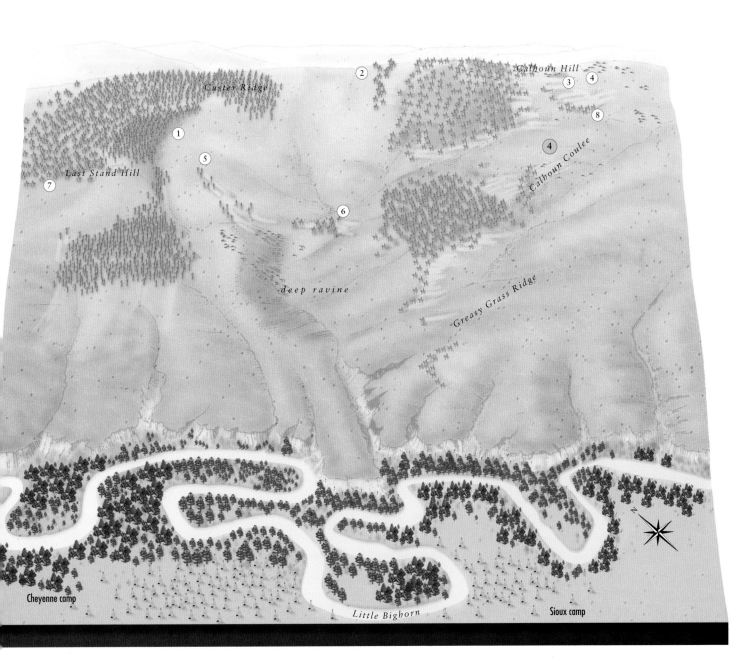

Custer Ridge

Calhoun Hill

Calhoun Coulee

Last Stand Hill

deep ravine

Greasy Grass Ridge

Cheyenne camp

Little Bighorn

Sioux camp

Battle of Little Bighorn
Phase 3
25 June 1876

1. Custer divides his command of 600 men into 3 groups, he then leads his own group northwest along the ridges above the Little Bighorn River. Meanwhile the other 2 groups are beaten off by Indian forces isolating Custer and his men

2. Custer's force moves in loose company formations along the ridge deep in Indian controlled territory, contact with Reno and Beufeau is lost. Large Indian forces move across the Little Bighorn River

3. Indian forces under Crazy Horse and Gall move to surround Custers 212 cavalry men, and begin their attack

4. The Indian attack rapidly overwhelms the companies to the east and south of Custer's position, the few survivors collect around Custer for a last stand

The progression of the Battle of the Little Bighorn. Custer's troops were completely overwhelmed by the Cheyenne and Sioux warriors.

A fanciful vision of "Custer's Last Stand" at the Battle of the Little Bighorn.

Major Marcus Reno set the battle in motion with his attack on the southern end of the Indians' camp.

Cheyennes, and Brulés and Oglalas under Crazy Horse. Then Gall arrived with Hunkpapa, and Sans Arc warriors. Custer was surrounded on a high, grassy ridge. By 5pm, his 215 men had been wiped out, among them his brother, Tom. Rain In The Face, a Hunkpapa previously captured by Tom Custer, cut out his heart and ate it.

Meanwhile, Benteen saw Reno's predicament and rode to his relief. Hearing gunshots from downstream, the two officers realized that Custer was engaged. Against orders, Captain Thomas Weir led his company toward Custer. He was followed by Reno, but they were pinned down while Custer and his command were destroyed. Reno's men retreated to the bluff, where they lost eighteen more killed and forty-three wounded. Fending off several assaults, Reno was eventually rescued by Terry and Gibbon on June 27; he was lucky not to have been overrun like Custer.

In the aftermath of the Battle of the Little Bighorn, U.S. forces regrouped and began harassing and pursuing Indians, resulting in several engagements. On July 17, a group of Cheyennes were defeated at Warbonnet Creek, and a fight at Slim Buttes in September led to the capture of some Tetons. The Battle of Dull Knife (November 25) routed the Northern Cheyenne, while in January 1877, Crazy Horse was beaten at Wolf Mountain; in May, Lame Deer's Lakota were defeated in Montana. The war ended officially on July 16, 1877, and sick, cold, and hungry warriors gradually surrendered. Sitting Bull fled to Canada, but returned in 1881; in 1885, he joined Buffalo Bill's Wild West Show.

Sitting Bull, holy man and war chief of the Sioux, with his adopted son, One Bull. They went into exile together to Canada after the victory at the Battle of Little Big Horn.

IMPRISONING THE WEST

TO PROTECT WHITE SETTLEMENTS, INTERESTS, AND OVERLAND TRAILS FROM INDIAN ATTACKS, THE U.S. ARMY BUILT A NETWORK OF FORTS ALONG THE FRONTIER.

The United States' peace policy attempted to place all Native Americans on reservations, to separate them geographically from white settlements, trails, and railroad construction. The reservations would be the forum for a white civilizing mission of the Indians. During and after the Civil War, every military campaign in the West and Southwest forced the Indians onto reservations, or made them return there if they fled. Reasons for restricting Indian movement included stimulating the expansion of trade, along the Santa Fé Trail for example, and protecting the immigrants who flooded into Kansas and the West after 1854. Tribal lands were being crossed increasingly by stage and mail routes, and by railroad crews laying track. To pursue all these policies, a network of forts was built along the frontier, moving ever westward as more Indian lands were acquired.

Another major problem facing the West was the vast number of miners chasing new mineral finds. In 1858, there was the Pike's Peak Gold Rush, while in 1875, prospectors discovered gold in the Black Hills. Between 1859 and 1860, about 40,000 miners and squatters encroached upon territory occupied by the Arapaho and Cheyenne, who numbered only 5,000. Such incursions into lands considered inviolate by treaty, and the consequent extra pressure on game supplies, led to violence and war. The 1858 gold rush caused the hostilities that culminated in the Sand Creek Massacre, while the 1875 incident led to the Battle of the Little Bighorn. Elsewhere, in 1866, the Fetterman Massacre resulted from the U.S. government's attempt to defend the Bozeman Trail between Fort Laramie and Bozeman so that Montana miners could be supplied. The construction of Forts C.F. Smith, Philip Kearny, and Reno provoked Red Cloud's War.

Constant hostility led to the construction of many forts for a variety of reasons. Fort Leavenworth, in Kansas, was built to protect the Santa Fé and Oregon trails, and later the Kansas Pacific Railroad. It was also where the African-American 10th Cavalry was raised. Fort Riley on the Smoky Hill Trail, in northeast Kansas, was used as a staging post to protect the frontier, while Fort Larned on the Santa Fé Trail acted as an Indian Bureau agency, and provided escorts for mail coaches and wagon trains. Fort Hays, in western Kansas, on the railroad between Kansas City and Denver, Colorado, protected rail gangs on both the Kansas Pacific and Union Pacific railroads. Fort Dodge was a camping ground and supply depot for wagon trains, and Fort Harker, in central Kansas, was a major distribution depot for the southwestern forts in Colorado, Arizona, and northern Texas. It also protected the Butterfield Overland Despatch Company routes.

Fort Benton, Montana, exemplifies the activities of many forts. Established on the upper Missouri River, it was intended to implement the 1855 Lame Bull's Treaty. The terms of this treaty restricted the Blackfeet to lands around the Hellgate, Musselshell, and Milk rivers in return for $20,000 worth annually of useful goods and services, plus another $15,000 annually to promote Christianization and civilization through instructional farms, schools, and farming equipment. The fort became an agency distributing these goods and services, which the Indians often possessed already, or were disliked by them, such as coffee and rice. As buffalo numbers dwindled, however, the Blackfeet became increasingly dependent upon the fort for government supplies. Fort Benton not only became a distribution point for supplies, but also served as a focal point of the Missouri route to the Columbia River and Pacific Northwest by the Mullen Road. In addition, the agency was a staging post for wolf hunters, prospectors, merchants, whisky traders, and migrant settlers.

A second fort, Shaw, was built on the Sun River, northwest Montana, in 1867 to assuage white fears of the Blackfeet, who were beset by cattle ranchers. In 1873 and 1874, President Grant had the reservation's southern border moved to the north of the Missouri and Marias rivers, and Birch Creek without federal payment. Tensions grew and culminated in an unfortunate attack on the friendly Blackfeet camp of Chief Heavy Runner in 1870. Known as the Baker Massacre, after Major Eugene Baker who led the cavalry detachment involved in the dawn assault, this fight led to the death of 173 Indians, while 140 women and children were abandoned on the prairie to fend for themselves in the Montana winter.

As the nineteenth century progressed, the number and range of the buffalo contracted. Indiscriminate killing by white hunters played a major part in this, but the Indians themselves contributed to the decline. One result was that Indians became more reliant on supplies provided by the government, tying them to the agencies.

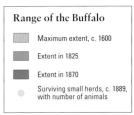

Range of the Buffalo

- Maximum extent, c. 1600
- Extent in 1825
- Extent in 1870
- Surviving small herds, c. 1889, with number of animals

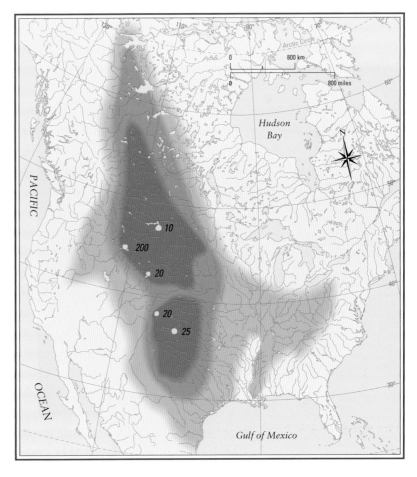

GHOST DANCE AND WOUNDED KNEE

BEATEN, RESENTFUL, AND CONFINED TO THEIR RESERVATIONS,
THE NORTHERN BANDS OF NATIVE AMERICANS GRASPED AT ONE
LAST, FORLORN HOPE OF RETURNING TO THE OLD WAYS.

Wovoka, the Paiute shaman
whose revelation gave rise to
the Ghost Dance religion.

In 1889, a part-Christian Paiute mystic, Wovoka, had a revelation while sick with fever. Son of another mystic, Tavibo, Wovoka incorporated his father's teachings with a vision that came to him during an eclipse of the sun, and spread a gospel ultimately known as the Ghost Dance religion. The revelation enabled him to meet his ancestors, and he received instructions from the Great Spirit— he must forget fighting and work for the white man, and dance the traditional Round Dance. The dance and ideas spread rapidly among the Indians of the Plains and Southwest, appealing to the traditional notion of warrior society that the spiritual world would inform the physical world.

One Lakota, Kicking Bear, visited Wovoka in Nevada. Upon returning to his reservation, he ignored Wovoka's teaching that good behavior would be rewarded in the afterlife; he and others thought that the white man could be eliminated because Indians could make special Ghost Dance shirts that would stop bullets. A religious, apocalyptic fervor spread through the Lakota reservations, and white officialdom banned the Ghost Dance in 1890. The fearful U.S. government even sent over half the Army to the reservations.

Eventually, the Ghost Dancers, some 3,000 Lakota, Oglala, and Sicangus from the Rosebud reservation, moved out and made camp in a remote region of the Badlands, in southwest South Dakota. They had chosen a natural fortress known as the Stronghold. Trouble really started when Sitting Bull broke his peace pipe, saying that he would fight and kill all whites. A party of forty Indian police was sent to arrest the chief before he left for the Stronghold, but a bitter fight broke out between them and 160 Ghost Dancers. Eventually, troops of the 8th Cavalry rescued the police, but Sitting Bull had been shot dead

Indian Wars in the West 1850–1900

0   200 km

0   200 miles

In the second half of the nineteenth century, the West was a tinderbox where armed conflict between the Indians and Army could erupt anywhere and at any time. Pushed around, cheated, and dispossessed, the Indians were fighting desperately against overwhelming odds to retain their homes and their way of life.

Meanwhile, General Nelson Miles, commander of the Division of the Missouri, ordered the arrest of Big Foot, a Miniconjou. Big Foot had already left the Cheyenne River in South Dakota for Pine Ridge in the south. He had been asked there not by Ghost Dancers, but by Red Cloud and other pro-white reservation Indians who wanted peace and stability. Miles dispatched Major S.M. Whitside with the 7th Cavalry to bring in Big Foot, and they found him at Porcupine Creek, some 30 miles (48 kilometers) east of Pine Ridge. No resistance was offered, and the Indians were ordered to make camp 5 miles (8 kilometers) to the west at Wounded Knee Creek. Colonel James Forsyth arrived, took charge, surrounded the camp with his 500 soldiers, and mounted four rapid-fire Hotchkiss machine guns on a bluff overlooking the camp. The Lakota numbered 120 men, and 230 women and children.

On December 29, Forsyth sent soldiers into the camp to disarm the men. Few weapons were offered up, but body searches of men and women revealed guns. In one scuffle, a shot was fired. Shooting began on both sides, the soldiers using their single-shot Springfields, while the Lakota replied with repeating rifles. Some Indians were gunned down, some ran for their families, and

THE BIRTH OF OKLAHOMA

IN 1885, THE NATIVE AMERICANS OCCUPYING INDIAN TERRITORY THOUGHT THAT THEY WOULD NOT BE REQUIRED TO MOVE AGAIN. THE UNITED STATES GOVERNMENT HAD OTHER IDEAS.

Groups of white settlers were squatting on Indian reservations, and these "Boomers" prompted commercial interests to pressure the government to allow further development of Indian lands. Congress passed The General Allotment (Dawes) Act in 1887. The legislation proposed that the reservations should be broken up and a 160-acre (65-hectare) holding, or allotment, be given to each Indian head of family. This would turn the Indians into farmers, strip the chiefs of their powers, and finally assimilate the Indians into white culture.

The Act authorized surveys of reservations, the preparation of a tribal consensus, and then division of the land. The Five Civilized Tribes, the Osage in Oklahoma, and the Seneca in New York were exempt. An Indian taking an allotment became a U.S. citizen, but the land was held in trust for twenty-five years, during which time the owner could neither lease, sell, nor will the land. The Dawes Act was modified in 1891, when each adult received an 80-acre (32-hectare) holding, and the Commissioner of Indian Affairs was allowed to lease allotments to white farmers.

In 1889, there were two significant developments. Congress established a separate federal court at Muskogee for the Indian Territory, defining the territory as that land bordered by the states of Kansas, Missouri, Arkansas, Texas, and New Mexico Territory. On April 22, the Unassigned Lands, in the southwestern part of Indian Territory, were opened to settlement by non-Indians, and over 50,000 settlers moved in during a single day. In May 1890, Indian Territory was reduced to the reservations belonging to the Five Civilized Tribes, together with those reservations in the far northeastern portion of the original territory. The remainder, including all the reservations in the Cherokee Outlet, became Oklahoma Territory.

Surplus lands of the Cheyenne and Arapaho were opened to settlement on April 19, 1892. The Cherokee Outlet, and the surplus lands of the Tonkawa and Pawnee reservations were thrown open on September 16, 1893, and those of the Kickapoo on May 25, 1895. The invasion of the Cherokee Outlet saw 100,000 people surrounding the area. There was a 4-mile (6-kilometer) line of people on horseback, in wagons, hacks, and carriages, and on bicycles, all waiting for the signal to homestead. Such wild settler races and scrambles were repeated as the lands were homesteaded in a disorganized fashion. However, disposal of the surplus lands of the Comanche-Kiowa and Wichita-Caddo reservations was accomplished by prior registration, each settler taking part in a land lottery.

The 1898 Curtis Act promoted sweeping changes in Indian Territory. It established tribal courts, and authorized the Dawes Commission to make allotments to the Five Civilized Tribes and eradicate tribal government without tribal consent. In all, 15.79 million acres (6.39 million hectares) were allotted to 101,506 tribal members, including 2,582 whites married to Indians, and 23,405 African-Americans who had been slaves before 1863.

Seeing their land holdings being steadily eroded, the Five Civilized Tribes organized a convention to write a constitution and asked to be allowed into the Union as the state of Sequoyah. This notion was rejected by Congress. The original treaties of removal signed by the Five Civilized Tribes had promised them lands in perpetuity. The Choctaw Treaty stated, *"No part of the land granted them shall ever be embraced in a territory (non-Indian) or state."*

In 1907, Congress approved a law that combined Indian Territory and Oklahoma Territory into the new state of Oklahoma. Legacies of the allotment policy are the checkerboarding of small reservations and many allotments that are too small to be economically viable. Another ironic outcome is that the Osage reservation, which was created in 1866 from a small slice of the large Cherokee Nation, is now the largest in Oklahoma.

Settlers preparing to take part in a land run. These "races" for land were started on the hour that a territory was opened for settlement, and usually the land was allocated on a "first come, first served" basis.

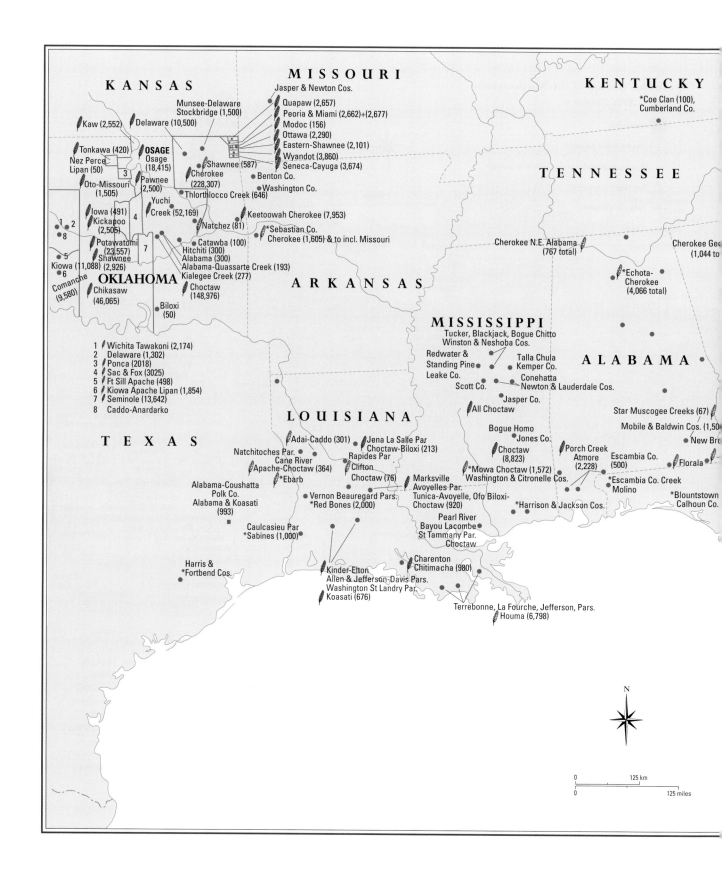

KANSAS

Munsee-Delaware
Stockbridge (1,500)

Kaw (2,552)
Delaware (10,500)

Tonkawa (420)
Nez Perce
Lipan (50)
OSAGE
Osage
(18,415)

Oto-Missouri
(1,505)
Pawnee
(2,500)

Cherokee
(228,307)
Shawnee (587)

Thlorthlocco Creek (646)

Yuchi
Creek (52,169)

Iowa (491)
Kickapoo
(2,505)
Natchez (81)

Potawatomi
(23,557)
Shawnee (2,926)
Catawba (100)
Hitchiti (300)
Alabama (300)
Alabama-Quassarte Creek (193)
Kialegee Creek (277)

Kiowa (11,088)
Comanche
(9,580)
OKLAHOMA
Chikasaw
(46,065)
Choctaw
(148,976)
Biloxi
(50)

1 Wichita Tawakoni (2,174)
2 Delaware (1,302)
3 Ponca (2018)
4 Sac & Fox (3025)
5 Ft Sill Apache (498)
6 Kiowa Apache Lipan (1,854)
7 Seminole (13,642)
8 Caddo-Anardarko

TEXAS

MISSOURI

Jasper & Newton Cos.

Quapaw (2,657)
Peoria & Miami (2,662)+(2,677)
Modoc (156)
Ottawa (2,290)
Eastern-Shawnee (2,101)
Wyandot (3,860)
Seneca-Cayuga (3,674)

Benton Co.

Washington Co.

Keetoowah Cherokee (7,953)

Sebastian Co.
Cherokee (1,605) & to incl. Missouri

ARKANSAS

MISSISSIPPI

Tucker, Blackjack, Bogue Chitto
Winston & Neshoba Cos.

Redwater &
Standing Pine
Leake Co.
Talla Chula
Kemper Co.
Conehatta
Newton & Lauderdale Cos.

Scott Co.

Jasper Co.

All Choctaw

LOUISIANA

Bogue Homo
Jones Co.

Choctaw
(8,823)

Porch Creek
Atmore
(2,228)

Adai-Caddo (301)
Jena La Salle Par
Choctaw-Biloxi (213)

Natchitoches Par.
Cane River
Apache-Choctaw (364)
Rapides Par.
Clifton
*Ebarb
Choctaw (76)

Alabama-Coushatta
Polk Co.
Alabama & Koasati
(993)

Vernon Beauregard Pars.
*Red Bones (2,000)

Marksville
Avoyelles Par.
Tunica-Avoyelle, Ofo Biloxi-
Choctaw (920)

*Mowa Choctaw (1,572)
Washington & Citronelle Cos.

Escambia Co.
(500)
*Escambia Co. Creek
Molino
Florala

*Blountstown
Calhoun Co.

*Harrison & Jackson Cos.

Caulcasieu Par
*Sabines (1,000)

Pearl River
Bayou Lacombe
St Tammany Par.
Choctaw

Harris &
*Fortbend Cos.

Kinder-Elton
Allen & Jefferson-Davis Pars.
Washington St Landry Par.
Koasati (676)

Charenton
Chitimacha (980)

Terrebonne, La Fourche, Jefferson, Pars.
Houma (6,798)

KENTUCKY

*Coe Clan (100),
Cumberland Co.

TENNESSEE

Cherokee N.E. Alabama
(767 total)

Cherokee Geo
(1,044 to

*Echota-
Cherokee
(4,066 total)

ALABAMA

Star Muscogee Creeks (67)
Mobile & Baldwin Cos. (1,50

New Br

N

0   125 km
0   125 miles

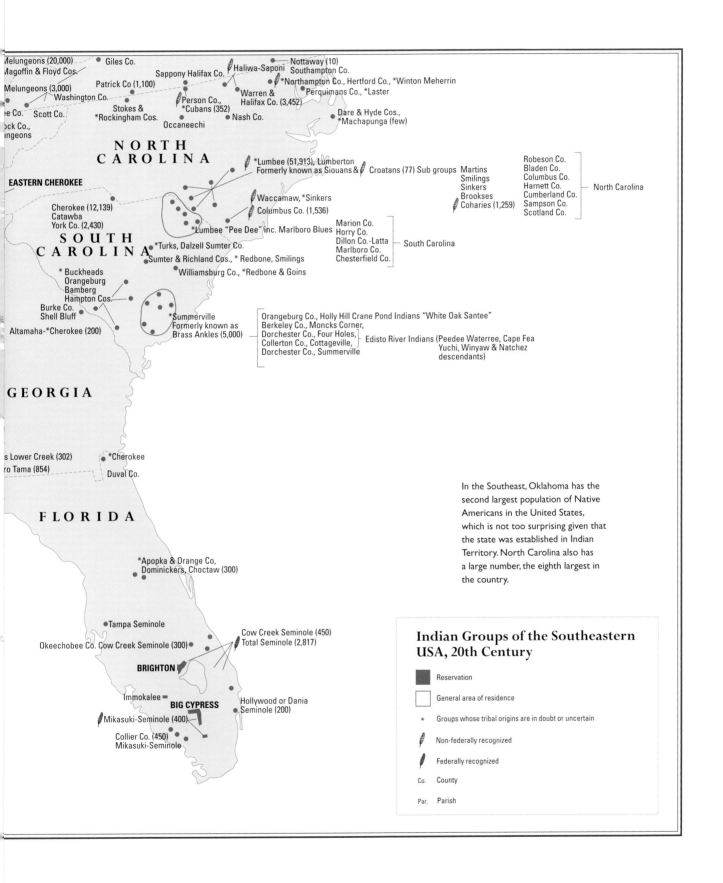

Melungeons (20,000)
Magoffin & Floyd Cos.
Melungeons (3,000)
Washington Co.
Giles Co.
Patrick Co (1,100)
Scott Co.
ock Co.,
ngeons
ee Co.
Stokes &
*Rockingham Cos.
Occaneechi
Sappony Halifax Co.
Person Co.,
*Cubans (352)
Nash Co.
Haliwa-Saponi
Nottaway (10)
Southampton Co.
*Northampton Co., Hertford Co., *Winton Meherrin
Perquimans Co., *Laster
Warren &
Halifax Co. (3,452)
Dare & Hyde Cos.,
*Machapunga (few)

NORTH CAROLINA

EASTERN CHEROKEE

Cherokee (12,139)
Catawba
York Co. (2,430)

SOUTH CAROLINA

*Lumbee (51,913), Lumberton
Formerly known as Siouans &
Croatans (77) Sub groups
Waccamaw, *Sinkers
Columbus Co. (1,536)
*Lumbee "Pee Dee" inc. Marlboro Blues
*Turks, Dalzell Sumter Co.
Sumter & Richland Cos., * Redbone, Smilings
Williamsburg Co., *Redbone & Goins

Martins
Smilings
Sinkers
Brookes
Coharies (1,259)

Robeson Co.
Bladen Co.
Columbus Co.
Harnett Co.
Cumberland Co.
Sampson Co.
Scotland Co.
— North Carolina

Marion Co.
Horry Co.
Dillon Co.-Latta
Marlboro Co.
Chesterfield Co.
— South Carolina

* Buckheads
Orangeburg
Bamberg
Hampton Cos.
Burke Co.
Shell Bluff
Altamaha-*Cherokee (200)

*Summerville
Formerly known as
Brass Ankles (5,000)

Orangeburg Co., Holly Hill Crane Pond Indians "White Oak Santee"
Berkeley Co., Moncks Corner,
Dorchester Co., Four Holes,
Collerton Co., Cottageville,
Dorchester Co., Summerville
Edisto River Indians (Peedee Waterree, Cape Fea
Yuchi, Winyaw & Natchez
descendants)

GEORGIA

s Lower Creek (302)
ro Tama (854)
*Cherokee
Duval Co.

FLORIDA

In the Southeast, Oklahoma has the second largest population of Native Americans in the United States, which is not too surprising given that the state was established in Indian Territory. North Carolina also has a large number, the eighth largest in the country.

*Apopka & Orange Co,
Dominickers, Choctaw (300)

Tampa Seminole
Okeechobee Co. Cow Creek Seminole (300)
BRIGHTON
Cow Creek Seminole (450)
Total Seminole (2,817)
Immokalee
BIG CYPRESS
Mikasuki-Seminole (400)
Collier Co. (450)
Mikasuki-Seminole
Hollywood or Dania
Seminole (200)

Indian Groups of the Southeastern USA, 20th Century

▪ Reservation
☐ General area of residence
* Groups whose tribal origins are in doubt or uncertain
Non-federally recognized
Federally recognized
Co. County
Par. Parish

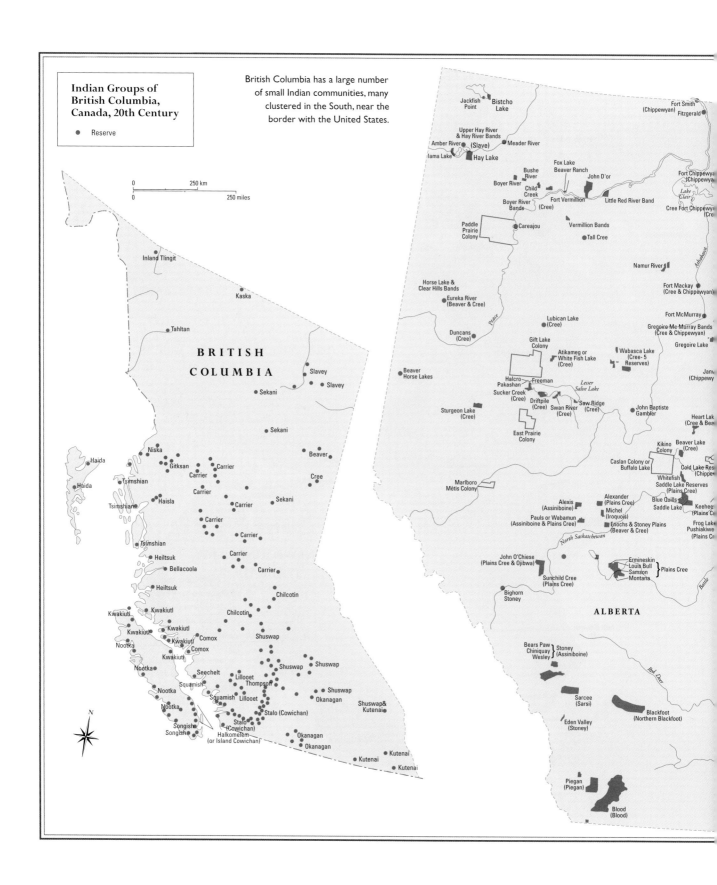

Indian Groups of British Columbia, Canada, 20th Century

- Reserve

British Columbia has a large number of small Indian communities, many clustered in the South, near the border with the United States.

0   250 km
0   250 miles

BRITISH COLUMBIA

ALBERTA

Inland Tlingit
Kaska
Tahltan
Slavey
Slavey
Sekani
Sekani
Beaver
Cree
Sekani
Haida
Haida
Niska
Gitksan
Carrier
Carrier
Tsimshian
Carrier
Haisla
Carrier
Tsimshian
Carrier
Tsimshian
Heiltsuk
Carrier
Bellacoola
Carrier
Heiltsuk
Chilcotin
Kwakiutl
Kwakiutl
Chilcotin
Kwakiutl
Kwakiutl
Comox
Shuswap
Nootka
Kwakiutl
Comox
Kwakiutl
Shuswap
Shuswap
Seechelt
Lillooet
Thompson
Squamish
Shuswap
Nootka
Squamish
Lillooet
Okanagan
Nootka
Stalo (Cowichan)
Shuswap & Kutenai
Songish
Stalo (Cowichan)
Songish
Halkomelem (or Island Cowichan)
Okanagan
Okanagan
Kutenai
Kutenai
Kutenai
Kutenai

Jackfish Point
Bistcho Lake
Fort Smith (Chippewyan)
Fitzgerald
Upper Hay River & Hay River Bands
Amber River   (Slave)   Meader River
Iama Lake   Hay Lake
Bushe River
Fox Lake Beaver Ranch
John D'or
Fort Chippewya (Chippewya
Boyer River
Child Creek
Lake Clair
Boyer River Bands
Fort Vermillion (Cree)
Little Red River Band
Cree Fort Chippewya (Cre
Paddle Prairie Colony
Careajou
Vermillion Bands
Tall Cree
Namur River
Horse Lake & Clear Hills Bands
Fort Mackay (Cree & Chippewyan)
Eureka River (Beaver & Cree)
Fort McMurray
Lubican Lake (Cree)
Gregoire Me Murray Bands (Cree & Chippewyan)
Duncans (Cree)
Gregoire Lake
Gift Lake Colony
Beaver Horse Lakes
Atikameg or White Fish Lake (Cree)
Wabasca Lake (Cree- 5 Reserves)
Janv (Chippewy
Halcro Pakashan Freeman
Sucker Creek (Cree)
Lesser Salve Lake
Saw Ridge (Cree)
Driftpile (Cree)
Swan River (Cree)
John Baptiste Gambler
Heart Lak (Cree & Bea
Sturgeon Lake (Cree)
Kikino Colony
Beaver Lake (Cree)
Caslan Colony or Buffalo Lake
Cold Lake Res (Chippe
East Prairie Colony
Whitefish Saddle Lake Reserves (Plains Cree)
Marlboro Métis Colony
Alexis (Assiniboine)
Alexander (Plains Cree)
Blue Quills Saddle Lake
Keehee (Plains C
Michel (Iroquois)
Pauls or Wabamun (Assiniboine & Plains Cree)
Enochs & Stoney Plains (Beaver & Cree)
Frog Lake Pushiakiwe (Plains C
North Saskatchewan
John O'Chiese (Plains Cree & Ojibwa)
Ermineskin Louis Bull Samson Montana
} Plains Cree
Sunchild Cree (Plains Cree)
Batk
Bighorn Stoney
Bears Paw Chiniquay Wesley
Stoney (Assiniboine)
Red Deer
Sarcee (Sarsi)
Blackfoot (Northern Blackfoot)
Eden Valley (Stoney)
Piegan (Piegan)
Blood (Blood)

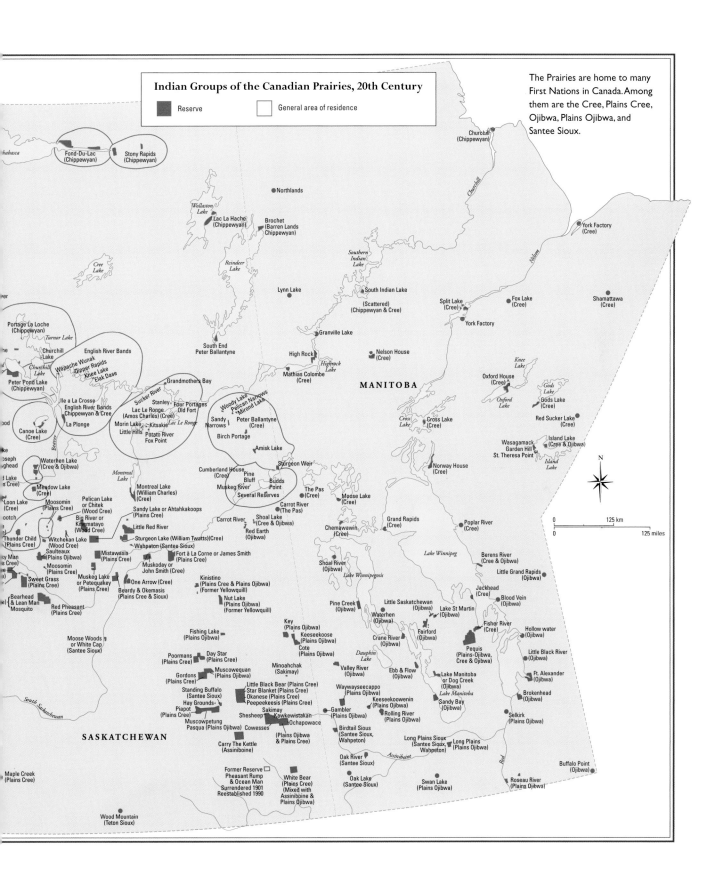

Indian Groups of the Canadian Prairies, 20th Century

Reserve   General area of residence

The Prairies are home to many First Nations in Canada. Among them are the Cree, Plains Cree, Ojibwa, Plains Ojibwa, and Santee Sioux.

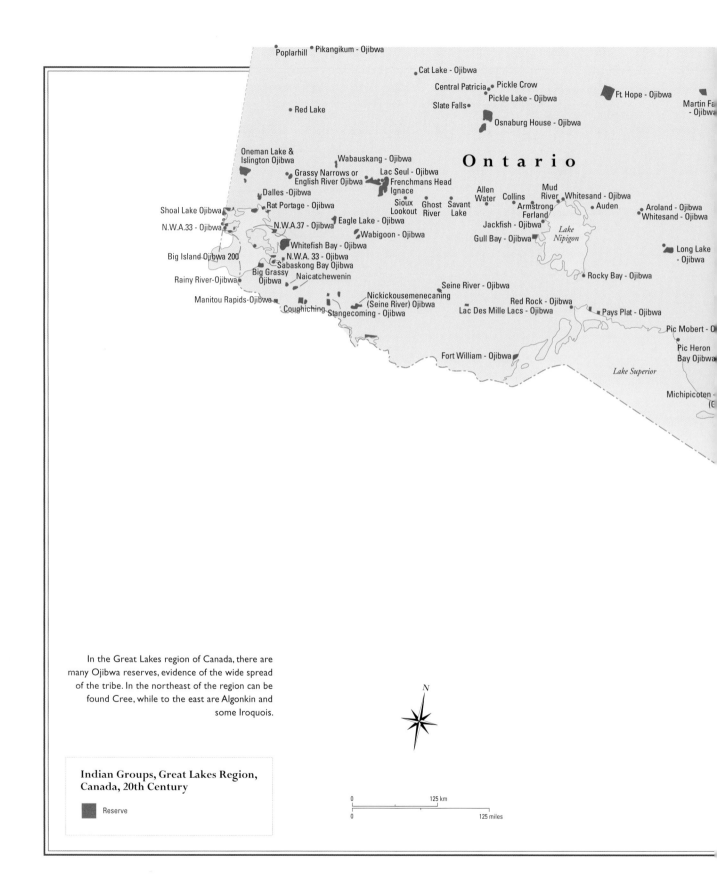

In the Great Lakes region of Canada, there are many Ojibwa reserves, evidence of the wide spread of the tribe. In the northeast of the region can be found Cree, while to the east are Algonkin and some Iroquois.

Indian Groups, Great Lakes Region, Canada, 20th Century

Reserve

Map labels:

Poplarhill • Pikangikum - Ojibwa

Cat Lake - Ojibwa

Central Patricia • Pickle Crow
Pickle Lake - Ojibwa
Slate Falls •

Ft. Hope - Ojibwa

Martin Fa - Ojibwa

Red Lake

Osnaburg House - Ojibwa

Ontario

Oneman Lake & Islington Ojibwa

Wabauskang - Ojibwa

Grassy Narrows or English River Ojibwa

Lac Seul - Ojibwa
Frenchmans Head
Ignace

Allen Water   Collins

Mud River   Whitesand - Ojibwa

Dalles -Ojibwa

Sioux Lookout   Ghost River   Savant Lake

Armstrong Ferland

Auden   Aroland - Ojibwa
Whitesand - Ojibwa

Rat Portage - Ojibwa

Shoal Lake Ojibwa

Jackfish - Ojibwa

N.W.A.33 - Ojibwa

N.W.A.37 - Ojibwa   Eagle Lake - Ojibwa

Lake Nipigon

Wabigoon - Ojibwa

Gull Bay - Ojibwa

Long Lake - Ojibwa

Whitefish Bay - Ojibwa

Big Island Ojibwa 200

N.W.A. 33 - Ojibwa
Sabaskong Bay Ojibwa

Rocky Bay - Ojibwa

Big Grassy Ojibwa   Naicatchewenin

Rainy River-Ojibwa

Seine River - Ojibwa

Red Rock - Ojibwa

Manitou Rapids-Ojibwa

Nickickousemenecaning (Seine River) Ojibwa
Coughiching   Stangecoming - Ojibwa

Lac Des Mille Lacs - Ojibwa

Pays Plat - Ojibwa

Pic Mobert - O

Pic Heron Bay Ojibwa

Fort William - Ojibwa

Lake Superior

Michipicoten - (G

N

0   125 km
0   125 miles

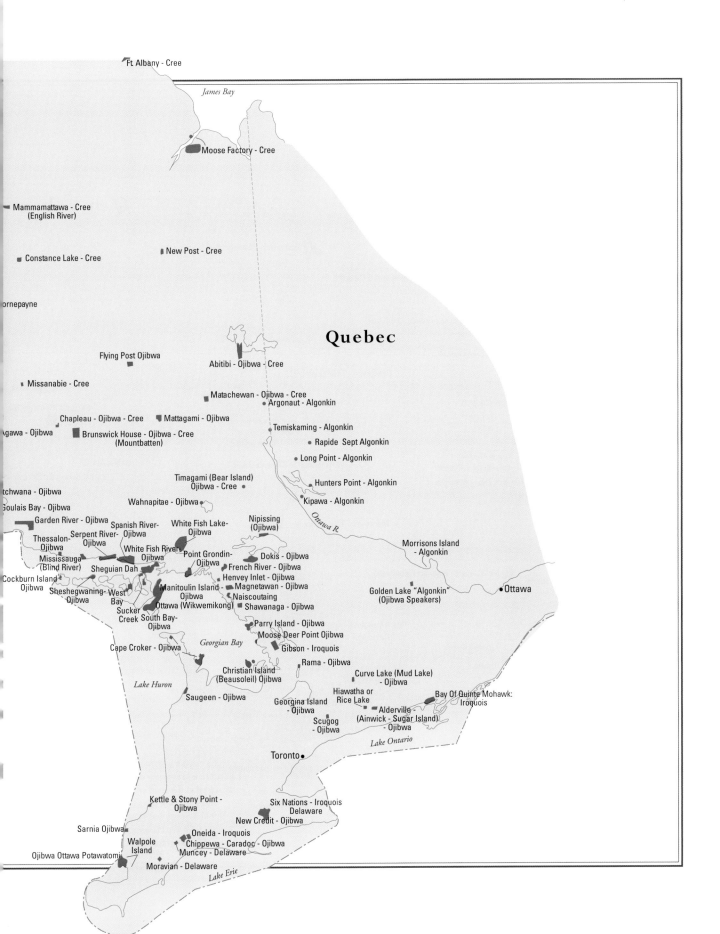

Ft. Albany - Cree

James Bay

Moose Factory - Cree

Mammamattawa - Cree
(English River)

New Post - Cree

Constance Lake - Cree

ornepayne

Quebec

Flying Post Ojibwa

Abitibi - Ojibwa - Cree

Missanabie - Cree

Matachewan - Ojibwa - Cree
Argonaut - Algonkin

Chapleau - Ojibwa - Cree   Mattagami - Ojibwa

Temiskaming - Algonkin

Agawa - Ojibwa   Brunswick House - Ojibwa - Cree
(Mountbatten)

Rapide Sept Algonkin

Long Point - Algonkin

Timagami (Bear Island)
Ojibwa - Cree

Hunters Point - Algonkin

tchwana - Ojibwa

Wahnapitae - Ojibwa

Kipawa - Algonkin

oulais Bay - Ojibwa

Garden River - Ojibwa   Spanish River-   White Fish Lake-   Nipissing
Ojibwa   Ojibwa   (Ojibwa)

Ottawa R.

Serpent River-
Thessalon-   Ojibwa
Ojibwa   White Fish River -   Point Grondin-
Ojibwa   Ojibwa   Dokis - Ojibwa

Morrisons Island
- Algonkin

Mississauga   Sheguian Dah   French River - Ojibwa
(Blind River)   Henvey Inlet - Ojibwa
Cockburn Island -   Sheshegwaning-   West   Manitoulin Island   Magnetawan - Ojibwa   Golden Lake "Algonkin"   Ottawa
Ojibwa   Ojibwa   Bay   Ojibwa   Naiscoutaing   (Ojibwa Speakers)
Sucker   Ottawa (Wikwemikong)   Shawanaga - Ojibwa
Creek   South Bay-
Ojibwa   Parry Island - Ojibwa
Moose Deer Point Ojibwa
Cape Croker - Ojibwa   Gibson - Iroquois

Georgian Bay   Rama - Ojibwa

Christian Island   Curve Lake (Mud Lake)
(Beausoleil) Ojibwa   - Ojibwa

Lake Huron   Hiawatha or   Bay Of Quinte Mohawk:
Rice Lake   Iroquois
Saugeen - Ojibwa   Georgina Island   Alderville -
- Ojibwa   (Ainwick - Sugar Island)
Scugog   - Ojibwa
- Ojibwa

Lake Ontario

Toronto

Kettle & Stony Point -   Six Nations - Iroquois
Ojibwa   Delaware
New Credit - Ojibwa
Sarnia Ojibwa   Oneida - Iroquois
Walpole   Chippewa - Caradoc - Ojibwa
Island   Muncey - Delaware
Ojibwa Ottawa Potawatomi   Moravian - Delaware
Lake Erie

Boarding Schools

DURING THE LATE NINETEENTH CENTURY, THE UNITED STATES GOVERNMENT ADOPTED AN EDUCATION POLICY DESIGNED TO ASSIMILATE NATIVE AMERICANS BY "KILLING THE INDIAN AND SAVING THE MAN."

The techniques used by Major Richard H. Pratt in reeducating seventy-two male prisoners of war, mostly Cheyenne, at Fort Marion, St. Augustine, Florida, were applied to an Indian boarding school he founded in 1879, at an abandoned military post in Carlisle, Pennsylvania. There, he enroled 169 students recruited from the High Plains Sioux. Pratt's educational philosophy was laid down in his book, *Battlefield and Classroom: Four Decades with the American Indian, 1864–1904*. Twenty-five such schools followed, handling 20,000 Indian male and female children from dozens of tribes. In its final year, 1917, Carlisle had students from fifty-eight tribes.

The U.S. government thought that Indian children could be saved and become a ready source of labor, a vital commodity for the spreading industrial society. Little or no understanding of indigenous educational methods was sought by white people. Among Native Americans, play, experience, and the example of elders comprised the normal teaching environment. However, the boarding schools cut off Indians' hair, gave them white people's clothes and names, and ordered the daily routine via the bell. Only English could be spoken. Strict discipline, military drill, poor-quality staff, violence, and verbal abuse were common. The culture shock sometimes broke minds, leading to alcoholism or suicide. Humiliation and degradation killed self-respect, dignity, and the human spirit.

The notion of removing Indian children from tribal contamination is ironic, considering the diseases encountered at school. Tuberculosis, measles, and influenza killed many, and trachoma spread rapidly in the early twentieth century. Some schools maintained their own cemeteries. Overwork, malnutrition, cruel punishments, poor training, and insufficient clothing permeated these Dickensian institutions. Sometimes, when sickness broke out, pupils were sent home, where they infected their brothers and sisters.

However, the portrayal of all boarding schools as inhuman hellholes would be incorrect. Some students overcame all difficulties, flourishing in an environment that they were determined to face bravely and use to the best effect. Children from different nations forged bonds in adversity, despite the variety of languages, cultures, and geographical origins. Later, some married. Cross-cultural exchanges facilitated the growth of a united Native American consciousness, and the realization that new methods were required to keep their sovereignty when confronting American domination and cultural imperialism.

One student, Luther Standing Bear (c. 1868–1939), a Brulé Sioux, returned to his reservation, where he assisted at the government school. He held a number of jobs, wrote essays and articles, and contributed four significant books with the aid of a niece. His novels were not just autobiographical, but also a method of confronting the prejudicial stereotype of the Indian as being a savage who needed to be assimilated into white society. His books are far more important than his roles in films, for example, *The Santa Fé Trail* (1930). He advocated Indian rights and urged America to see the Native American world as a human world.

Another success story is that of Wa Tha Huch, Bright Path, otherwise known as Jim Thorpe (1887–1953). Of mixed ancestry (Sauk and Fox, Potawatomi, Kickapoo, Menominee, Irish, and French), Thorpe always considered himself an Indian at Carlisle. He was a brilliant football player, and he won two gold medals for the decathlon and pentathlon at the 1912 Olympic Games in Sweden. In 1913, he signed a contract to play as a professional for the New York Giants baseball team, later moving to the Boston Braves. He also played professional football in Ohio. For fifteen years, he played baseball in the spring and football in fall.

A group of Native American children at a government boarding school. The aim of such schools was to "kill the Indian and save the man". Often, that meant preparing the children to be a source of cheap labor for menial work.

Some Native Americans rejected the enforced education. Sometimes the Hopi hid their children from government agents, soldiers, and missionaries. In 1895, Chief Lomahongewa and eighteen Hopi men chose imprisonment at Alcatraz rather than give up their children. A variety of problems were generated by the schools. Phoenix Indian School (built 1892) failed to develop industrial skills among its students. Instead, the school channeled its charges into menial, unskilled jobs on local farms; the school authorities often forced local Indian children to attend the school to ensure a pool of cheap labor. Changes did not occur until 1935. Buffalo Woman, a Hidatsa woman, maintained that, within the tribe, girls were carefully monitored by their mothers and did not become pregnant before marriage. When the reservation schools began, so did unmarried pregnancies.

Generally speaking, Native Americans feared that their children would acquire new values of materialism and lose their culture. Moreover, parents missed their children. Interestingly, the boarding schools contributed to the creation of Pan-Indianism, a number of boarding-school graduates becoming militants in the 1960s.

THE SOCIETY OF AMERICAN INDIANS

FORMED BY A GROUP OF INDIAN ACADEMICS IN 1911, THE SOCIETY OF AMERICAN INDIANS HAD THE AIM OF EDUCATING THE PUBLIC ABOUT THE ACHIEVEMENTS OF NATIVE AMERICANS.

Charles A. Eastman was active in matters dealing with Indian rights. In 1903, President Theodore Roosevelt assigned Eastman the responsibility for revising the allotment method of dividing tribal lands. This was to become an internal problem for The Society of American Indians.

The Society of American Indians came into being after much discussion among a group of Indian academics. Led by Fayette Avery McKenzie, an Ohio State University sociologist, these notable Native Americans included Carlos Montezuma (Yavapai), Charles A. Eastman (Santee), Sherman Coolidge (Arapaho), Charles E. Daganett (Peoria), Minnine Kellogg (Oneida), Arthur Parker (Seneca), and Gertrude Simmons Bonnin (Yankton). These people organized the first national Indian conference in the fall of 1911.

Some members of the society believed that strengthening tribal values was vital, but most of them favored complete assimilation. Historian Arthur Parker urged Native Americans *"to strike out into duties of modern life and find every right that has escaped them before."*

The society allowed individual, not tribal, membership, and offered associate membership to non-tribal people. By 1913, enrolments had reached 619, with some 400 associates. Many tribes were represented, the majority of members emanating from the Plains and the Great Lakes-New York region. This fact is probably explained by the society holding its conferences in the Midwest. Western support developed over the next few years. The society was committed to the notion of collective tribal action and became a vehicle for the demand of U.S.

citizenship for Native Americans.

Those who held office in the society were generally assimilationists. Many had been educated at the Carlisle Indian Industrial School, designed to wean its students from Indian culture. Especially significant were the high-powered Native American women, who had strong personal agendas and radical approaches. Bonnin (Zitkala Sa) edited the society's *American Indian* magazine, and fought against peyote and for citizenship. She also criticized white civilization and wanted reservations with self-sustaining communities; she broke with the society in 1912. Kellogg was strongly opposed to the Bureau of Indian Affairs' economic and educational policies, unlike her colleagues. Other important women were Emma D. Johnson Goulette, Marie L.B. Baldwin, and Rose B. LaFlesche.

The task of the society was to educate the public about the achievements and hopes of Native Americans, and its publications were sent to universities and libraries throughout the United States. The national conferences commissioned reports, but the numbers attending gradually declined, from around 200 to a handful in the 1920s. One of the major problems faced by the society was the difference of opinion held by members with such strong personalities, notably over U.S. intervention in World War I. In this respect, divisions between traditionalists, progressives, and the undecided were made manifest.

Gertrude Simmons Bonnin was the editor of the society's *American Indian* magazine. She helped organize the first national Indian conference in the fall of 1911.

The society was pulled in various directions, but it had strong relations with the Bureau of Indian Affairs, which resulted in criticism that it was the BIA's stalking horse. Many BIA Indian employees were members. Into these divisions were thrown American objectives in World War I, as proclaimed by President Woodrow Wilson. One of these was "the self-determination of subject peoples." Many Indians hoped that this principle would lead to a relaxation of BIA policies, but opinions differed on how to approach the war. Some Native Americans volunteered for combat, considering that this action would progress assimilation and win U.S. citizenship. Other Indians claimed that the lack of citizenship negated wartime obligations, and they resisted the war, either actively or passively. Arthur Parker and Carlos Montezuma exemplified these respective reactions. Parker tried to ensure draft registration of New York Indians, while Montezuma attempted to persuade tribal leaders to ignore the draft.

The citizenship question became crucial, and the society promoted a campaign for universal Native American citizenship, which finally was granted by the 1924 Indian Citizenship Act. When this was passed by Congress, it was hailed as a victory by all of the society's factions, but the organization virtually collapsed after achieving its goal. However, the society provided valuable experience for the Indian urban middle class, which supplied members to succeeding pan-Indian organizations. Other inter-tribal groups were formed, such as the All Pueblo Council (1922), which successfully opposed the Bursum Bill giving rights to squatters on the Rio Grande. The Grand Council Fire of Native Americans was founded in 1923, the Indian Association of America in 1932, and the Indian Confederation of America in 1933. This tradition of activism eventually resulted in the National Congress of American Indians (1944) and the later, more youthful, Red Power Movement.

TRIBAL ENTERPRISES

WHILE AGRICULTURE HAS BEEN THE TRADITIONAL ACTIVITY OF NATIVE AMERICANS, MANY TRIBES HAVE TURNED TO MORE RELIABLE AND LUCRATIVE MEANS OF BOOSTING INCOME.

Despite many tribes owning gaming halls, today most remain in a cycle of poverty. Indeed, many nations are paying off debts incurred in establishing casinos. Thus, many tribes and bands have attempted economic diversification. Agriculture has been a mainstay of Indian life, but finances are required for irrigation, and capital investment and farm incomes have dropped. Moreover, there is not enough tribally owned land for a thriving, independent, agricultural economy. Therefore, such tribes as the Northern Cheyenne lease out land for grazing and farming.

Major economic resources are minerals and oil under tribal lands, but much oil was stolen during early exploitation, as the 1981 Linowes Commission discovered. Coal mining has damaged tribal lands and water resources; the Northern Cheyenne have refused access to their estimated 23 billion tons of coal, in case their culture and values are destroyed. Some tribes established the Council of Energy Resource Tribes (CERT) to gain real control over their resources, managing them in the face of capitalist greed. The Jicarilla Apache, and the Fort Peck Assiniboine and Sioux tribes have drilled independently and successfully for oil. Meanwhile, the Navajo have a joint arrangement with private industry to operate a Dineh powerplant.

The Apache have been particularly successful in their economic ventures. The Naishan and Chiricahua depend on grazing and agriculture, while other bands run lumber and recreational industries. The Northern Paiute rely on agriculture, and some who inhabit the Warm Springs Reservation, living with Sahaptin and Chinook speakers, used the reservation corporation to establish fishing and plywood industries. The corporation was financed by compensation monies for the flooded Celilo Falls fishery. Now, these confederated tribes own an electricity producing dam, the Kah-Nee-Ta resort complex, and

Opposite: A Navajo woman at work on a loom. The Navajo are renowned for their weaving skills, among several other crafts.

two radio stations. Fishing is important to all tribes around Puget Sound, and Washington State has twenty-eight tribally owned fish hatcheries; the Muckleshoot, with 1,000 enrolled members, own two, at Keta Creek and the White River.

The Colorado River tribes, mainly Mojave, are financed by riverfront property rentals, the recreational Aha Quin Park, and over 90,000 acres (36,000 hectares) farmed for cotton, alfalfa, wheat, lettuce, and melons. Other notable tribal industries are run by the Pima, who have three industrial parks for the production of aluminum, concrete, and telecommunications equipment. They also run the Gila River Arts and Craft Center, commercial recreational facilities, and the Firebird International Raceway Park dragstrip. In addition, the Pima own a 120-acre (49-hectare) boat racing lake. In Oklahoma, the Miami run a trucking line for transporting their oil and fuel throughout the United States. The Hopi rely on arts and crafts, especially silverwork, textiles, and kachina dolls. They also run gas stations. The Lakota own the Lake Traverse plastic-bag plant, and a factory at Devil's Lake manufactures military camouflage material.

The Inupiat of Alaska still go whaling, but are subject to International Whaling Commission quotas. The communal participation in whaling and its rituals forms the bedrock of Inupiat society and culture, without which the people would lose their character. A spectacular aspect of the development of tribal income are the 7,500 or so Native American ironworkers in Canada and the United States. Among these are Akwesasne Mohawks from the New York State St. Regis Reservation and Caughnawaga Mohawks from the Kahnawake Reservation in Ontario. Working as steel erectors for bridge and skyscraper construction, these "skywalkers" helped build Toronto's CN Tower, the Golden Gate Bridge in San Francisco, and the New York World Trade Center.

Despite some economic improvements, Native Americans remain the poorest ethnic group in the United States, with a high unemployment rate on reservations; the 1990 census showed 30.9 percent as living in poverty, that is individuals earning less than $6,300 annually. Only gaming is likely to improve conditions. For example, Foxwoods, in Connecticut, plans to support 20,000 jobs with an annual payroll of $480 million. Adding indirect employment to the total, Foxwoods will probably underpin $6 billion of jobs in the early twenty-first century.

Legalized gambling on reservations began with a 1976 court case, in which the U.S. Supreme Court ruled that states do not have regulatory jurisdiction over Native American tribes. Other court rulings said that states could not prevent tribes from pursuing gaming activities. In 1988, the Indian Gaming Regulatory Act was passed into law, legalizing gambling for profit by Native American tribes on their self-governing lands. Today, the tribally owned casinos are flourishing.

Native Americans run some 100 high-stake bingo operations and over sixty casinos in more than twenty states. About 180 tribes own bingo halls, and 20–25 tribes run high-stake bingo operations producing from $100,000 to $1 million each month. By 1993, over sixty-three tribes were running high-stake casino establishments. Gaming revenue will probably be used by more tribes as they build new facilities. The highest concentrations of gaming activities are in Arizona, New Mexico, California, Wisconsin, and Minnesota. The first really big operation to open was Foxwoods in Ledyard, owned by the Mashantucket Pequot in southeast Connecticut. They began with high-stakes bingo on the reservation, then opened a casino in 1992. Built with a $55 million loan, the casino repaid the debt within seven months of opening and now produces $3 million daily. Today, the Foxwoods Resort comprises five casinos with over 300,000 square feet (28,000 square meters) for gaming, a 3,000-seat bingo hall, the 1,450-seat Fox Theater, thirty restaurants, and three hotels. The casino pays 20 percent of its slot-machine profits to the state of Connecticut.

The range of tribes involved in gaming is extraordinary: the Apache, Cherokee, Chinook, Coeur d'Alene, Coleville, Kickapoo, Standing Rock Sioux, Cheyenne-Arapaho, Coquille, Pechanga, Oglala Sioux, San Manuel, Seminole, Turtle Mountain Band of Chippewa, and Oneida are all represented. The Apache Gold Casino Resort operates 500-plus slot machines, and offers bingo, keno, and racebook. There is a championship golf course, a hotel, a covered rodeo pavilion, an RV park, restaurants, a convention center, cabaret, gift shops, a convenience store, and a BMX track. In contrast, facilities are more limited at the Oglala owned Prairie Wind Casino on the Pine Ridge Reservation in South Dakota. The casino operates a variety of slot machines, while table games include three-card poker and blackjack.

The development of gaming has generated much needed revenue to provide loans for other tribal businesses, to fund tribal land purchases, to give full medical and dental coverage to tribal members, and to finance scholarships and education. The Cabazon Band of Mission Indians in California uses gaming revenue to develop employment opportunities, as well as for welfare, housing, and educational purposes. In addition, the band has built a biomass-fueled electricity generating plant and a 950-unit housing development. Furthermore, reservation gaming boosts economic development by providing jobs for non-Indians and helps boost tourism.

The downside of gambling is that occasionally it provokes conflict within tribes, between modernizers and traditionalists. In 1990, for example, violence broke out in the St. Regis Akwesasne Reservation in upstate New York. The Mohawk Warrior Society saw gaming as a means of increasing economic independence and obtaining sovereignty from white society, while traditionalists and tribal officials opposed it. On the Oneida reservation in New York State, a bingo hall was destroyed in a disagreement between tribal factions. Disputes with state governments have been rife. Some states fear that competition from Indian gaming will have an adverse effect on non-Indian casinos and lead to a decline in state tax revenues. Court cases have ensued, but states argue that the 11th Amendment bars tribes from suing them.

A sign in front of the Apache Gold Casino and Resort, located in San Carlos, Arizona. The Casino is owned and run by the local Apache tribe, and includes gaming, restaurants, and a hotel.

THE INDIAN NEW DEAL

THE 1930S SAW THE IMPLEMENTATION OF THE INDIAN REORGANIZATION ACT, WHICH SECURED A NUMBER OF RIGHTS FOR NATIVE AMERICANS. THESE INCLUDED THE RIGHT TO TRIBAL SELF-GOVERNMENT.

By 1933, during the Great Depression, large areas of Native American tribal lands had become privately owned, as a consequence of the Dawes Act and similar legislation. When President Roosevelt was elected, he was determined to end his country's economic crisis and began introducing legislation to this end. He was unaware of Indian issues, but trusted his Indian Commissioner, John Collier, who served from 1933 to 1945. New Deal laws were passed for the United States and the Indians.

In 1934, Collier put forward the Indian Reorganization Act (IRA), otherwise known as the Wheeler-Howard Act, which sought to reverse the Dawes Act. The bill was too radical for Congress, but certain elements of it were enacted. First, tribal governments could be created, but with limited powers, and tribes could accept or reject the IRA by a referendum. The land provisions of the Dawes Act were abolished, but the Indians of Oklahoma were outside the provisions of the new Act. An unfortunate feature was that Alaskan Indians could not have access to credit loan funds. Financial appropriations were considerably increased for Native American education, as were loans to tribal corporations for economic development, although these monies were intended to help assimilate Indians into white society, rather than stimulate and preserve Indian society. Thus, overall, the IRA was a compromise between encouraging Indian independence and assimilation.

The next stage in the IRA's life was for each reservation to accept or reject it. The plebiscite resulted in 174 Native American bands or tribes (some 129,750 people) accepting, while seventy-eight tribes (approximately 86,365 people) rejected its application to their reservations. Important tribes like the Crow, Navajo, Assiniboine, Fort Peck Lakota, Klamath, Crow Creek Lakota, and the Wyoming Arapaho voted against the IRA. The unfortunate outcome of this decision was that they now had no right to adopt a tribal constitution under an IRA protectorate, nor did they qualify for land-purchase and economic-development loans. One estimate suggests that ultimately only one third of those eligible for IRA benefits actually qualified for them.

Collier persevered in his attempts to spread the benefits of the IRA. In 1936, he managed to get passed the Alaska Reorganization Act and the Oklahoma Indian Welfare Act, which ensured that the most important IRA provisions were extended to Indians of those regions.

Another success was the 1935 Indian Arts and Crafts Act, which promoted artists and craftsmen to such an extent that two major exhibitions were held, one at the 1939 World's Fair in San Francisco, the other at the Museum of Modern Art in New York in 1941. Two key figures involved in the Indian Arts and Crafts Board, established under the Act, were Rene d'Harnoncourt, chairman until 1961, and the Cherokee Lloyd Kiva New, who became chairman in 1972. Both were prominent in promoting Indian controlled cultural institutions.

Also established was the Indian Civilian Conservation Corps (CCC), which has helped preserve forested regions and worked to upgrade ranges in the northern Plains, the Great Basin, and the Southwest.

Two groups of Native Americans were vociferous in their antagonism toward the IRA. One, the Five Civilized Tribes of Oklahoma, tended to favor integration into white society. The other group was the Navajo, who were forced to cull their sheep under a conservation program aimed at protecting ranges and pastures. Those Navajos with small flocks were wiped out economically, while all were forced to witness rotting sheep carcasses because no programs existed to sell the meat. On the other hand, the Mescalero Apache established a business committee that canceled grazing leases so that they could run their own cattle on the reservation; the Mescaleros' yearly income grew from $18,000 to $101,000 in three depression years. In 1963, the business committee borrowed finance from New Mexico banks to buy the Sierra Blanca ski resort. They also built a fish hatchery, a resort hotel, golf courses, and an industrial park. The Jicarilla Apache benefited from oil company exploration fees, while the tribal council published newspapers and ran an alcoholism program.

When John Collier proposed the Indian Reorganization Act in 1934, many Indians, like this Chippewa in Wisconsin, were struggling to survive through farming. Although agriculture is still a mainstay of Indian life, the Act made it possible for the tribes to exploit many resources previously denied them.

NATIVE AMERICANS IN WORLD WAR II

LARGE NUMBERS OF NATIVE AMERICANS SERVED IN THE U.S. MILITARY DURING WORLD WAR II, MAKING A GREAT, AND AT TIMES UNIQUE, CONTRIBUTION TO THE COUNTRY'S WAR EFFORT.

Native Americans saw action in all branches of the U.S. armed forces during World War II, but those who served in the Marines, some of them Navajo code talkers, have received the most publicity. However, the 45th (Thunderbird) Infantry Division had the highest proportion of Indian soldiers of any division. It was involved in amphibious landings on Sicily, at Salerno and Anzio, and in southern France. Indians also served with distinction in the 4th and 88th Divisions, the 19th and 180th Infantry Regiments, the 147th Field Artillery, and various Oklahoma National Guard units.

Several traditions imbued Native Americans as warriors. Mental and spiritual strength, the ability to ignore thirst, and enthusiasm for battle have made Indians formidable fighters throughout history. Warriors also attained status within their families and communities. Moreover, military service provides education and decent pay, and can satisfy the spirit of adventure. Reputedly, Indians excelled at bayonet fighting, marksmanship, and scouting. Indeed, one Lakota soldier, Kenneth Scisson, a member of an American commando unit, killed ten Germans on one patrol.

The scale of Native American enlistment during World War II was greater as a percentage of their total number than any other ethnic group. Of 350,000 Native Americans, 44,000 saw military service. The Pueblos provided 213 men, 10 percent of their 2,205 population; nearly all able-bodied Ojibwa at the Grand Portage Reservation enlisted, while the Navajo contributed 3,600 men. One quarter of the New Mexico Mescalero Apache enlisted, rather than wait for their draft cards. Several hundred Indian women also served as WACs, WAVEs, and Army Medical Corps nurses. Native Americans in the Army often hit the headlines, but three times as many served in the Navy, and one, Oklahoma Cherokee

Joseph (Jocko) Clark, an Annapolis graduate, made the rank of admiral. The Air Corps generally took Indians from the more assimilated tribes in Oklahoma, Texas, and Wisconsin. In addition, over 40,000 Indian men and women left their lands to take up war related work.

An all-Navajo Marine Corps signal unit encoded messages in their own language, evolving translations of military and naval terms. Orders could be transmitted over the radio by voice, and the Japanese never cracked the code. For example, the code for "Saipan" was "dibeh (sheep) wo-la-chee (ant) tkin (ice) bi-so-dih (pig) wo-la-chee (ant) nesh-chee (nut)." Code talkers chose alternative Navajo words for the most common used letters in English—E, T, A, O, I, and N. Thus, the letter "A" could be represented by be-la-sana (apple). Military terms included "dive-bomber" (gini, chicken hawk), "submarine" (besh-lo, iron fish), "cruiser" (lo-tso-yazzie, small whale), and "brigadier general" (so-a-la-ih, one star).

A group of Comanche code talkers of the 4th Signal Company, U.S. Army during World War II. Indians from many tribes made this special contribution to the war effort, helping to ensure secure communications.

By the end of the war, over 400 Navajos had become code talkers. They were used first in 1942 on Guadalcanal, but were especially effective on Iwo Jima. There, six Navajo radio nets sent and received over 800 messages during the first forty-eight hours of the assault. When the Marines raised the Stars and Stripes on Mount Suribachi, the Navajo relayed the message, "Suribachi" (sheep, uncle, ram, ice, bear, ant, cat, horse, itch). The next day, the small American flag was replaced by a large one for the benefit of photographer Joe Rosenthal, whose image became an icon of the war. Among the five men shown raising the flag was Ira Hayes, a Pima, born on the Gila Reservation in Arizona.

The Navajo Code was kept secret until the 1969 reunion of the 4th Marine Division Association in Chicago. The code talkers are now honored by a sculpture in Phoenix Plaza, Phoenix, Arizona.

Combat honors can be a measure of extraordinary bravery in the face of the enemy, especially the award of the Medal of Honor. One Indian recipient of this award was First Lieutenant Jack Montgomery, a Cherokee, who was with the Thunderbirds near Padiglione, Italy. Alone, he attacked three enemy positions that had pinned down his platoon. He mopped up the enemy and took prisoners. Another Medal of Honor winner was Van Barfoot, a Choctaw and second lieutenant in the Thunderbirds, who was at Anzio during the breakout to Rome. On May 23, 1944, he wiped out two machine-gun nests and captured seventeen German soldiers. Later that day, he repelled a German tank assault, destroyed a German artillery piece, and carried two wounded commanders to safety.

THE FATE OF THE INUIT

WITH THEIR WAY OF LIFE AND ENVIRONMENT UNDER ATTACK, THE INUIT PEOPLES OF THE FAR NORTH HAVE HAD TO BAND TOGETHER TO MAKE THEIR VOICES HEARD.

On April 18, 2002, four Canadian soldiers were killed in Afghanistan by "friendly" fire. To commemorate these men, and those injured by the incident, Canadian soldiers built an *inuksuk* (a stone marker). The *inuksuk* is traditionally used by Inuit hunters to help them find their way. The national Inuit organization in Canada, the Inuit Tapiriit Kanatami, stated that, when considering a new logo, it looked at many designs, including the maple leaf, but that the *inuksuk* had become a national soldiers' symbol. The organization's president, Jose Kusugak, said, "I think we're on the same wavelength." Were Inuit-white relations always so cooperative in the twentieth century?

Traditionally, Eskimos (Inuit, Inupiat, and Yup'ik) pursued a program of annual subsistence activities, generally fixed to animals' seasonal migrations. Their customs have been assailed by state educational policies, however, the Christian mission schools and boarding high schools having taught Inuits alien concepts, such as individuality, which opposes their essential cooperative community spirit. Other aspects of the white world that have damaged the Arctic peoples' way of life include gold mining, alcoholism, the International Whaling Commission, and the dumping of 15,000 pounds (7,000 kilograms) of radioactive material from Nevada. Ecological issues affecting the Inuit include mercury pollution on the Labrador and Québec coasts, and at Giaque Lake. Arsenic leaching has been discovered at Yellowknife, while caribou migration has been disrupted by the Dempster Lateral Pipeline. Further ecological damage has been caused by the Alaska Highway Pipeline. In addition, Alaska faces many problems caused by the oil industry.

In partial retaliation, the eight Alaskan Inuit whaling communities formed the Alaskan Eskimo Whaling Commission in an attempt to obtain an increase in their harvest quota from the International

Whaling Commission, with considerable success. Similar associations deal with the hunting of the walrus, sea otter, porcupine, and caribou. The Inuit have also developed cooperative agreements across state and national borders to monitor pollutants, and to manage and protect shared animal populations, such as water fowl, the polar bear, and walrus. Pressure-group activity, such as the Arctic Slope Native Association and the Northwest Alaska Native Association (formed in 1963 by Willie Hensley, later a senator), pushed for the Alaska Native Claims Settlement Act (ANCSA) of 1971. Indians, Aleuts, and Inuit received title to 40 million acres (16 million hectares) of land, a billion dollars in compensation, and mineral rights plus eventual shareholdings in mineral companies. The legislators assumed that the Native Americans were in a period of transition from subsistence to a modern lifestyle, however, and removed all hunting and fishing rights outside protected lands around villages. Thus, attacks on traditions still occur. Ironically, the Iglulik Inuit prefer all-terrain vehicles to dog sleds for traveling and hunting.

In 1977, the Inuit Circumpolar Conference (ICC) was established by Eben Hopson because he had been unsuccessful in convincing U.S. policy makers of the need to involve the Inuit in decisions affecting them. The ICC's first meeting took place in June of that year, bringing together, for the first time, Inuit from Alaska, Canada, and Greenland. In 1989, the Russian Inuit sent a delegation, and they became full members in 1992.

The ICC's aims are to strengthen Inuit regional unity, protect their culture and environment, and be an active partner in decision making in respect of the circumpolar region. In 1983, the ICC achieved non-governmental organization status with a formal voice at the United Nations. It works with the UN Working Group on Indigenous Peoples, and thereby helps monitor the status and conditions of similar peoples throughout the world. The ICC made an important contribution to the 1989 revision of the International Labor Organization Indigenous and Tribal Peoples' Convention. The institution has helped develop an Inuit Regional Conservation Strategy; shares in the Arctic Monitoring and Assessment Program initiated by the Finnish government in 1989; promotes and spreads the traditional knowledge of Inuit peoples, such as soapstone carving and beliefs in the spirituality of the natural world; and protects traditional economies based on whaling, seal hunting, fishing, and similar activities.

An Inuit hunting caribou. The traditional Eskimo lifestyle relied heavily on the annual migration pattern of such creatures, but increasingly this is being disrupted by industrial processes.

TRIBAL MUSEUMS AND CULTURAL CENTERS

TOWARD THE END OF THE TWENTIETH CENTURY, THE NUMBER OF TRIBAL MUSEUMS GREW AS NATIVE AMERICANS SOUGHT TO DEFINE THEIR IDENTITY AND CULTURE.

The character of museums displaying Native American artifacts and lifeways has changed over time. Thousands of museums collected Indian objects, together with the skeletal remains of many individuals. Before 1900, these were in non-Indian hands. After World War II, the U.S. government recognized that many sacred objects should be returned to tribal possession, like the Zuni war gods from the Denver Art Museum. The desire to allow Native Americans access to religious objects and sites was highlighted in the 1978 American Indian Religious Freedom Act. Legislation has encouraged the protection of historic sites, and the 1990 Native American Graves Protection and Repatriation Act requires federal institutions to return Native American human remains and artifacts to their respective peoples. This does not apply to the Smithsonian, however, although that institution has repatriated some 18,500 skeletal remains, including 756 to Alaska. The Smithsonian has also returned remains to the South Dakota Sisseton-Wahpeton Sioux, and may do the same for other tribes. Wampum belts have been sent to the Iroquois, while medicine bundles have been returned to the Navajo, Hopi, and Mohawk, as has a sacred pole to the Omaha. Other institutions, such as the University of Nebraska, have repatriated museum materials.

This more sensitive approach to Native American culture, religion, and lifestyles has been negotiated by non-Indian museums with Indians, who are now consulted about displays and museum aims. An even more significant outcome is the mushrooming number of Native American

An exhibition of Native American artifacts discovered by the Oxbow Archaelogists at the Chippewa Nature Center..

and Alaskan Native museums in the United States and Canada, from about forty in the 1980s to over 175 by 1992.

Tribally operated museums have two basic rationales. They allow groups to define their own identity and culture, and they meet the government's obligation to identify and preserve culture. Tribal museums help conserve historical sites and channel tourism, which aids the commercial development of archaeological sites. An example of this is the Makah Cultural and Research Center at Neah Bay, Washington, which has recreated Ozette Village.

The repatriation process requires a means of preserving and storing archaeological remains, which has prompted the establishment of more tribal museums. Such museums can also rekindle traditional skills, and promote old ways of passing on history and systems of belief. Museums have been helped by the Department of Commerce Economic Development Administration, which supports the construction costs of projects that focus on tourism, such as the Gila River Indian Arts and Crafts Center in Arizona. Native Americans realize that for them to control their destiny, the continuation and transfer of tribal knowledge is essential. Thus, managing culture, artifacts, archives and libraries, language, historical sites, and rituals and ceremonies is paramount.

Four basic types of museum exist. The first are tribally operated museums on reservations. These may be managed by tribal governments or advisory committees made up of community delegates. Second, there are some urban cultural and recreational centers that cover a variety of tribes. These give tourists a Native

Native Americans clothing displayed at the Hoard Historical Museum, Fort Atkinson, Wisconsin.

American perspective of history, and provide a showcase for Indian arts and crafts. The Daybreak Star Arts Center in Seattle exemplifies this type of not-for-profit, tax-exempt enterprise. A third type is a Native American controlled department located within another institution, such as the Southeast Alaska Indian Cultural Center in the U.S. National Park Service building in Sitka. Finally, a family or individually owned museum might be located on a tribal reservation. One such non-profit organization is the Lenni Lenape Historical Society in Pennsylvania.

Typically, tribal museums display prehistoric artifacts, tools, clothing, weapons, household goods, transport items, musical instruments, and ceremonial articles. Photographs and oral history recordings preserve a community's heritage, while opportunities are provided to research the museum's archives, genealogy, and linguistics. Exhibitions concerning creation myths, pre-European-contact lifestyles, art, and inter-tribal relationships are common. The wealthy Mashantucket Pequots in Connecticut will eventually possess the largest tribally owned museum in the United States, which will incorporate extensive exhibit galleries, a significant library, and archives.

ACKNOWLEDGMENTS

For Cartographic Press
Design, Maps and Typesetting: Jeanne Radford, Malcolm Swanston and Jonathan Young

The publishers would like to thank the following picture libraries for their kind permission to use their pictures and illustrations:

Corbis 10, 13, 14, 15, 21, 23, 26, 44, 46/47, 48, 50, 51, 53, 55, 56, 59 (top), 67 (left), 67 (right), 69, 104, 109, 110, 112, 114, 115, 117, 120, 124, 134, 140, 143, 145, 148 (large), 159, 173, 179, 196, 198, 200, 221, 241, 245, 253, 256, 266, 272, 274, 275, 281, 282, 287, 294, 320 (top), 322, 328, 335 (bottom), 351, 365, 371.
Photowest 11, 54, 292, 318, 320 (bottom).
Private and On-Line sources 22, 39, 40, 42, 43, 58, 59 (bottom), 62, 63, 66, 87, 88, 89 (top), 89 (side), 90, 93, 96, 97 (top), 97 (bottom), 99 (top), 99 (bottom), 100, 102, 105, 116, 129, 130, 131, 132, 136, 138, 146, 148 (top), 154, 160 (top), 160 (bottom), 163, 167, 168, 169, 176, 178 (top), 178 (bottom), 181, 183, 184, 185, 187, 202, 208, 210, 214, 215, 224/225, 228, 230, 233, 244, 248, 257, 258, 260, 276, 277, 278 (bottom), 284, 286, 288, 302, 303, 304, 305, 306, 309, 312, 313, 316, 327, 329, 330, 331 (top), 331 (bottom), 332, 335 (top), 337, 339, 345, 347, 365, 374, 382.
Rochester Museum and Science Center, Rochester, New York 31.
Library of Congress 33, 83, 216, 217, 259, 262, 265, 289, 300, 301, 310, 315, 326, 363.
Bildersburg, Hamburg 77.
Indiana University 79.
National Archive of Canada 85.
Getty Images 103, 234, 236, 267, 278 (top).
Bibliotheque des Arts, Paris 128.
Nacket Visitors Center 167.
Smithsonian Institute 175, 296, 307, 317, 346, 377.
Tippecaneo County Historical Association, Laffayette, Indiana 190.
Yale University 205.
Collection of Glenn and Lorraine Myers 212.
Washington University Art Gallery 222.
Denver Public Library 298, 299, 311.
Colorado Historical Society 299 (top).
National Archives and Records Administration (USA) 321, 359,
Nevada Historical Society 375.
Philbrook Museum of Art, Tulsa, Oklahoma 381.
Hoard Historical Museum, Fort Atkinson Historical Society, Wisconsin 383.
Christian F. Feest, Allenstadt, Germany 387.

Every effort had been made to contact the copyright holders for images reproduced in this book.
Any omissions are entirely unintentional, and the details should be addressed to Quantum Publishing.